D1475601

The Making
of an Economist

Studies in the History, Methods, and Boundaries of Economics

Series Editors
Axel Leijonhufvud and Donald N. McCloskey

The Making of an Economist, Arjo Klamer and David Colander

Carl Menger and the Origins of Austrian Economics, Max Alter

A History of Balance-of-Payments Theory, John S. Chipman

The Making
of an Economist

Arjo Klamer
and David Colander

Westview Press
Boulder • San Francisco • London

Studies in the History, Methods, and Boundaries of Economics

Copyright © 1990 by Westview Press, Inc.

Published in 1990 in the United States of America by Westview Press, Inc., 5500 Central Avenue, Boulder, Colorado 80301, and in the United Kingdom by Westview Press, Inc., 13 Brunswick Centre, London WC1N 1AF, England

Library of Congress Cataloging-in-Publication Data
Klamer, Arjo.
    The making of an economist/Arjo Klamer and David Colander.
        p.   cm.—(Studies in the history, methods, and boundaries of
economics)
    Includes bibliographical references.
    ISBN 0-8133-0697-3. — ISBN 0-8133-0698-1 (pbk.)
    1. Economics—Study and teaching (Graduate)—United States.
2. Economists—United States.   3. Graduate students—United States.
I. Colander, David.   II. Title.   III. Series.
HB74.8.K57   1990
330'.071'1073—dc20   89-37899
                                                                              CIP

Printed and bound in the United States of America

The paper used in this publication meets the requirements of the American National Standard for Permanence of Paper for Printed Library Materials Z39.48-1984.

10   9   8   7   6   5   4   3   2   1

To Arjo's daughter, Alexandra,
and David's son, Zachary Bo

Contents

List of Tables   xi
Preface   xiii
Acknowledgments   xvii

PART ONE
INTRODUCTION

1   The Nature of the Economics Profession   3

Economics as a Profession, 4
The Number of Economists, 7
Undergraduate Training, 9
Graduate Training, 11

2   The Making of an Economist   13

Profile of Students, 14
Interests of Students, 14
Differences Between Graduate Students and
   the Profession, 19
Distinctive Characteristics of Graduate Programs, 20
Some Thoughts About the Implications, 25
Conclusion, 27
Appendix 2A, 28
Appendix 2B, 29

**3   Reciting the *Kama Sutra* Under a Fig Tree:
Further Results from the Survey**   37

A Sampling of Some of the More Interesting
   Comments, 37
Comments Reinforcing the Survey Results, 38
Ranking Economists, 41
Likes and Dislikes, 44

What Is a Successful Economist? 46
Portrait of a Graduate Economics Student, 53

PART TWO
CONVERSATIONS WITH GRADUATE STUDENTS

4   Ambivalence and Security: MIT Students   59

First-Year Students, 59
Second-Year Students, 67
Third-Year Students, 72
Fourth-Year Students, 79

5   Diversity and Skepticism: Harvard Students   87

First-Year Students, 87
Third-Year Students, 100

6   Eclecticism and Concern: Columbia Students   109

First-Year Students, 109
First- and Third-Year Students, 112

7   Commitment and Loyalty: Chicago Students   127

First-Year Students, 127
Second-Year Students, 137
Third-Year Students, 144
Fourth-Year Students, 154

PART THREE
INTERPRETATIONS

8   A Case of Mistaken Identities, *Arjo Klamer*   169

Are They Technocrats? 170
Diversity, 172
Socialization, 176
Economists as Characters, 179
A Lost Generation? 183

9   **Workmanship, Incentives, and Cynicism,**
     David Colander   187

     Methodology and the Survey Results, 189
     What to Do About the Current State of Affairs, 194
     How Did Economics Evolve into Its Current State? 195
     Graduate and Undergraduate Economics Training, 196

Notes   201
About the Authors   207
Index   209

Tables

1.1   University ranking controlling for age and citation dispersion   10

2.1   The importance of reading in other fields   16

2.2   Interest of students by area   17

2.3   Perceptions of success   18

2.4   Economic opinions of graduate students compared to Frey Study of American economists   19

2.5   Opinions of economics as a science: comparison among schools   21

2.6   Economic opinions: a comparison among schools   22

2.7   Importance of economic assumptions   23

3.1   The five most-respected economists   41

3.2   Top most-respected economists   42

3.3A   What graduate students like   47

3.3B   What graduate students dislike   50

3.4   What makes a successful economist   54

Preface

"Where did he get his Ph.D.?" The question comes up all the time in the world of U.S. economists. It is a loaded question.

Graduate schools have reputations that rub off on their Ph.D.'s. Where you went to school is a signal of what type of an economist you are. Massachusetts Institute of Technology (MIT) is known for attracting the best students. A Ph.D. from MIT, therefore, means something like, "Ah, she must be bright." MIT is also known as solidly neoclassical with a Keynesian slant. Its Ph.D.'s are expected to be just that. Chicago stands for a conservative tradition in economics. Hearing "Chicago," most economists will think, "Oh, one of the Gary Becker–George Stigler–Robert Lucas crowd." (Older Ph.D.'s will evoke the reaction "Milton Friedman.") Ph.D.'s from the University of Massachusetts at Amherst will bring "radical" to mind, because that is the reputation of those schools. A George Mason Ph.D. will make one think "Austrian" or "public choice."

Such signaling can be unfair. An MIT student who studied with Michael Piore, a nonneoclassical economist, gets mislabeled. And the University of Massachusetts doesn't produce exclusively "radical" economists; good neoclassical adherents come from there, too. Fair or unfair, these labels are a fact of life. The colors of their graduate training follow economists wherever they go.

Approximately 150 schools offer Ph.D.'s in economics; of these, about 10 or 20 are considered elite. These elite schools dominate and shape the U.S. economics profession.

Our focus in this book is on graduate students at these elite institutions and what happens to them in the process of becoming economists. The students do the talking in this book. They speak out about their aspirations as economists and their expectations of the economics discipline, and they tell us what they discovered about economics during their graduate training.

The book is intended for three audiences: aspiring economists, economists, and the lay public. For the aspiring economists, the potential and current graduate students, the book offers a view of what the future holds. For economists, the book provides an in-depth look at a set of institutions that they know well and allows them to test their own presuppositions against what is reported here. For the lay public, the book allows a peek into the world of academic economists. The book is no "profscam" story. It is more objective, more balanced, than the peek people got into academia in Sykes's book, *Profscam*.[1]

The first impulse to write this book came during a conversation about a possible sequel to Klamer's *Conversations with Economists*.[2] It was Robert Solow who threw out the suggestion, "Why don't you talk with our graduate students?" A shared concern about the current state of economics was the next impulse for this venture. One day, after having endured an economics convention, the two of us sat down in a New York cafe and lamented the state of the profession: Why did we have this gut feeling that much of what went on there was a waste? We decided that looking into the training of economists would be one good way to find out exactly what was going on in the economics profession. And so we got started.

We knew from discussions with other economists that we weren't alone in our beliefs, but we also knew that we were going against the tide. Economics as a discipline has never been stronger, with thousands of students seeking its insights each year and millions of dollars in grants supporting its development. But such outward manifestations of success mask discontent. Much of the frustration economists feel is kept to themselves. Younger economists who complain don't advance in their careers. At times established economists stand up and admonish their colleagues to keep in mind that economics should be about the economy, not about topology or hyperspace. But they are ignored. The success of the profession confronts the critics of the profession.

We wanted to determine whether our views were shared by those just entering the profession—those who were not yet fully socialized into its folkways. We felt this group would be more objective than established economists. Once having entered the profession, one stops asking questions about its nature. And so we decided to do a survey of graduate students at elite schools to see what they thought and why they thought so. Doing a survey may sound a natural thing to do, but for economists it is unnatural. Surveying is not a technique that economists teach students; economists teach how to build models and conduct econometric tests, but not how to dirty one's hands by going out and asking people what is on their minds.

With the help of colleagues in the other social sciences, we designed a survey that we distributed among students at MIT, Harvard, Stanford, Chicago, Yale, and Columbia. We also conducted conversations with groups of students at MIT, Harvard, Chicago, and Columbia. The survey and the conversations provide the raw material for the book.

After what is now Chapter 2 appeared as an article in the *Journal of Economic Perspectives*,[3] it received strong reactions from people both inside and outside the profession. Most of these reactions focused on what the students perceived to be the conditions for success in the economics profession. The low ranking of "knowledge of economic literature" and "knowledge of the economy" confirmed our belief that economic research was becoming separated from the real world.

The survey results confirmed that the economics profession is divided and that one's graduate school is a good indicator of where one stands in relationship to economics and the economy. George Stigler is reported to have said that he is pleased with the results because they showed that only his Chicago students have good economic sense. Many others were dismayed. Our findings provoked discussion in a panel of the National Science Foundation and in the American Economic Association (AEA) and led to the AEA's appointment of a committee that spent hundreds of thousands of dollars to review graduate education in economics.

Of course, the AEA study committee is composed of a representative sampling of the elite of the profession. For such a committee to find something egregiously wrong with graduate training would be about as likely as the American Bar Association condemning the law school experience or the American Medical Association severely criticizing the medical school experience. It's possible, but we wouldn't bet on it.

Many of the major issues raised in our survey were brought out in our article, but we had significant material that could not be included there. Hence this book. Chapter 3 reports information that because of space limitations could not be included in the *JEP* article. Chapters 4, 5, 6, and 7 report conversations with MIT, Harvard, Chicago, and Columbia students. The information in these chapters breathes life into the statistics reported in Chapter 2. In the conversations, the students speak without much interference from us.

To make the survey and conversations meaningful to a wide population of readers, we have added an introductory chapter, Chapter 1, which provides a context for the survey and conversations. It describes the nature of the economics profession. Chapters 8 and 9 present our interpretations of the conversations. Because we discovered that each of us wanted to take a different direction, we decided to offer separate interpretations so we could each have our own views presented without the compromises collaboration imposes. Klamer's interpretation stresses the confusion of students as to what economists and their discipline are all about. Colander's stresses the conflict between the incentives for success within the profession and the workman's pride individuals take in their jobs. There are many other interpretations, we're sure, and it is our hope that this book will stimulate discussion about the meaning of our findings.

Arjo Klamer
David Colander

Acknowledgments

This book could not have been put together without the help of many people. Robert Clower, Metin Cosgel, Caroline Craven, Lee Cuba, Marion Just, Donald McCloskey, Chrystal Sharp, and Stephen Smith provided advice and assistance in the development and processing of the survey. For helpful comments on drafts of the *JEP* article as well as on the additional chapters in this book, we thank Bob Coats, Fred Dirks, Rendigs Fels, David Lindauer, Warren Samuels, Robert Solow, and Hal Varian. Helen Reiff provided wonderful editorial assistance and transcribed many hours of tapes. Spencer Carr was his usual helpful self as was Jane Raese, our project editor at Westview. Ida May Norton did a superb professional job of editing. We thank them all.

But most of all we thank the students who participated in the survey. This is their book and their story. We hope that our presentation does them justice.

A. K.
D. C.

PART ONE

Introduction

Surveys are not the usual way that economists gather empirical evidence. Thus, when we conducted a survey, it provoked a number of comments from the profession. Luckily for us, in response to some of the same concerns we had, the American Economic Association had recently founded a new journal, *The Journal of Economic Perspectives*, which was designed to discuss economic issues in a less technical manner. We presented the central results of the survey there; Chapter 2 is a reprint of that article. The questionnaire we developed is reproduced in Appendix 2B. Chapter 3 extracts some student comments from the questionnaire. Chapter 1 describes the nature of the economics profession to put the survey in context for the lay reader.

1

The Nature of
the Economics Profession

"How can I become an economist?" Imagine a student asking this question of her professor. And imagine she volunteers a few avenues herself. "Should I first go to Wall Street and learn how markets work?" Getting firsthand experience may sound like a good idea to her, but the professor will briskly dismiss the suggestion. "Well, maybe I should get a job in a real business—say, turning out automobiles." The answer will be "no" again: "That's not how you learn economics." She'll try one more time. "Well, how about if I read all the top economists of the past—John Stuart Mill, David Ricardo, Adam Smith?" The professor will say, "It wouldn't hurt, but it probably won't help." Now the student asks, "What should I do?" An honest answer would be, "Going to graduate school is the gateway to becoming an economist." Instead of asking "How?" she should ask "Where? Which graduate school?"

Graduate schools have not always held the key to becoming an economist. In the nineteenth century and even in the early twentieth century, the "How?" question was pertinent. Graduate schools in economics didn't exist, and in their absence, many different paths led to fame in economics. Take David Ricardo. He was not only a famous economist but also a London stockbroker, and later in his life a respected parliamentarian. John Stuart Mill wrote about economics while a bureaucrat in the East India Company for thirty-six years. Francis Edgeworth, the British economist who dreamed up the indifference and contract curves, taught logic and wrote about economics as well as ethics. William Stanley Jevons started his career in mineralogy and wrote a book on physics. Leon Walras wrote a novel and lived like a bohemian before he turned to the theory of economics. These people were not professional economists, because when they wrote there were no professional economists. Professionalization—specialization—came only later.

3

Economics as a Profession

As economic knowledge grew, the economics profession became more insulated. In the United States, academic economics came to dominate economics organizations and to define the nature of economists. As that happened, the real-world emphasis of economics, so noticeable in the nineteenth century, declined. Thus, when the student asked her professor how to become an economist, the professor thought of himself (and we mean himself—the economics profession is dominated by men) and his colleagues. An economist was someone absorbed in academic affairs, busy teaching and writing academic papers.

Today the economics profession has become sufficiently insulated from the real world that it is the subject of jokes and parodies. Just ask any economist what the can-opener joke is, and you'll get the answer. The joke is a satire of economists' predilection for assumptions. A somewhat less well-known, but nonetheless biting, satire of the profession was written by Axel Leijonhufvud: "The Econ tribe occupies a vast territory in the far North. Their land appears bleak and dismal to the outsider, and travelling through it makes for rough sledding." Leijonhufvud calls his parody "Life Among the Econ."[1] The notion of economists as a tribe and the image of economics as a far-off land that "appears bleak and dismal to the outsider" are bothersome, if not annoying, to many economists. As is true of any good parody, Leijonhofvud's comes uncomfortably close to reality.

Economists protect themselves by their language. Leijonhufvud writes: "The extreme clannishness, not to say xenophobia, of the Econ makes life among them difficult and perhaps even somewhat dangerous for the outsider." Jargon, secret codes, and various social procedures keep the outsiders out. Initiation rituals prevent easy entry. "The young Econ, or 'grad,' is not admitted to adulthood until he has made a 'modl' exhibiting a degree of workmanship acceptable to the elders of the 'dept' in which he serves his apprenticeship. Adulthood is conferred in an intricate ceremony the particulars of which vary from village to village."

Like most professionals, economists have a keen sense of who is "in" and who is "out." The Ph.D. after the name signals that the person is an insider (although economists are far more subtle than to place a pedigree after their names; rather, they let their Ph.D.-hood come up casually in conversation).

Like medical doctors, economists behave as professionals. Their articles have a professional format. Theorems, lemmas, and mathematics are in. English is out. Their professional language is at least as foreign to the public as medical jargon is to patients. In dealing within the profession, economists follow a professional code. Helping out colleagues, writing recommendations, traveling long distances to serve on panels—all are gestures to be expected from the professional economist. Much of the interaction within the economics profession is nonmarket interaction.

Like medical doctors, economists have their own institutions that sustain the profession. Their equivalent of the American Medical Association is the American Economic Association (AEA), which confers legitimacy on economists. This association is dominated by the elite graduate schools.

Most doctors work as doctors, applying their skills in the real world, whereas most elite economists don't work in the real world. True, the elite of the medical profession centers around universities, but the elite have their private practices, too. They keep their fingers in the pie, so to speak. Elite economists are more likely to stay within the academic institutions and use their skills to advance the knowledge of their peers. A few are for hire as consultants, textbook writers, or court witnesses, but such activities are looked down upon by the profession. Economists who dedicate their careers to such outside services for pay are treated with suspicion. Medical doctors derive professional status from their prestige in the community at large. In contrast, public prestige often hurts economists in their professional standing. For example, economists treat John Kenneth Galbraith, one of the best-known economists in the world today, with due respect, but do not encourage their graduate students to read his work. Many use "Galbraithism" as a term of derision. The rule seems to be, "If the public can understand the argument, the argument must be wrong."

Another difference between medical doctors and economists is that economists believe that extensive contact with the outside world compromises the scientific inquiry about that world; thus economists should avoid such contact. More than fifty years ago Wesley Mitchell, the founder of the National Bureau of Economic Research, warned his colleagues against the temptations that the outside world puts in their way:

> A cautious scientific inquirer is sometimes gravely disturbed by the confidence with which a businessman will ask his opinion upon some delicate problem and still more disturbed by the practical man's disregard of the limitations and conditions with which he feels it necessary to hedge his answers about. The time was when such folk as economists complained about the neglect of their findings by men of affairs. Now they are frequently called upon to advise about matters of which their knowledge is slight. They do not always decline the over-flattering invitations with firmness which befits a scientific conscience.[2]

The original purpose of Ph.D. programs was to create an environment in which students could dedicate themselves to the pursuit of knowledge free from outside distractions. In 1863, thirteen years before Johns Hopkins founded the first graduate school, the president of Harvard, Thomas Hill, ruminated about this ideal:

> Our Divinity School prepares its scholars to take charge of parishes; but where are our young men coming simply as lovers of truth, simply as scholars, for aid in exploring the highest realms of human thought? . . . Our Medical School prepares young men to enter into practice; even our Scientific School is largely technological, teaching the applications of science as much as science itself.[3]

Later, when graduate schools became firmly established institutions, fears spread that they would become like professional schools. In 1912 a dean at Princeton worried that graduate schools were attracting "men, not because they must be scholars, but because they want a job. Why is the degree made the be-all and end-all? It is beginning to be known like a 'union card' for labor."[4] In 1932 Dean Howard Lee McBain of Columbia expressed the same sentiment:

> Whether we like it or not, the Doctor's degree has come to have high commercial value. It is, in consequence, pursued by large numbers who have great interest in the degree but little or no interest in, or capacity for, genuine research. . . . The task is undertaken not for the sake of the subject but for the sake of the degree. Many of these "students plow and plug and ultimately win the coveted reward. It is their first and, so help them God, their last sally into this stupid business of research."[5]

These sentiments continue to be strong. As the survey results confirm, economists nowadays value pure theoretical research over applied research. They favor academic jobs over real-world jobs. Accordingly, economists do not perceive themselves as professionals in the way medical doctors do. They are foremost *academics.*

Because they are academics, economists are wedded to academic institutions. Their lives revolve around the academic rituals of department meetings, tenure decisions, academic journals, classes, students, summer and other grants, sabbaticals, academic or faculty councils, committee meetings, and so on. Their first commitment is to the communication behind the ivory towers. Some, with warm hearts, will venture into the public realm—flying to Washington to testify, serving on the Council of Economic Advisors, doing a consulting job here and there, or writing for the general public or students. But they run the risk of going too far. Too much public service will elicit among colleagues the reaction that the person has "given up," "copped out," or "stopped doing serious work." The disciplinary measure for senior academics is a downgrading in academic prestige; the as-yet-untenured members simply do not become tenured.

Similar downgrading awaits economists who fail to heed the separations between academic departments and trespass on the domain of other departments in pursuit of knowledge. One can switch from, say, game theory to linear programming of even to economic history, but incorporating anthropological theory or psychological theory as an economist is a taboo in most economics departments.[6]

The Number of Economists

The economics profession is controlled by elite academics, but they make up only a small percentage of the total number of economists. We estimate that in the United States the core elite is 500 to 600 strong, and on the periphery of the elite are another 1,500 economists. All have Ph.D.'s; most have academic appointments. The profession itself, however, is significantly larger and has a quite different makeup.

Precise numbers of economists are hard to come by. According to the Bureau of the Census definition, there are approximately 130,000 economists in the United States. This number includes not only academic economists but other individuals who report themselves as being economists. (It generally takes a Ph.D. to get an academic job as an economist but only a friendly employer to become an economist in business; there is no license required as for doctors and lawyers.) If the definition is limited to those with advanced degrees in economics—M.A.'s and Ph.D.'s—the figure falls to approximately 60,000 economists whose highest degree is the M.A. and 17,500 whose highest degree is the Ph.D. in the subject.[7]

Of the approximately 130,000 economists, 52 percent work in business and industry, 20 percent in academia, 15 percent in the federal government, and 8 percent in some other level of government (5 percent are "other").[8] Of those in business and industry, roughly 8 percent have Ph.D.'s, compared with roughly three-fourths in academia.[9] The economics profession—its common usage compels us to stick to this term—is a predominately male profession, increasingly so at higher education levels: Women's representation is 30 percent at the bachelor level, 23 percent at the master's level, and 14 percent at the doctorate level.

The average annual salary for all economists in 1982 was $35,000. In recent years, salaries have risen significantly. New Ph.D.'s who started their academic jobs in the fall of 1988 probably had initial job offers with pay somewhere in the $30,000–$40,000 range. Some economists supplement their income with consulting fees, which can range from $50 to $500 an hour.

What economists do depends on where they work. Academic economists teach, do extensive committee work at the college or university that employs them, and carry on "research," which generally takes the form of writing articles. To provide outlets for all the articles, there has been a steady increase in the number of economics journals, from 15 in 1920 to 112 in 1963 to well over 200 in 1980.[10] The focus on articles is different from that in other social science disciplines, such as history and political science, where researchers generally write books rather than articles. Writing articles is, however, common in physics and the other natural sciences.

Government economists' primary activity is providing background studies and advice for decisionmakers and reporting statistics. They do not write articles but usually write internal memos, studies, and reports that are not published. Much of their work is what is called "fire-fighting"—a quick, superficial consideration of a problem or proposal—but they also do in-depth studies that require a larger view and a longer time to prepare. Such studies often play a role in the shaping of future governmental policy.

A small number of economists work for independent research institutes (think tanks), which are a type of university without students. Examples are the Brookings Institution, the Rand Corporation, the National Bureau of Economic Research, the Heritage Foundation, and the American Enterprise Institute. At these institutions, the research is more policy-oriented than is research done at universities, but is more academic than that done in government. Their publication outlet is often books or pamphlets, and these institutions play a significant role in new policy initiatives in government.

Business economists are the least likely to have advanced degrees in economics, and those who do are often trained in business schools rather than in graduate schools in economics. Their output is generally represented by memos or briefings held for other officers in the firm. For most business economists, forecasting is the primary responsibility.

The difference between what economists in different areas do is demonstrated by the small transition among areas. The flow of economists between academia and business is insignificant; between 1979 and 1981, for example, only 130 moved from one to the other. The transition that does take place is lopsided, with 120 economists making the switch from academia to business; only 10 made the opposite move.

A few business and government economists join the American Economic Association. The AEA has about 20,000 members, the majority of whom are academics. In 1985 the job-listing service of the AEA showed 2,075 openings posted with the association, of which nearly two-thirds were for academic positions. Four-year colleges and universities with graduate programs accounted for roughly 80 percent of those openings.

As we have stressed before, reputations of the schools matter a great deal in the academic world. They affect the chances the schools' Ph.D.'s have in the job market and dictate the academic standing of their faculties. Making it to the top as an academic economist is hard to do without a Ph.D. from one of the top twenty schools. Most economists define "making it to the top" as getting a tenured position at one of the top twenty schools. As could be expected, the precise ranking of what schools make up the top twenty is in dispute. Good criteria simply do not exist. One criterion often used is the number of citations the faculty gets in academic journals. This produces the ranking shown in Table 1.1.

Undergraduate Training

Our student at the beginning of this chapter is 1 out of 30,000 undergraduate students who graduate with a major in economics each year (a relatively small group if one considers that about one million or so students a year take introductory economics). Thirty thousand is about 2 percent of all college seniors. At liberal arts colleges, however, economics majors are a much higher percentage of total college enrollment, often comprising 25–30 percent of all seniors. The reason is that most liberal arts economics majors are actually business majors in disguise. These students have no intention of becoming economists; they are planning to go into business, with banking, finance, and general management the most popular fields. Only 2 percent of the majors are working as economists two years after graduation. Because business is not an acceptable liberal arts major, students major in the closest thing to it—economics.

Economics majors are above average academically, with average combined SAT scores of 1216, compared with a nationwide average of about 890. Their average GPA (grade point average) is 3.23 in economics courses and 3.18 overall (on a 4-point scale).[11]

There are three core areas in the undergraduate training: macroeconomics, microeconomics, and statistics and econometrics. After studying the core courses, students choose among specialties, such as public finance, international trade, money and banking, corporate finance, industrial organization, political economy, and history of economic thought. The types of special courses offered vary from school to school and tend to depend upon the interest of the faculty.

Table 1.1
University ranking controlling for age and citation dispersion

	Number of Citations Controlling for Age and Dispersion*	Rank Controlling Only for Age	Rank Controlling for Dispersion
1. Harvard	500	1	1
2. Princeton	366	2	5
3. Chicago	364	3	2
4. MIT	277	5	3
5. Pennsylvania	271	7	4
6. Stanford	245	4	6
7. Yale	230	6	8
8. Wisconsin-Madison	214	9	7
9. UC-Los Angeles	201	11	10
10. Columbia	180	8	12
11. Berkeley	175	13	9
12. Michigan	168	16	11
13. Northwestern	160	16	11
14. Rochester	131	18	14
15. Washington	110	21	16
16. Maryland	107	12	19
17. Minnesota	103	20	13
18. Virginia	102	30	20
19. New York University	92	15	18
20. Illinois	88	24	21
21. USC	76	14	22
22. VPI	74	17	27
23. Michigan State	68	23	23
24. Cal Tech	68	25	26
25. Duke	66	36	17
26. George Washington	64	26	25
27. Johns Hopkins	60	29	29
28. Washington	60	39	24
29. UC–San Diego	59	27	33
30. Purdue	58	22	38
31. Boston	55	28	32
32. Massachusetts-Amherst	51	19	34
33. Brown	50	37	34
34. Cornell	48	32	28
35. UC–Santa Barbara	44	35	31
36. Arizona	42	33	36
37. Ohio State	37	38	35
38. Texas-Austin	36	34	37
39. Claremont	24	31	39
40. Colorado-Boulder	10	40	40

*Where the number of citations is identical, ranking was by magnitudes after the decimal point.
Source: Paul Davis and Gustav F. Papanek, American Economic Review, 74 (March 1984), p. 228.
Reprinted by permission of the American Economic Association.

Graduate Training

Of the 30,000 economics majors, only a minute percentage pursue graduate degrees, and those who do have often gone on to something else before they enter graduate school. Graduate school enrollment is supplemented by foreign students and noneconomics majors (among whom many are mathematics majors). Foreign students make up approximately 30 percent of the graduate student body. Most of the students who begin graduate school in economics choose not to complete it, so the number of Ph.D.'s is significantly smaller than the number of first-year graduate students. The annual output of M.A.'s is about 1,800 and of Ph.D.'s is about 800.

The doctorate normally requires the full-time concentration of the student for four years. Formal requirements are limited in number: The candidate must (1) achieve a specified level of competence in core fields; (2) demonstrate competence in four fields of study in economics; (3) submit and defend a dissertation that represents a contribution to knowledge; and (4) be in residence for a minimum of two years. Candidates differ in their rates of progress, depending on their abilities, their backgrounds, their interests, and their preparation. Normally, however, the satisfaction of all requirements except the dissertation is completed by the end of the second year.

The first two years of graduate study are composed of course work. What is taught in these graduate courses is quite different from what is taught in undergraduate school. There is much greater emphasis on technical issues. Most undergraduate schools teach a mix of common sense and lowbrow theory that might be called neo-Marshallian and neo-Keynesian economics. This lowbrow theory uses supply/demand geometric tools. In graduate school, a highbrow theory—neo-Walrasian economics—is taught. This highbrow theory is more precise, but has far less institutional richness than does undergraduate economics. The focus of graduate school courses is on issues such as search theory and dynamic disequilibria, and a typical course will use highly technical mathematical tools and concepts. One might say that graduate school builds vertically from undergraduate education rather than linearly: It formalizes concepts the student met in undergraduate study—teaching new tools that can be used to analyze the same issues more carefully rather than teaching how to make better use of the undergraduate tools.

At the end of two years, students generally take comprehensive exams. If they pass, they become ABD's (all but dissertation done). The third year of graduate study consists of some course work, but emphasis is on workshops or seminars in which students develop ideas into papers that are to form the basis for writing a dissertation. The fourth year is spent writing a dissertation, which should be a contribution to knowledge in a particular subfield. The minimum length of time required to earn a Ph.D. is three years. Usually it takes six or seven years, although often in the final two or three years the students are also working full-time.

The central focus in this book is on the graduate education of a small group of economists—those at elite schools. It is the members of this core group who shape what economics is and what economists do. Each year roughly 100 individuals graduate who have a chance of joining this core group, and nearly all come from these elite institutions. Only a few will ultimately be recognized as the movers and shakers in the discipline.

As previously mentioned, the academic elite is small. It numbers about 500 or 600 and has maybe 1,500 more on the fringes. These are the economists who are committed to academic pursuits. They communicate with each other mainly through scholarly articles in academic journals and by conferring in seminars and conferences. Their work is the stuff that students of economics will have to learn. Being part of that core is the aspiration of most academic economists. Mindful of that goal, undergraduate advisers understandably tell students to go to graduate school if they want to become serious economists. Once in graduate school, students will discover that getting into the academic elite is what graduate education is all about.

The Making
of an Economist

As economists, we have an interest in and individual knowledge of the initiation process that turns students into professional economists. However, other than anecdotal evidence, very little in the way of data exists. This chapter is a step toward providing insight into that process.

There are differing opinions about graduate economic education; most are privately expressed. However, some do surface, usually the most critical. For example, Robert Kuttner,[1] summarizing the views of critical economists such as Wassily Leontief and John Kenneth Galbraith, writes: "Departments of economics are graduating a generation of *idiots savants*, brilliant at esoteric mathematics yet innocent of actual economic life." Our study of graduate education provides some data to help in assessing such views.

Besides being of general interest, information on the making of economists is important to the sociological and the rhetorical approach to economic methodology.[2] The graduate school experience plays an important role in determining economic discourse; it certifies economists as professionals; it establishes economists' views of argumentation and guides them as to what is important to study and what is not. To understand economic discourse, one should have a good sense of the professionalization of economists that occurs in graduate school.

We obtained our data from questionnaires distributed to graduate students at six top-ranking graduate economics programs—the University of Chicago, Columbia University, Harvard University, Massachusetts Institute of Technology, Stanford University, and Yale University—exploring who current graduate students are and what they think about

This chapter originally appeared in the *Journal of Economic Perspectives* (Fall 1987): 95–111. Reprinted, with minor changes, by permission of the American Economic Association.

economics, the economy, and graduate school. The 212 respondents were relatively equally divided by year of study. (See Appendix 2A for a discussion of the questionnaire and methodology.) We followed up our survey with a series of interviews. We present the information gained from the questionnaire in four sections, keeping our editorial discussion to a minimum.

Profile of Students

The typical graduate student in economics at these selected institutions is a 26-year-old, middle-class, nonreligious white male who is involved in a long-term relationship. (In our sample 18.9 percent were female; there was one Hispanic and no blacks.) Most had attended highly competitive undergraduate colleges and came from relatively well-to-do families. More than half (54 percent) of their fathers and 23 percent of the mothers had advanced degrees; the average family income was approximately $50,000. Eighty-seven percent majored or concentrated in economics as undergraduates, 28 percent in mathematics, 24 percent in other social sciences, 15 percent in the humanities, and 9 percent in the natural sciences. (Students could have both a major and a concentration.) For most students (63 percent), graduate work in economics was their only choice of career when they applied. Those who contemplated alternatives considered policy-related work or law school. Part of the reason for such clear focus is that 50 percent of the students had worked, traveled, or studied in another graduate field before they began their economics graduate program.

George Stigler has remarked that economics tends to make individuals conservative.[3] At least at this stage of their career, that was not the case with our respondents. In terms of political views, 47 percent considered themselves liberal, 22 percent moderate, 15 percent conservative, and 12 percent radical. (Four percent were "other.") Thus, at least for students at the top schools, the majority see themselves as predominantly liberal.

Interests of Students

When asked an open question as to what they most liked and disliked about graduate school, 36 percent stated they most liked the intellectual environment and 24 percent said they liked the courses and research. As to the things they liked least, the majority of comments focused on the heavy load of mathematics and theory and a lack of relevance of the material they were learning. Whatever their reservations, only 6 percent said they would definitely not do it again; 21 percent were unsure.[4]

In terms of future jobs, 53 percent were planning to pursue an academic career, 33 percent were planning to go into policy-related work, 17 percent into business, 8 percent into research institutes, and 2 percent into journalism.[5] These results are roughly consistent with an unpublished study by the National Science Foundation, which found that 60 percent of all new economics Ph.D.'s plan to enter academia.[6] Our lower percentage may be accounted for by the difference in the sampled populations: graduate students versus new Ph.D.'s. The difference would then suggest that students not planning to enter academia are more likely to drop out.

The academic jobs the students desired were primarily at research universities. Forty-one percent wanted to be at a major university fifteen years from now, 32 percent at a policy-oriented research institute, 16 percent at a good liberal arts college, 11 percent at a major research institute, and 9 percent in the private sector. The students confirmed these preferences in the interviews. As one student said: "That's definitely not the thing to do—to walk into [a well-known professor's] office and announce that you want to teach at [a major liberal arts college]."

Not all of the 53 percent had academia on their mind when they entered. In our conversations, several students referred to peer pressure and the opinion of their professors as important factors in their decisions. When alternatives to a career at a major institution came up in a conversation among fourth-year students, the students emphasized the problems. One student noted, "It is very hard [to go into a public policy job] when a lot of friends, and certainly the faculty, are judging you by how good a job you get. When you want to succeed in their eyes, you get a job at a major university. It is very hard to chuck all this and be a failure in the eyes of all those people who have been very important in the last four years."

If graduate schools are graduating *idiots savants* who have no interest in policy, it is not because students enter graduate school with no interest. The majority of students (53 percent) considered a desire to engage in policy formation very important in their decision to attend graduate school; only 17 percent considered such a desire unimportant. The other significant reason for attending graduate school was enjoyment of their undergraduate major in economics (53 percent); 13 percent considered that unimportant. During graduate school 71 percent worked as teaching or research assistants, 11 percent worked as consultants, and 11 percent did political work. (Some students did more than one kind of work.) Thirty-four percent were already in the process of writing scholarly papers for publication.

In the survey as well as in our conversations, concern about the relevance of economics dominated. When asked what the major factor

Table 2.1
The importance of reading in other fields

	Very important	Important	Moderately important	Unimportant
Mathematics	41	32	21	6
History	34	34	24	8
Political science	24	30	33	13
Sociology	16	29	35	21
Philosophy	15	27	27	15
Psychology	9	20	44	27
Computer science	8	26	35	30
Physics	2	6	27	64

in their choice of dissertation topic was, or would be, there was a focus on wanting to do relevant work. When asked about the factors that influence the choice of the dissertation, the majority (67 percent) stated that they wanted to understand some economic phenomenon. Seventeen percent said that getting the dissertation done was an important reason, while 4 percent mentioned the applicability of certain mathematical or econometric techniques.

Jacob Viner once said that "men are not narrow in their intellectual interests by nature; it takes special and rigorous training to accomplish that end." Based on our survey, we can conclude that graduate economics education is succeeding in narrowing students' interests. Most of the respondents had wide interests, but class work left little time to follow up these other interests. We asked them how important to their development as an economist readings in various fields would be; their responses are shown in Table 2.1. Even though most graduate students believed that reading in areas such as history and political science, and to a lesser extent, sociology and philosophy, was important for their development as economists, we found from our interviews that most did not undertake such reading because they lacked the time.

Another indication of the narrowing process is that students also felt that graduate school gave them little opportunity for interdisciplinary discussions. Even though 60 percent said they had frequent interactions with students or scholars in other disciplines, only 13 percent thought those interactions intellectual.

The interests of our respondents (ranked by percentage of students having great interest) are given in Table 2.2. In terms of interest among areas within economics, our respondents mirrored a hierarchy that Benjamin Ward argued exists, although there were some notable exceptions.[7] Microeconomics and macroeconomics coincide with Ward's sug-

Table 2.2
Interest of students by area

Area	Great interest	Moderate interest	No interest
Macro	42.6	43.5	13.9
Political economy	36.1	38.0	25.5
Micro	35.7	48.3	15.9
International	30.5	43.8	25.7
Industrial organization	30.1	45.1	24.8
Money and banking	28.0	41.1	30.9
Development	26.0	42.3	31.7
Labor	24.6	40.1	35.3
Econometrics	22.4	55.7	21.9
Public finance	18.9	47.6	30.5
History of thought	18.7	50.2	30.6
Law and economics	10.6	40.1	47.3
Comparative	9.3	42.4	48.6
Urban	5.4	27.0	67.6

gested hierarchy of the profession. Econometrics is lower but has a significant amount of moderate interest. Economic development and industrial organization ranked higher than Ward suggested they would. Political economy (not found in Ward's classification) received significant interest. (Political economy would include both neoclassical political economy, such as public choice, and Marxist political economy.)

One of the objectives of our study was a better understanding of the perceptions of their discourse that students acquire in graduate school. For that reason, we asked them what abilities will likely place students on a fast track. That question provided some of the most dramatic results of our survey.[8] We presented students with possible abilities that they ranked as shown in Table 2.3.

Knowledge of the economy and knowledge of economics literature do not make an economist successful, according to graduate students. Forty-three percent believed that a knowledge of economics literature was unimportant, while only 10 percent felt that it was very important. Sixty-eight percent believed that a thorough knowledge of the economy was unimportant; only 3.4 percent believed that it was very important. The attitude about the importance of knowledge about the economy was confirmed in our interviews. The following typical comment was given in response to a question about what students thought of class work:

One of the questions of your survey was, "What puts students on the fast track?" and if I remember correctly, one of the choices was "general

Table 2.3
Perceptions of success

	Very important	Moderately important	Unimportant	Don't Know
Being smart in the sense of being good at problem solving	65	32	3	1
Excellence in mathematics	57	41	2	0
Being very knowledgeable about one particular field	37	42	19	2
Ability to make connections with prominent professors	26	50	16	9
Being interested in, and good at, empirical research	16	60	23	1
Having a broad knowledge of the economics literature	10	41	43	5
Having a thorough knowledge of the economy	3	22	68	7

knowledge about the economy." You can walk in off the street and take the courses and not know what the Fortune 500 is and blaze through with flying colors. You can also come in and know the difference between subordinated debentures and junk bonds and fail miserably.

Clearly these results raise significant questions about the nature of graduate school, what is being taught, and the socialization process that occurs. The issues raised here are complicated ones, but the results suggest that these issues need to be addressed by the profession.

In the questionnaire, we did not ask whether students like what they perceive in graduate school, nor are graduate students necessarily the ones to ask. As Robert Solow stated when commenting on this paper, "To say that something is wrong with graduate education is to say that something is wrong with the economics profession."

For what it is worth, the interviews suggested a definite tension, frustration, and cynicism that, in our view, went beyond the normal graduate school blues. There was a strong sense that economics was a game and that hard work in devising relevant models that demonstrated a deep understanding of institutions would have a lower payoff than devising models that were analytically neat; the facade, not the depth of knowledge, was important. This cynicism is not limited to the graduate school experience, but is applied also to the state of the art as they perceive it. A fourth-year student stated:

We go to the money workshop. You'd think that for our edification the faculty would bring in supposedly some of the best young people throughout

Table 2.4
Economic opinions of graduate students compared to Frey Study of
American economists

| | | Graduate students | | | | American economists | |
	yes	yes but	no	not[a] sure	yes	yes but	no
Fiscal policy can be an effective tool in stabilizing policy.[b]	35	49	11	5	65	27	8
The FRB should maintain a constant money growth.	9	34	45	12	14	25	61
A minimum wage increases unemployment among young and unskilled workers.	34	39	18	9	68	22	10
Tariffs and import quotas reduce general economic welfare.	36	49	9	6	81	16	3
Inflation is primarily a monetary phenomenon.	27	33	29	11	27	30	43
Wage-price controls should be used to control inflation.	1	17	73	9	6	22	72
Worker democracy will increase labor productivity.	13	40	22	24	—	—	—
The market system tends to discriminate against women.	24	27	39	10	—	—	—
The capitalist system has an inherent tendency toward crisis.	8	23	59	13	—	—	—
The income distribution in developed nations should be more equal.	47	32	14	7	40	31	29

[a] The survey of Frey, *et al.* did not allow the "not sure" option.
[b] The question as formulated in the Frey survey is; Does fiscal policy have a stimulative impact on a less than fully employed economy?

the country to give macro talks about their current research. All of us go, week after week, and come back and just laugh at their big reputations. What they do is usually very complicated and very implausible.

Differences Between Graduate Students and the Profession

Bruno Frey and his colleagues recently surveyed the beliefs of U.S. economists.[9] Our questionnaire included questions similar to theirs, allowing us to compare their reponses for U.S. economists with ours for graduate students. Table 2.4 compares the two sets of results. As can be seen in this percentage comparison, graduate students tend to qualify their conclusions, especially about the role of quotas and tariffs and the effectiveness of fiscal policy, much more than do most U.S. economists.

Distinctive Characteristics of Graduate Programs

In an insightful study of the economics profession, George Stigler and Claire Friedland pose this question: "Are the major centers of graduate instruction in the U.S. 'schools' in the sense of leaving distinctive imprints upon their doctorates?" They examine the citation practices from 1950 to 1968 of economists who received their doctorates between 1950 and 1955. Stigler and Friedland find "genuine differences among the universities in the attention and respect paid to various scholars." But the differences are so small, according to them, they they do not provide evidence for the existence of divergent schools of economic thought.[10]

Unlike the study by Stigler and Friedland, our survey does not cover research interests after graduate school, but it gives insight into the opinions that graduate students hold. The results shown in Table 2.5 demonstrate that graduate schools, particularly Stigler's own University of Chicago, have distinctive characteristics. For example, differences come out clearly in the answers to questions about economics as a science.

The "Total" column in Table 2.5 reveals that the scientific status of economics is clearly in doubt among students. A majority deny two key elements of any objective science: the distinction between positive and normative economics and agreement on fundamental issues. However, those views are not evenly distributed among schools. For example, if MIT and Harvard are excluded, a small majority would conclude that economists do agree on fundamental issues.

The response indicates that Chicago students are most convinced of the relevance of neoclassical economics, and Harvard students least convinced. Apart from the Chicago students, the majority of graduate students question the possibility of separating positive and normative economics. In fact, three-quarters of those at MIT and five-sixths of those at Harvard deny the distinction between positive and normative economics. Chicago accepts it; other schools have bare majorities against.

The differences among schools are brought out more clearly when we compare the opinions of students at various schools on economic opinions in Table 2.6 and on the importance of economic assumptions in Table 2.7. These two tables strongly support the hypothesis that Chicago constitutes a "school" that is distinct from other schools. It

Table 2.5
Opinions of economics as a science: comparison among schools

	Chicago	MIT	Harvard	Stanford	Columbia	Yale	Total
Neoclassical economics is relevant for the economic problems of today.							
strongly agree	69	31	20	34	24	33	34
agree somewhat	28	56	56	60	68	60	54
disagree	3	11	22	6	8	8	11
no clear opinion	0	2	2	0	0	0	1
Economists agree on fundamental issues.							
strongly agree	3	4	2	2	4	13	4
agree somewhat	47	31	27	51	48	33	40
disagree	44	60	68	43	44	47	52
no clear opinion	6	4	2	4	4	7	4
There is a sharp line between positive and normative economics.							
strongly agree	22	7	9	9	0	7	9
agree somewhat	38	16	4	30	32	33	23
disagree	34	73	84	55	52	60	62
no clear opinion	6	4	2	6	16	0	6
Economics is the most scientific social science.							
strongly agree	47	27	9	27	36	13	28
agree somewhat	28	36	43	31	24	47	39
disagree	9	24	30	23	28	40	19
no clear opinion	16	13	18	19	12	0	14

seems to be a creed at Chicago that inflation is primarily a monetary phenomenon, with 100 percent agreeing with the proposition. At Harvard, 46 percent disagree. Likewise, it seems a creed at MIT that fiscal policy can be an effective tool for stabilization, with no student disagreeing. At Chicago, 44 percent disagree.

The differences are also significant in the responses to the microeconomic questions. Chicago students have a significantly higher degree of confidence in the market than do students at other schools. Harvard shows most variety in the answers, with a significant number of the students skeptical of the market.

The "Total" column in Table 2.7 shows that most graduate students found the rationality assumption important, but were cautious about the rational expectations hypothesis. Only 17 percent considered the hypothesis very important, while 25 percent considered it unimportant.

Table 2.6
Economic opinions: a comparison among schools

	Chicago	MIT	Harvard	Stanford	Columbia	Yale
Fiscal policy can be an effective tool in stabilizing policy.						
strongly agree	6	48	30	30	54	60
agree with reservations	34	51	65	52	38	33
disagree	44	0	2	9	8	7
no clear opinion	16	2	2	9	0	0
The Fed should maintain a constant growth of the money supply.						
agree	41	0	7	2	4	0
agree with reservations	44	27	24	39	50	21
disagree	9	60	57	44	33	64
no clear opinion	6	13	11	15	13	14
A minimum wage increases unemployment among young and unskilled workers.						
agree	70	24	15	36	38	33
agree with reservations	28	53	41	40	25	27
disagree	3	11	35	19	21	13
no clear opinion	0	11	9	4	9	27
Tariffs and import quotas reduce general economic welfare.						
agree	66	38	20	32	38	33
agree with reservations	34	42	56	51	54	60
disagree	0	13	11	9	8	7
no clear opinion	0	4	13	9	0	0
Inflation is primarily a monetary phenomenon.						
agree	84	7	15	23	29	13
agree with reservations	16	44	26	45	25	40
disagree	0	36	46	23	33	33
no clear opinion	0	11	11	10	13	13
The market system tends to discriminate against women.						
agree	6	24	44	11	38	27
agree with reservations	19	22	20	38	21	53
disagree	69	40	26	43	33	13
no clear opinion	3	13	11	9	8	7
The distribution of income in developed nations should be more equal.						
agree	16	52	54	52	46	60
agree with reservations	50	30	33	24	37	20
disagree	19	9	13	17	9	20
no clear opinion	15	9	0	7	9	7

Table 2.7
Importance of economic assumptions

	Chicago	Harvard	MIT	Stanford	Total
Rationality assumptions					
very important	78	35	44	58	51
important in some cases	22	51	44	36	41
unimportant	0	14	9	6	7
no strong opinion	0	0	0	0	1
Rational expectations					
very important	59	14	0	9	17
important in some cases	38	45	71	53	53
unimportant	0	38	18	32	25
no strong opinion	3	2	7	6	5
Price rigidities					
very important	6	37	38	26	27
important in some cases	56	54	56	65	60
unimportant	38	7	4	4	10
no strong opinion	0	2	0	4	3
Imperfect competition					
very important	16	47	51	38	40
important in some cases	72	47	44	60	55
unimportant	9	7	0	2	4
no strong opinion	3	0	2	0	2
Cost mark-up pricing					
very important	0	7	9	11	9
important in some cases	16	48	62	41	46
unimportant	50	26	18	33	26
no strong opinion	34	19	9	15	18
Behavior according to conventions					
very important	0	16	18	4	4
important in some cases	31	55	69	64	25
unimportant	31	9	2	4	57
no strong opinion	38	20	11	28	15

The assumption of imperfect competition and the assumption of price rigidities ranked higher than the rational expectations assumption.

Looking at the breakdown among schools, we see that Chicago students, compared with students in other schools, demonstrate the greatest commitment to neoclassical economics, with significant support for the rational expectations hypothesis and relatively less interest in the assumptions of price rigidity, imperfect competition, and cost mark-up pricing. (One could also say that other schools demonstrate little support for Chicago ideas. As one third-year MIT student noted, "There are no Lucas types [at MIT].") It is particularly striking that not a single MIT student thinks the rational expectations assumption is very important.

Chicago was unique in other areas as well. For example, only 19 pecent of the Chicago students perceive a significant tension between their course work and their interests. This number contrasts with an average of 42 percent for the other schools. No stress is reported by 60 percent at Chicago, compared with an average of 28 percent at the other schools.

While Chicago definitely constitutes a specific school, there is nonetheless some evidence that other programs do too. Were we to generalize, we would say that Harvard students appear to be most skeptical, whereas Stanford students place themselves in the spectrum of opinions between Chicago and MIT students.

The fact that Chicago represents a different school does not mean that the school shapes the students to its image. The students could have been self-selected. We tested this possibility in two ways. First, we asked students to compare their beliefs before graduate school with their beliefs now in regard to certain issues such as the relevance of neoclassical economics, whether a sharp line can be drawn between positive and normative economics, and whether economics is the most scientific of the social sciences. No clear-cut conclusion emerged from these questions. Approximately 50 percent of the students felt that they had not changed their minds in graduate school. Among those who did change their minds, for the total sample of all schools there was no clear-cut movement toward or away from the beliefs associated with that school.

Looking at the data by school, however, one can detect a slight pattern, especially at Chicago. For example, at Chicago 44 percent did not change their view about the relevance of neoclassical economics from what it was before graduate school. The 56 percent who did change their mind were divided as follows: 3 percent thought it less relevant, and 53 percent thought it more relevant. This is in direct contrast to other schools. For example, at MIT 62 percent of the students believed that they did not change their view of the relevance of neoclassical economics from what it was before graduate school, but those who did change their mind were split: 22 percent thought neoclassical economics more relevant, 16 percent thought it less relevant.

Another example can be seen in students' beliefs about how scientific economics is. Forty-seven percent of the Chicago students did not change their mind; 34 percent thought economics more scientific; 19 percent thought it less scientific. At MIT 71 percent of the students did not change their mind on this question; 7 percent thought it more scientific; 22 percent thought it less scientific. These data suggest that schools tend to reinforce previously held positions.

Although we did not ask questions about previous beliefs on economic policy, we were able to separate answers to questions by year of study and thereby capture changes in views that occurred after the first year.

This provided a second test, although its results are inconclusive because the study was done in the spring, and it is possible that first-year students could have already been influenced by the school. Still, this test also suggests that self-selection is important but that some adjustment and reinforcement of views occur at graduate school. For example, at MIT 66 percent of first- and second-year students agreed that inflation was a monetary phenomenon, whereas only 42 percent of fourth- and fifth-year students agreed. (At Chicago 100 percent agreed in all years.) But the comparison also presented some anomalies. For example, at Harvard 26 percent of first- and second-year students felt that inflation was primarily a monetary phenomenon, while 53 percent of fourth- and fifth-year students believed that it was.

Answers to the two other questions provide a good sense of the reinforcement of views that occurs in graduate school: 58 percent of first- and second-year Chicago students believed that fiscal policy could be effective, but only 36 percent of the fourth- and fifth-year students believed that it was. At Harvard and MIT all but one student in all years agreed that fiscal policy is effective. In response to a question about the minimum wage, all Chicago students in all years believed it increased unemployment; of Harvard students in the first and second year 45 percent disagreed; in the fourth and fifth year only 24 percent disagreed.

Our conclusion from these two incomplete tests is that although some adjusting to the school view does occur in graduate school, unless the changes occur in the first year, the predominant factor in determining the beliefs of a graduate school student is self-selection. Graduate schools modify those beliefs somewhat, but often reinforce previously existing views.

Some Thoughts About the Implications

Reporting the data is one thing; interpreting them is another. We were especially struck by a series of tensions that emerged in the making of economists. Graduate students are interested in policy; most entered economics because they hoped it would shed light on policy. In the early years when they learn techniques and basic skills, the application to policy is limited; this causes some frustration for the students, as shown in the following conversations:

STUDENT 1: It seems to me that we spent six weeks in the macroeconomics course where we did a lot of algebra, we took a lot of derivatives, but we never really talked about how applicable these models were, how reasonable these assumptions were.

STUDENT 2: I don't think we get policy at all in our courses. Well, there's theory of commercial policy, but we don't really get policy in that. We get questions like what's the optimum tariff.

Some students argued for the advantage of specializing in technique. Other students disagreed, as can be seen in the following exchange:

STUDENT 3: I think there are two things going on. One is the first year we're getting equipped [with the basics]. I think it's very important to make sure that we cover an agenda of items. And I think there's another feeling—I've seen this in a quote of Solow's—that policy is sort of for simpletons. If you really know your theory, the policy implications are pretty straightforward. It's not the really challenging meat-and-potato stuff for a really sharp theorist. I think that's another reason why they don't spend much time on applications.[11]

STUDENT 4: Not necessarily. I feel that the implementation of policy is a much trickier question than those people give it credit for. A guy like [names an instructor], for instance, on the faculty here, is very concerned with that sort of thing, and I get the impression that he's almost sneered at for caring about the institutional problems that come along with implementing theoretical results. And there are very few other people on the faculty whose work takes that sort of thing into consideration.

The other students agreed.

To make it through the first two years of graduate school, students have to focus on technique. Thus, the graduates are well trained in problem solving, but it is a technical approach, which has more to do with formal modeling techniques than with real-world problems. To do the problems, little real-world knowledge of institutions is needed, and in many cases such knowledge would actually be a hindrance because the simplifying assumptions would be harder to accept.

Students come into graduate school wanting economics to be relevant, and they are taught theory and techniques that point out the complexity of the problems. But they quickly come around; they perceive the incentives in the system. They are convinced that formal modeling is important to success, but are not convinced that the formal models provide deep insight into or reflect a solid understanding of the economic institutions being modeled. Believing this, they want to be trained in what the profession values. Thus we find that students who believe they are not being taught the most complicated theory feel deprived and unhappy because they worry about the ability to compete.

The value students place on learning technique can be seen clearly in the interviews with students at Columbia. In response to a question about how they and the faculty would respond to bringing in a higher level of theoretical economists, they stated:

STUDENT 1: If you ask me, that's [the absence of a high-level theoretical economist] one of the weaknesses of Columbia when we go into the job market. We don't have a high-level theorist here.

STUDENT 2: What do you mean—like pure money theory?

STUDENT 1: In micro. Micro theorists, topology—we don't have anyone like that here. We don't touch it.

Does that bother you?

STUDENT 3: Yes, it worries me greatly because I'm interested in micro theory. That's what I want to do.

STUDENT 1: It's a liability not to understand foundations.

STUDENT 2: I kind of think that math for math's sake is nice—just to learn the math—and then it's a good way of thinking. And then maybe some of it might be relevant to economic ideas.

The likely reason for students' transformation into technique-oriented individuals is that most of them aspire to academic jobs. They know that tenure depends on publication in the right journals. They logically choose a course of study that is most likely to lead to their goal of succeeding in that intermediate goal. Knowing a technique that can be applied to ten areas can lead to ten articles; knowing a specific area well might lead to one or two articles. Thus, students see little incentive to know the literature in an area or to have institutional knowledge of a particular area. This emphasis does not reflect their lack of concern about policy; it reflects the perceived incentives in the system. Novelty in approach, not slogging through enormous amounts of data or becoming an expert in the literature, is important.

Conclusion

We are not saying that graduate education in economics is bad or good. We are merely stating how students perceive the incentives and providing a possible explanation for why those incentives exist. If we are correct in our explanation, these incentives are the inevitable result of other aspects of the economics profession that we have not considered here. It is not because of the interest of students. Thus, it seems that some very real socialization process is going on. In our conversations, the students frequently brought up the subject themselves, often using the notion of socialization:

STUDENT 1 (A FOURTH-YEAR STUDENT): I came into economics with little economics and math and felt very much that I was being socialized into something and put through a wringer of linear algebra. After the first two years it has been fabulous. The thesis-writing process has been really fun.

STUDENT 2 (A FIRST-YEAR STUDENT): The first year seems to shape the rest of our career as an economist. It is really disturbing. We are moving into something but nobody really knows what that is, except that they were socialized in this way of thinking by people who got their Ph.D.'s five years ago. It's like being brainwashed. You are deprived of sleep. You are subjected to extreme stress, bombarded with contradictory notions, and you end up accepting anything.

STUDENT 3 (ANOTHER FOURTH-YEAR STUDENT): I feel that I have been socialized into the profession, into its way of thinking. When I came here I would have sworn that I was to go straight into political work. I was reasonably skeptical of these hoity-toity articles in academic journals where the thing to do is to get an academic position, write papers for journals, and the idea is that those who can't do economics do policy. ("Or teach at a liberal arts school," added another student.) Now the research side is more valuable, or maybe it is that I view that as the thing I am supposed to be doing.

Others present confirm this experience.

Our attempt in this chapter was to provide some empirical data that allow us better to understand the process that shapes economists. Certain results seem unambiguous and worth repeating. Specifically, there is a significant variety of opinions among graduate economics students and among the schools in the survey, and there definitely seems to be a Chicago school of economics. There are also tensions between the emphasis on techniques and the desire to do policy-oriented work. What students believe leads to success in graduate school is definitely techniques; success has little to do with understanding the economy, nor does it have much to do with economic literature. We hope that this information leads to discussion within the profession of whether this focus is good or bad.

Appendix 2A
Methodology of the Questionnaire

In 1985, 812 doctorates were awarded in economics. Judging from incomplete figures, we estimate that the six schools in our study awarded approximately 110; thus those of our sample schools represent about 14 percent of the total.

The questionnaire was distributed in the spring of 1985. The total number of respondents was 212 from an estimated population of 600–800, an approximate 25–30 percent response rate, normal for this type of study. There were 31 questions that the students took anywhere from 15 minutes to more than an hour to answer. The distribution of respondents by year was roughly equal: first, 24.5 percent; second, 20.8 percent; third, 21.7 percent; fourth, 14.2 percent; and fifth or more, 18.9 percent. We followed up our survey with a series of interviews.

The questionnaires were distributed at the six schools in two ways. Where possible (at all schools except Yale and Columbia), they were placed in individual student mailboxes. At Yale and Columbia they were distributed by a few selected individuals. This accounts for the lower response rate and adds a possible bias in the coverage at those schools; we therefore eliminated them in certain cross-school comparisons. Determining the total size of the student population is difficult because schools list individuals who have not finished dissertations as active students even though they may not be active students: still, the response rate was about 40 percent at Harvard, MIT, Chicago, and Stanford. The response rate at Yale and Columbia was lower, but because the results of the survey were not far out of line with the results from the other four schools, it seems reasonable to conclude that the results from these schools are valid.

The potential for bias in these surveys does, however, exist. Technically oriented students may be less likely to answer questionnaires. In our survey there were, for example, relatively few Asian students, who are believed to be more technically oriented than the typical U.S. student. Thus, as with all empirical research, the results must be interpreted with care.

Appendix 2B
Questionnaire for
Graduate Students in Economics

Background

1.   1. Age: _____   2. Sex: _____   3. Nationality: _____

      4. Ethnic Background: _____
      5. Are you involved in a long term relationship?   Yes / No
      6. Do you have children?   Yes / No
      7. Do you consider yourself religious?   Yes / No
         Denomination? _____

2.   1. Occupation of mother _____

      2. Education of mother _____

      3. Occupation of father _____

      4. Education of father _____

      5. Political orientation of father (check one)
         [ ] conservative; [ ] moderate; [ ] liberal; [ ] radical; [ ] don't know

6. Political orientation of mother (check one)
[ ] conservative; [ ] moderate; [ ] liberal; [ ] radical; [ ] don't know

7. In which of these groups did your parents' combined income from all sources fall last year before taxes? (check one)
[ ] Under $20,000
[ ] $20,001–40,000
[ ] $40,001–70,000
[ ] $70,001–100,000
[ ] Above $100,000
[ ] I really don't know

3. Which college(s) did you attend?   Name   Dates
                             1.
                             2.

   Undergraduate major: _____

   Other fields of concentration: _____

   Significant extracurricular activities in college:

4. Did you begin graduate work in economics immediately after earning your B.A.?   Yes / No
   If not, what did you do in between?

5. When did you first consider economics as a career?

6. At the time you were considering graduate work in economics, did you have alternative plans?   Yes / No

   If yes, what other options did you consider seriously?

7. a. How important were the following factors in your decision to do graduate work in economics?
   (3. very important; 2. somewhat important; 1. unimportant)

   1. enjoyed undergraduate classes in economics   3   2   1
   2. desire to engage in policy formulation   3   2   1
   3. good grades in economics classes   3   2   1
   4. advice of my undergraduate teachers   3   2   1
   5. acceptance by a good graduate school   3   2   1
   6. wanted to get a job in academia and economics
      seemed to offer the best possibility   3   2   1
   7. economics seemed the most relevant field given my
      intellectual interests   3   2   1
   8. political reasons   3   2   1

b. What other factor was very important?

c. Of the above factors, which (one, two, three) was/were the most important in your decision?

Graduate School

8.   In what year of graduate school are you? Check one.
[ ] first; [ ] second; [ ] third; [ ] fourth; [ ] fifth or more

9.   Did you receive a fellowship for graduate school in your first year?   Yes   No
If yes, which one? _____
Percentage of total financial need covered by fellowship? _____
How did you finance the expenses not covered by the fellowship?

10.   In which of the following activities, besides studying, are you currently engaged? (Check all applicable alternatives.)
[ ] research assistantship
[ ] teaching assistantship
[ ] consulting
[ ] the writing of scholarly papers for publication
[ ] political work
[ ] volunteer work
[ ] sports
[ ] other significant activities. Please specify:

11.   We would like you to consider the following statements and compare your current opinion with the one you held before you began graduate school. Circle the most appropriate numbers.
(4. strongly agree; 3. agree somewhat; 2. disagree; 1. no clear opinion)

CURRENT	STATEMENT	BEFORE
4 3 2 1	The study of neoclassical economics is relevant for the economic problems of today	4 3 2 1
4 3 2 1	Economists agree on the fundamental issues	4 3 2 1
4 3 2 1	We can draw a sharp line between positive and normative economics	4 3 2 1
4 3 2 1	Learning neoclassical economics means learning a set of tools	4 3 2 1
4 3 2 1	Economics is the most scientific discipline among the social sciences	4 3 2 1

12.   Can you think of any elements of graduate school that have been or are stressful for you? Circle one. (4. very stressful; 3. stressful; 2. moderately stressful; 1. not stressful)

coursework   4   3   2   1
your financial situation   4   3   2   1
relationships with faculty   4   3   2   1
relationships with students   4   3   2   1
doing the mathematics   4   3   2   1
finding a dissertation topic   4   3   2   1
maintaining a meaningful life
   outside graduate school   4   3   2   1
conflict between course content
   and your interests   4   3   2   1

13.   What do you like most about graduate school?

      What do you dislike most about graduate school?

14.   Where have you learned most about economics? Check one.
      [   ] in the classroom
      [   ] in seminars
      [   ] by reading assigned readings on your own
      [   ] by reading unassigned readings on your own
      [   ] in discussions with other students
      [   ] in your job as a research assistant
      [   ] teaching a section of principles or being a teaching asst.
      [   ] other. Specify:

15.   Rate the following fields with respect to your degree of interest. Circle one. (3. Of great interest to me; 2. of moderate interest to me; 1. Of no interest to me)

Microtheory   3 2 1   Macrotheory   3 2 1   Econometrics   3 2 1

Intern. Trade   3 2 1   Public Fin   3 2 1   Mon & Banking   3 2 1

Labor   3 2 1   Ind. Organ.   3 2 1   Law & Econ   3 2 1

Urban Econ   3 2 1   Econ Devel   3 2 1   Comp Econ Syst   3 2 1

Hist of Thought   3 2 1   Political Econ 3 2 1

In which fields are you, or will you be, specializing?

16.   Which professors in the graduate program are at the moment most important for you? (Please give name and field, and specify briefly the reason)
      1.

      2.

      3.

17. How important to your development as an economist would you, if you had the time, consider readings in or discussions about topics in the following fields? Circle one.
(4. very important; 3. important; 2. moderately important; 1. unimportant)

Mathematics	4 3 2 1	Computer Science	4 3 2 1
Physics	4 3 2 1	Political Science	4 3 2 1
Sociology	4 3 2 1	Psychology	4 3 2 1
Philosophy	4 3 2 1	History	4 3 2 1

18. Do you have frequent interactions with graduate students or scholars in other disciplines?   Yes / No

If yes, are those interactions primarily intellectual or social?
intellectual [ ]   social [ ]

19. What has been, or probably will be the major factor in your choice of the dissertation topic? Check one.
[ ] the suggestion of a teacher
[ ] the desire to understand some economic phenomenon
[ ] the desire to get the dissertation done, and thus the feasibility of the topic
[ ] the application of certain mathematical or econometric techniques; the economic topic is of secondary importance
[ ] other. Specify:

20. a. Indicate your political orientation:
[ ] conservative; [ ] moderate; [ ] liberal; [ ] radical
[ ] politics is unimportant to me

b. Did your political views change in graduate school?   Yes / No

c. If yes, in what way?

21. If you had to do it over again, would you go to graduate school in economics?

Yes / No / Unsure

Would you go to the same graduate school?   Yes / No / Unsure
If not, why?

About being an economist

22. Which economists (dead or alive) do you respect most? Please specify the characteristics that you admire in each of them.

    1. _____   Characteristics:

    2. _____   Characteristics:

    3. _____   Characteristics:

23. Do you consider the role that economists currently have in society relevant?   Yes / No / Uncertain
    Why?

24. Which characteristics will most likely place students on the fast track? Circle one.
    (4. Very important; 3. Moderately important; 2. Unimportant; 1. I don't know)

being smart in the sense that they are good at problem solving	4	3	2	1
being interested in, and good at, empirical research	4	3	2	1
excellence in mathematics	4	3	2	1
being very knowledgeable about one particular field	4	3	2	1
ability to make connections with prominent professors	4	3	2	1
a broad knowledge of the economics literature	4	3	2	1
a thorough knowledge of the economy	4	3	2	1

    Other (specify):

25. What is your idea of a successful economist? (Specify the characteristics.)

26. Will you pursue an academic career after graduate school?
    Yes / No / Unsure

    If no or if unsure, what other career might you pursue?

27. Where do you hope to be 15 years from now?
    [ ] at a major university
    [ ] at a good liberal arts college
    [ ] at a major research institution
    [ ] at an institution that is indirectly involved in economic policy making
    [ ] in the private sector (specify: _____)
    [ ] other. Specify: _____

About Economics

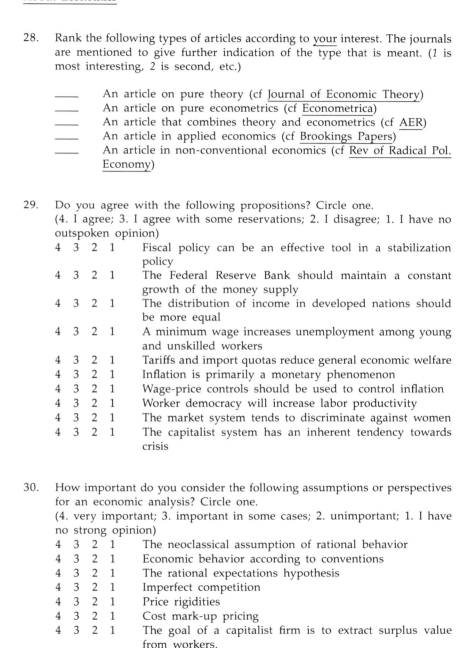

28. Rank the following types of articles according to your interest. The journals are mentioned to give further indication of the type that is meant. (*1* is most interesting, 2 is second, etc.)

____ An article on pure theory (cf Journal of Economic Theory)
____ An article on pure econometrics (cf Econometrica)
____ An article that combines theory and econometrics (cf AER)
____ An article in applied economics (cf Brookings Papers)
____ An article in non-conventional economics (cf Rev of Radical Pol. Economy)

29. Do you agree with the following propositions? Circle one.
    (4. I agree; 3. I agree with some reservations; 2. I disagree; 1. I have no outspoken opinion)
    4 3 2 1   Fiscal policy can be an effective tool in a stabilization policy
    4 3 2 1   The Federal Reserve Bank should maintain a constant growth of the money supply
    4 3 2 1   The distribution of income in developed nations should be more equal
    4 3 2 1   A minimum wage increases unemployment among young and unskilled workers
    4 3 2 1   Tariffs and import quotas reduce general economic welfare
    4 3 2 1   Inflation is primarily a monetary phenomenon
    4 3 2 1   Wage-price controls should be used to control inflation
    4 3 2 1   Worker democracy will increase labor productivity
    4 3 2 1   The market system tends to discriminate against women
    4 3 2 1   The capitalist system has an inherent tendency towards crisis

30. How important do you consider the following assumptions or perspectives for an economic analysis? Circle one.
    (4. very important; 3. important in some cases; 2. unimportant; 1. I have no strong opinion)
    4 3 2 1   The neoclassical assumption of rational behavior
    4 3 2 1   Economic behavior according to conventions
    4 3 2 1   The rational expectations hypothesis
    4 3 2 1   Imperfect competition
    4 3 2 1   Price rigidities
    4 3 2 1   Cost mark-up pricing
    4 3 2 1   The goal of a capitalist firm is to extract surplus value from workers.

31. Do you use the neoclassical notion of individual optimizing behavior when you think or talk about non-economic issues?
     [ ] Very often   [ ] Infrequently   [ ] Never

Your name (optional): ———————————————

If you are willing to be interviewed in depth, please give your address, telephone number and convenient times to call you.

David Colander
Arjo Klamer
April 1985

3

Reciting the *Kama Sutra* Under a Fig Tree: Further Results from the Survey

Questionnaires and surveys are faulty sources of data: Questions inevitably have implicit values within them, the options allowed within the questions are limited, and there's no guarantee that people are answering truthfully. Having been trained as economists to doubt the results of surveys, we approached our own survey skeptically. We nevertheless used it because it was the only source of quantifiable information available—and unless the information could be quantified, we felt it would get no hearing by the profession. But we also recognized the limitations of survey data.

To help the respondents flesh out their numerical choices, and to help us infuse the tabulated numerical results with the breath of life, we invited written comments on any question and included a number of questions that required written answers. In this chapter we consider a sampling of the responses.

A Sampling of Some of the More Interesting Comments

It is often reported that economists can't write. This may be true, but many of the graduate students in our survey wrote pithy, eloquent, and cryptic comments. One of the cryptic comments that we found highly expressive was from the Chicago student who said his idea of a successful economist was someone "who can recite the *Kama Sutra* forwards and backwards while sitting in the lotus position under a sacred fig tree."

Another expressive comment came in reply to our question, "Which professor has been most important?" The student left it blank but wrote, "It has not been an inspiring year." Another student named Kenneth Boulding, John Kenneth Galbraith, and E. S. Schumacher as the three economists he most admired, then added, "But isn't it sad? These are the same ones I liked before I came to graduate school, where they were never mentioned."

Another telling remark was written in the margin by the question asking where students learned the most about economics. The student wrote, "In all seriousness, I have learned the most from Klamer's book *Conversations with Economists*, because it provided a context for the myriad of models I have studied. Columbia does not lay a backdrop when teaching economics."

Other comments were telling in other ways. In answer to the question, "What other significant activities do you have?" one student wrote, "Trying to be a good father and spouse. Though that may sound frivolous, it actually takes a lot of time to be fair to my wife and good to my two kids." That graduate school can make a student believe such efforts are frivolous is, in our view, revealing.

Comments Reinforcing the Survey Results

The written comments gave us a better sense of the numerical results reported in Chapter 2. For example, it is apparent from the survey that Chicago students are more conservative than students at many other schools. This view was reinforced by written comments that suggested to us that the numbers alone underestimated how conservative, or at least how libertarian, Chicago students are. For example, one Chicago student who checked "conservative" as his political orientation wrote, "Libertarian. Why is there no category for us? We are not really conservatives." A number of Chicago students made similar comments; one student who checked "liberal" added, "In Denmark I was considered conservative, although my orientation hasn't changed." In a comment on the political orientation of his parents, another Chicago student who had checked "moderate" put in parentheses, "Less conservative than I am."

Students at other schools had fewer comments about political orientation, although those who did comment strengthened the results of the survey. One Yale student who checked "liberal" wrote, "I'm very unhappy with that description, but 'radical' would also not be accurate." Another Yale student checked "conservative" and added, "but with a healthy degree of skepticism."

The survey results also reinforced the findings in other questions. For example, few Chicago students commented on the question about the use of the neoclassical notion of individual optimizing. Almost all of them contented themselves with checking "very often." (One added, "Everyone does.") Other schools were quite different; for instance, far fewer Yale students answered that same question "yes," and those that did displayed a sense of cynicism. Their comments about using the optimizing model included

- Yes, I am brainwashed.
- Infrequently—usually ironically.
- Very often, in spite of myself.
- Frequently, but only as a joke.

The Yale students also expressed a stronger degree of cynicism than did Chicago students in regard to the fast-track question. Some Yale comments were

- My answer represents my beliefs about how things actually work, not how they should work.
- Self-confidence, good math background, and the lack of critical thinking are important.

Chicago students didn't display cynicism. They had few problems with the way things were.

Students at the other schools wrote proportionately fewer comments than did Yale students on their view of the fast track and of the use of the optimizing model, and those comments were mixed. One Columbia student who acknowledged frequently using individual optimizing made us wonder if the cynicism at Yale was more widespread than we thought. His admission was accompanied by the remark, "We refer to this as being burned out."

We had expected the students to display a relatively strong ambiguity about the policy relevance of economics, but when we tabulated the returns, that expected result didn't come through. More than 50 percent thought economics was relevant. In the comments, however, one of the reasons became clear: Our question was ambiguous, and students interpreted it in a number of ways. Many who answered that economics is relevant for policy expressed concern about the nature of that relevance in their comments. One student who answered "yes" wrote, "Economic theory has practical policy relevance. It may not be right, but it has an effect. It is relevant." Another said that "for better or worse, [influential people] believe that economists have important knowledge and accept many of our opinions."

Some of the other notable answers included

- Half no, half uncertain. Economists should not be (or become) a self-perpetuating club of closet mathematicians seeking to quantify the world; or, worse yet, they should not harbor thoughts along the lines of "If it's not quantifiable, then it's not economics" or "not relevant." Mathematics is a tool of economists. Economics is not a mathematical game.
- Uncertain. Economists are used as instruments to polish and focus policies that politicians already have; [economists] serve as commentators and as proselytizers for positions. So, in that sense, they are relevant. But as far as influencing people's decisions independently of politicians (and I should say independently of people and corporations who suit their own prejudice), they don't seem to have much of a role.
- Yes, but it seems less and less clear why anyone should bother to listen to them since their insight into reality seems to be diminishing with each new wave of graduate students that hits the job market.
- Yes, every so often we hit upon something very important, worth all the other blind alleys we go down.
- Yes, in the same sense that, say, lawyers, or other professional sophists, are relevant.
- Yes, in the sense that economists are not irrelevant. I am not sure that this involvement is always constructive.
- Yes, relevant, but dangerous.
- Yes, because people let us mess things up.
- Uncertain. Economists have succeeded in demonstrating that they don't really know much about what they're supposed to know about and consequently have lost influence politically. Academically, I think that an unfortunate amount of what goes on in the name of academic research is little more than mental masturbation.

There were many more comments conveying the same ideas, but these were the most expressive.

Not all of the responses questioned the relevance of economics. Once again, Chicago students wrote few qualifying comments. For them, economics is relevant in a highly positive way. One student wrote, "Yes. A safe and pleasant journey through the oceans of life is one where the captain knows his ship and the waters. Today we must take this role, such that to create the conditions that will permit all individuals

Table 3.1
The five most-respected economists

	Stanford	Columbia	Yale	Chicago	MIT	Harvard	Total
J. M. Keynes	7	11	6	0	17	17	58
Kenneth Arrow	23	0	3	0	0	9	35
Paul Samuelson	7	0	0	4	10	5	26
Karl Marx	5	0	3	0	5	10	23
Adam Smith	5	3	0	8	2	0	18

to pursue their well-being and in that race increase the social pie." We couldn't decide whether or not he was being facetious.

Ranking Economists

Rankings are fun and, if not taken too seriously, can provide some insight into the economics profession. One of the questions we asked (question 22) was, "Which economists (dead or alive) do you respect most?" The five economists listed most often by graduate students are presented in Table 3.1.

This overall list is not surprising. What is surprising is the distribution of votes among schools. Keynes ranked high at all schools except Chicago, where he doesn't make the top ten. There is no consistency among schools in ranking the others. Kenneth Arrow is second, mainly because of his strong showing at Stanford, where he teaches. Samuelson scored high at MIT, where he teaches. Marx made the list because of Harvard, and Smith made it because of Chicago. Table 3.2 presents the most-respected economists as seen by the graduate students at the various schools.

What Do the Rankings Tell Us?

Our question "Which economist (dead or alive) do you respect most?" was purposely vague. We wanted to see how students would choose between living and dead economists. Living economists won by far; they represented about 70 percent of the top economists mentioned. Of course, this view reflects what the students are taught; their schools do not emphasize the writing of earlier economists. If students knew of them, it was from their undergraduate education or outside reading.

Characteristics of Respected Economists

The characteristics students listed for economists they admired were similar to what we expected.

Table 3.2
Top most-respected economists[a]

Stanford	Columbia
1. Kenneth Arrow (23)[b]	1. J. M. Keynes (11)
2. J. M. Keynes (7)	2. Adam Smith (3)
3. Paul Samuelson (7)	3. Milton Friedman (3)
4. Joseph Schumpeter (5)	4. Gunnar Myrdal (3)
5. Karl Marx (5)	5. Ronald Findlay (2)
6. Adam Smith (5)	6. Gerard Debreu (2)
7. Robert Solow (4)	7. Gary Becker (2)
8. Joseph Stiglitz (4)	8. Joan Robinson (2)
9. Milton Friedman (4)	
10. Amartya Sen (4)	

Yale	Chicago
1. J. M. Keynes (6)	1. Robert Lucas (9)
2. Karl Marx (3)	2. Adam Smith (8)
3. Kenneth Arrow (3)	3. Milton Friedman (7)
4. James Tobin (3)	4. Gary Becker (6)
5. David Ricardo (3)	5. Paul Samuelson (4)
6. John Hicks (2)	6. Sanford Grossman (4)
7. Karl Lewis (2)	7. Eugene Slutsky (3)
8. Kenneth Boulding (2)	8. George Stigler (3)
	9. Martin Feldstein (2)
	10. Gerard Debreu (2)
	11. Sherwin Rosen (2)

MIT	Harvard
1. J. M. Keynes (17)	1. J. M. Keynes (17)
2. Paul Samuelson (10)	2. Karl Marx (10)
3. Karl Marx (5)	3. Kenneth Arrow (9)
4. Robert Solow (5)	4. James Tobin (6)
5. Joseph Schumpeter (3)	5. J. K. Galbraith (5)
6. Arthur Okun (3)	6. Paul Samuelson (5)
7. Stanley Fischer (2)	7. Karl Polanyi (3)
8. Adam Smith (2)	8. Michael Spence (3)
9. J. K. Galbraith (2)	9. Robert Lucas (3)
10. Jerry Hausman (2)	10. Amartya Sen (3)
11. Joseph Stiglitz (2)	
12. Thorstein Veblen (2)	
13. George Akerlof (2)	
14. Oliver Hart (2)	

[a]We report only the "top" economists who received two or more votes. At Columbia and Yale only eight economists received two or more votes. More than ten are listed where a tie existed.

[b]Numbers in parentheses represent the number of times the economist was mentioned.

Keynes. John Maynard Keynes was admired for roughly the same reasons at all schools: his ability to make a radical departure from past theory and the scope of his vision. One student asked, "How can one be interested in Keynesian macro and not admire Keynes?" Some students seemed to take Keynes's nontechnical approach as a plus, making comments such as "not a mere model-maker," "mathematical skill is not overexploited," and "technically very capable, but able to express ideas to lay people." One student admired Keynes "because of his courage in confronting a great social problem directly without binding intellectual preconceptions not supported by fact, and the brilliance and integrity with which he forged tools to cope with it."

Arrow. Kenneth Arrow, like Keynes, was respected for the seminal nature of his work and for the breadth of his interest and knowledge. Unlike Keynes, he received high marks for being mathematically rigorous. Students who listed Arrow seemed to be especially impressed with the combination of mathematical rigor and his social concern and philosophical awareness. According to one student, Arrow is "imaginative, open-minded, clever, insightful, intuitive. And a nice guy besides." How much better can it get?

Samuelson. The characteristics students admired in Paul Samuelson were his mastery of theory, his intelligence ("sheer brains," as one student put it), and his use of math. More than Arrow and Keynes, Samuelson is viewed as an economist's economist, valued for his "widespread influence on the profession" and for being "the consummate master of theory." One student's justification for naming Samuelson was simply, "Need I say more?"

Marx. As could be expected, students admired Karl Marx for his deep concern about real-world questions. One student wrote that she admired him "for his political cunning." But they also respected his economics. According to one student, Marx is "a better economist than people give him credit for—especially in areas of technology and development." Another student mentioned his "breadth, intellectual intensity, and the timelessness of his work."

Smith. One Chicago student acknowledged Adam Smith "the founding father." According to another, he "got the ball rolling." Originality and the breadth of his thinking were the qualities mentioned most often. One student respected Smith for his "ability to analyze as a modern economist."

Important Professors

Although some professors were named in the most-respected rankings also, we had a different purpose in asking our question, "Which professors in the graduate program are the most important to you?" Most students at the thesis stage chose their thesis adviser or the individuals who taught courses in their particular field; others named the person likely to be their thesis adviser. Some of the general comments as to why they thought a professor important are instructive.

- I liked him for his humanism, grasp of the material, and wit.
- I liked him because he is willing to discuss my work.
- Willingness to question the given assumptions of neoclassical theory. I admire his originality and innovativeness.
- I admire him because of his rigorous, clear expositions.
- I like him because he's wise and personable; because he makes learning enjoyable; and because he's taught me how to think.
- My adviser. He is the only serious faculty member we've met this year who acted as if women were human beings. Without any effort, that is.
- He uses methods I don't like, but he's open to argument and thinks on a theoretical level. He's willing to debate on a deeper level than most.

There were a few answers we find hard to forget. One frank, cynical person answered, "Whoever will be on my orals committee." Another, as we mentioned above, left blanks, saying, "It has not been an inspiring year."

Likes and Dislikes

What do students like and dislike about graduate school? Do their likes and dislikes differ among schools? To answer that question, we asked students the question directly. Their answers reveal both similarities and differences among schools.

The MIT students especially liked the intellectually stimulating environment in their department. They liked "talking to smart people" and "learning new theories and ideas." The dislikes of MIT students centered around the narrowness and lack of relevance of the economics taught to them and the stifled social life. Students singled out "the strain graduate school puts on personal and family relationships," and more than one was in accord with the student who said, "[I] feel isolated from the rest of the world." Many mentioned the pressure, and quite a few complained of the emphasis on techniques.

Like the MIT students, Harvard students are attracted by the intellectual stimulation of graduate school, but unlike the MIT students, they emphasize the freedom that they experience—the freedom "to study what

I want," "to chart my own intellectual development," and to "be my own boss." In sharp contrast to the likes of MIT students, neither the faculty nor fellow students appear on the list of what the Harvard students like—in fact, faculty and fellow students were mentioned as reasons for disliking graduate school. One student in particular was bothered by the "non-intellectual and anti-intellectual fellow grad students," and another alleged that he unwillingly found himself "hanging out with nerds."

The Yale students echo much of what the students at the other schools like about graduate school. They cite intellectual stimulation, freedom, and interaction with fellow students. In the dislike column, the Yale students had more extensive comments. Fear that they are doing something quite irrelevant looms large. They speak of the "disconnection with the real world," "the fetishism of formalism and the consequent lack of intellectual exploration among many of the professors and students," and "lack of discussion about what we're studying—we treat ideas like techniques."

Opportunity and freedom are the terms that Stanford students use most often to indicate what they like about graduate school. A few mention their fellow students and the faculty. One likes graduate school for "being at the center of the profession—not ideologically but in practical terms; being in the midst of a lot of state-of-the-art research, with access to a lot of unpublished research and a *very* good library."

Pressure is the big concern of Stanford students. They cite the pressure of course work, of limited money, of choosing a dissertation topic, and especially of limited time. A few students complain about the lack of respect students get from faculty. Irrelevance and the emphasis on formal mathematical reasoning get mentioned, but not as often as at the other schools, especially Harvard and Yale.

More than any of the other students, Columbia students stress learning new tools and ideas as the reason for liking graduate school. A few mention the relationships with fellow students and professors.

Professors also get some abuse. There are complaints about "bad teachers" and "the constant lack of interest and lack of support and lack of respect from the bulk of professors toward the students." Pressure and the level of abstraction are other complaints that come up more than once.

Like the MIT and Harvard students, the Chicago students stress the intellectual stimulation as the reason they like graduate school. Fellow students and faculty get mentioned a few times in a positive sense, but not as often as in the MIT sample. Chicago students complain that studying makes immense demands on their time and mental energy. One student expresses a common sentiment: "The stress; the time constraint. There's nowhere near enough time, it seems, for anything—my intellectual interests, my personal life, everything is subjugated to the program." Chicago students share this gripe with the MIT students (Harvard students hardly brought it up). Chicago students are less bothered than other students by the lack of relevance and the emphasis on mathematics and techniques.

Table 3.3A presents a collage of answers from the various schools as to what students like about graduate school. Table 3.3B presents a similar compilation about their dislikes.

What Is a Successful Economist?

We found the answers to the question "What is your idea of a successful economist?" revealing. They tell us loud and clear that there is a big discrepancy between students' perceptions of what the profession values (see Table 2.3 in Chapter 2) and their own values.

The majority of MIT students think of professional standards when they articulate what they consider a successful economist to be. Yet most students want to see professional proficiency combined with knowledge of and interest in the real world. Several students mentioned social concern as a standard.

Nearly all Harvard students consider the applicability to the real world of what economists do to be crucial. They also want to see a "broad interest" and the ability to communicate economics to outsiders. Only a few seem to consider professional standards as important as MIT students do.

Chicago students have diverse views of the successful economist. The prototype would be an intuitive economist searching for the truth, publishing his or her findings in top journals, and being well paid for the work.

Yale students are not significantly different from Chicago students in their view of success, even though they are significantly different in other aspects. A successful economist would understand the economy and be able to "explain important economic phenomena."

Stanford students focus slightly more on rigor than do Chicago or Yale students. For them, a successful economist would be "a careful, rigorous thinker" who could "blend theoretical explanations with a set of facts."

Columbia students have similar views. For them, the person would be "someone who is able to combine a good intuitive grasp of the workings of the economy with a knowledge of the formal econometric tools."

Table 3.3A
What graduate students like

MIT	Harvard
• Talking to smart people.	• Freedom to chart my own intellectual development.
• Stimulating faculty and peers; exposure to new ideas and methods.	
• The intellectual stimulation and the growth of one's knowledge.	• Having much free time.
	• The people.
• At this moment I am very disappointed in my graduate studies, so I cannot say there is something I like about them.	• Freedom to study.
	• The flexible schedule.
	• The cooperative atmosphere (among my group of female colleagues).
• High quality of students and faculty.	• The general university environment.
• The chance to study phenomena I've not fully understood.	• The opportunity to work as a research assistant for a professor.
• One can bounce theories off one's colleagues, who can respond.	• The intellectual stimulation and freedom to follow my own interests.
• Getting out.	• Do not have to work regular hours.
• Stimulating and intellectual environment.	• The opportunity to try out new ideas and methods without being irreparably ridiculed (as opposed to after graduate school).
• Talking with smart people.	
• Ability to read and study what I'm interested in—at least since generals.	
	• The intellectual atmosphere.
• The freedom to work and think about important problems in an environment that permits close contact with excellent faculty and students.	• Doing serious intellectual work.
	• The challenge.
	• Access to new ideas.
	• Learning new things.
• The intellectual stimulation.	• Freedom to study what I want.
• I'll leave here with a set of tools, good credentials, and membership in a profession whose methods and assumptions are not seriously examined by the general public; hence, I'll have disproportionate influence in public questions.	• Freedom.
	• The intellectual environment.
	• I can't think of anything I like about graduate school; it has even turned me off the whole subject from time to time.
	• The intellectual environment.
• Studying economics.	• The opportunity for continual learning.
• Exposure to science's knowledge frontier.	• Being my own boss.
• Learning new theories and ideas.	• Doing what I want to do.
• Being in an environment where the goal is intellectual achievement.	• Intellectual stimulation.
• Contact with new ideas and with people.	
• The intellectual challenge.	
• The challenge and quality of the course work.	

(continues)

48

Table 3.3A What graduate students like (*continued*)

Chicago	Yale
• The feeling that I am doing what I want to; that I am getting credentials. The professors and students take economics seriously.	• Original research.
• Exposure to recent research on the environment; chance to think and manage my life without a boss.	• Stimulating atmosphere.
	• Doing my own research.
• The interaction with other students.	• The lack of structure of my day.
• The intellectual stimulation.	• I keep my own hours; informality; independence.
• The yearning to pursue original research. (This is also the most difficult.)	• Completing the requirements.
• The constant mental stimulation both from the course demands and other, particularly foreign, students.	• Looking back at my accomplishments and making friends.
• The freedom to do what you want to do; work on problems in depth without external time limits.	• The other students' occasional moments of scholarly passion.
• The challenge of acquiring so-called tools of mathematics, the sense of accomplishment, and using a particular model to analyze a real-life situation.	• You get to sleep a lot, and the women find us intellectuals attractive.
• It is a chance to work with an intelligent and motivated group of people who are interested in economics. Then there are people who are interested in work they are doing and some of whom are at the very frontier of research.	• The intellectual stimulus.
	• The (occasional) feeling of doing interesting and worthwhile research.
	• When I get a glimpse of actually understanding, or at least believing that I do.
	• The opportunity to debate theoretical and policy issues with people who really understand and care about these issues.
	• Conversations with fellow students.
	• Nothing.

(continues)

Table 3.3A   What graduate students like (continued)

Stanford	Columbia
• Schedule flexibility.	• Not having a full-time job; being able to pursue intellectual interests.
• Constant exposure to new and highly varied points of view.	• Learning tools in economics.
• Flexible schedule; some ability to design own research.	• The vast knowledge at my reach.
• Personal autonomy.	• The opportunity to study subjects that are important thoroughly, without hand-waving and ignoring large areas, and the opportunity to hear people who are doing this sort of study talk and answer questions.
• Academic freedom and flexibility.	
• The ability to study things I find important without outside interference.	
• The peer group and intellectual atmosphere—I like always to think and question.	• I like to observe the world's future economists learning tools of the trade. Some are very uncritical; some are questioning.
• A chance to think about interesting things without day-to-day demands for results.	• Knowing the good works of economics.
• The opportunity to learn and investigate new topics.	• Freedom of thought.
• Being at the center of the profession—not ideologically but in practical terms; being in the midst of a lot of state-of-the-art research, with access to a lot of unpublished research and a very good library. I feel as if I have my hands on the pulse of the profession.	• Learning intricate and involved models and applying those to the real world.
	• Learning the material.
	• The camaraderie and friendship developed.
	• Doing empirical work.
	• The recognition of new tools.
• Stimulating atmosphere.	• The focus on the discipline.
• My fellow students.	• Courses are very useful and informative. They open doors to understanding journal articles.
• Good technical training.	
• Exposure to stimulating people, new ideas, conversations.	• Contact with my professors and other students.
• Environment at Stanford provides so many opportunities for intellectual advancement.	• Learning the core companionship.
• Ability to pursue advanced studies in depth.	• The opportunity to study in areas of my interest once the first year is finished.
• Exposure to the best in the profession.	• Associating with other students, intelligent people who share interests.
• Learning how to teach!	• Learning a mode of analysis rigorously.
	• Learning economics.
	• Have enjoyed the work and the erudition of some professors.

Table 3.3B
What graduate students dislike

MIT	Harvard
• Time spent doing problem sets. • Stifled social life. • The narrow focus of the department and discipline. • The lack of relevance to the real world; graduate studies take away from the real world. • It is a sort of vicious circle—academicians who produce academicians, all engaged in spending most of their time talking about very abstract problems. • Course work is silly and boring. • Emphasis on methodological technique. • The emphasis on mathematical tools and technique. • The economics is far too mathematical, far too little real-world oriented. • Actually, the math is not the bad part; it is the attempt to fit economics into inappropriate mathematics. • The narrow focus, first of studying only economics and second of studying only economics as it is practiced today. • The closed society and absence of humor. • The pressure, though somewhat self-induced. • It destroys my self-esteem. As a consultant, on the outside, I'm a honcho from MIT; here I'm a peon who can't get the time of day from some professor, can't find a thesis topic, won't get a good job—all this, in turn, makes it tougher to work and reinforces my feelings of inadequacy. • The pressure and feeling of dependency. • Departmental politics. • Strain it puts on personal and family relationships. • Petty political maneuvering and competition to impress faculty. • Stress of uncertainty. • All other dimensions of myself have been neglected. • Feeling isolated from the rest of the world. • Pressure. • Vocational pressure and informational void. • Life is too centered around economics. • The social life here: there is none.	• The Harvard atmosphere. • The non-intellectual and anti-intellectual fellow grad students. • Lack of relationship with faculty. • Not having time to read the things I find most relevant and interesting in economics. • Emphasis on game-playing in your work. • Having to do irrelevant requirements, which leads to a non-serious attitude to work among students. • I find it hard to find the meaning or usefulness of what I'm learning. • Being vastly in debt. • Hanging out with nerds. • Makes it hard to lead a normal life. • By necessity, most grad students lead a narrow existence. Their single-mindedness makes it difficult to develop and maintain meaningful friendships. • The world would not be an overwhelming problem, except that due to the sheltered grad school the environment inhibits access to outside relationships. • It simply prolongs adolescence. • The faculty and their lack of interest in education (as opposed to their interest in creating carbon copies of themselves). • I have never met a more selfish egocentric group of people in my life. • A subtle but noticeable pressure to conform to certain professional roles. • Feeling like I'm over thirty but not grown up. • Feeling of not doing anything. • The over-reliance of the field on formal models. • I think that the constrained optimization approach to mathematical economics has very little relevance for analyzing the real economy; therefore, I find it difficult to get motivated to spend hours and hours learning this form of model. Consequently, it becomes stressful and tedious. • Jumping through hoops.

(continues)

Table 3.3B What graduate students dislike (*continued*)

Chicago	Yale
• The stress; the time constraint. There's nowhere enough time, it seems, for anything—my intellectual interests, my personal life, everything is subjugated to the program.	• Reading journal articles.
	• Comprehensives.
	• Low pay for T.A.'s.
• Little application to real-world problems; the irrelevance of course and dissertation subject matter to policy questions; and the increased use of high-level mathematics.	• Either I didn't understand or didn't believe what I learned in class. The antiseptic approach to social problems. No philosophical guidance.
• It is lonely in that professors and students are busy pursuing their own interests and have little time for discussion or exchange of ideas in a relaxed atmosphere.	• Economics (in both senses).
	• A feeling of doing uninteresting and worthless research; feeling of never quite having free time. There are always things that one ought to be doing.
• Writing the damn thesis. Working on my dissertation. This particular school distances faculty.	• Lack of discussion about what we're studying. We treat ideas like techniques.
• Being on limited funds.	• Aestheticism or formalism and the consequent lack of intellectual exploration among many of the professors and students.
• Speed at which we are assumed to assimilate information. Professors uninterested in teaching.	• Lack of breadth, insight, and intellectual activity among the faculty.
• People are boring. Nobody has time for anything or anyone else. Everybody works too much, enjoys others too little. I'm not sure when I'll finish.	• The fear that much of what I'm spending my time on is ultimately irrelevant.
	• The disconnection with the real world.
• Students and faculty have a poor relationship.	• The narrow classes consisting of thoughtless banging through a series of models.
• Sometimes too theoretical, with little relevance. Worry if I should have majored in economics.	• Lack of discussion about what we study; we treat ideas like techniques. (I'm hoping that will change after the first year.)
• The fear that being a student is not a socially productive activity.	• The fetish of formalism and the consequent lack of intellectual exploration among many of the professors and students.
• The severe intellectual, emotional, time and financial demands it imposes on every aspect of your life; the continuous stress to become smarter and the paralyzing fear that you're working as hard as possible but not making any significant headway; the abysmal thought of not being able to finish for many years beyond what you originally planned and struggling all the while; the conflict of needing to spend every minute doing economics while realizing that this is an almost destructive choice.	• The lack of breadth, insight, and intellectual daring among the faculty (and, to a lesser extent, the students).
	• The disconnection with the real world.
	• Everything. [This from the same person who wrote "nothing" under "most liked."]
	• The over-reliance of the field on formal models. (I sometimes change my mind about this.)
• The strength of graduate school is also its weakness: too much of life is concentrated on economics.	• I don't enjoy much learning about basic neoclassical theory, although I realize that it is quite important and it can be interesting as a problem in and of itself. But I always thought economics was supposed to be about policy.
• Too ivory-tower. Don't apply tools to studying the world as much as I'd like.	

(continues)

Table 3.3B   What graduate students dislike (*continued*)

Stanford	Columbia
• The number of hoops that we need to jump through.	• The pedantic attitude of quasi-intellectuals.
• Pressure—constant boy-do-I-work-hard complaints from others make one feel as if economics is all that matters. I'm tired of people saying they don't have time to do things because of work.	• As far as learning tools are concerned, it is o.k., but we should also learn some economics. So with the flood of math and economics, economic content seems to have gone down.
• Pressures to meet professional standards that, in my mind, have closed the discipline to many pertinent issues. Standards not on quality of scholarship but on types of questions that may be asked and approaches that may be used.	• The themes they are teaching are way too abstract. With all the complications of the math, we lose contact with the real world, and, after all, we are studying the behavior of individuals in a social context.
• Dealing with theory which has become mathematically technical far beyond its foundations in the real world (so-called).	• The constant lack of interest and lack of support and lack of respect from the bulk of professors towards the students. The abuse of students by their professors; the constant failure to be explicit about underlying premises and their range of applications on the part of the professors.
• Lack of respect by faculty and department administration. Lack of financial support (especially after fourth year).	
• Lack of a good social life, especially interaction with good students from other departments, especially humanities and the other social sciences.	• I dislike the abstractions from reality; although I recognize the need for abstractions and forming some type of a coherent discipline, we must never forget that we are modeling the world and that modeling in and of itself is not economically relevant.
• Course requirements so onerous that I feel I have no time to do my own research.	• Financial constraints; bad teachers.
• No money.	• In-between social period between undergraduate and the real world.
• The stress involved in picking a dissertation topic; the isolation inherent to the research process; the uncertainty about the time to completion.	• Poor lecturers, of whom there have been thankfully few.
• (1) The ease with which one can become isolated doing individual research; and (2) the premium that appears to be placed on highly abstract and technical theoretical work.	• Professors who ignore life outside of the school. • Taking courses. • Exams and the grading system. • Not enough free time to pursue my real interests in economics.
• Lack of respect for interests of students.	• The pressure for a dissertation.
• Over-emphasis on formal mathematical reasoning. Lack of critical discussion in most classes. Splits in the faculty. How hard it is to explain what I do to "ordinary" people!	• The pressure of passing the exams. • The attitude of some of the faculty in handling of some of the core courses.
• Lack of structure in the curriculum, despite extensive requirements. Instructors teaching in a sequence rarely coordinate the material each will cover. Despite interesting insights, the courses sometimes fail to connect up, or give a clear impression of how things fit into the larger body of thought to which they belong.	• Sacrifice it implies. • The regimen of the curriculum; the lack of significant interaction with faculty following course work; dealing with faculty; lack of interaction with faculty.

As was the case with their likes and dislikes, individuals' views of what makes a successful economist were varied, and our short summary cannot do justice to that variety. Table 3.4 presents a collage of the views from the different schools.

Portrait of a Graduate Economics Student

These comments, together with the survey results, paint a portrait of the students in economics graduate education. It's a group portrait; to us, it's a favorable (though diverse) portrait of the students and an unfavorable picture of economics education. We see a group of intelligent, sympathetic, caring, and sincere students who find themselves in an academic situation where they are presented with a highly challenging field of study—but one of dubious relevance to reality. In that field of study, most of them believe, technique overrides common sense, but it is a successful field and a field in which a participant can achieve gratifying success. At the same time, that field is one in which a participant who doesn't know the technique doesn't advance.

Students know this. At schools like MIT where they feel they are learning the latest techniques, the students feel secure; they will be able to play the game. At schools where they don't feel they're getting the most up-to-date techniques, the students feel concern that they won't be equipped to play the game. So even as they call for relevance, they recognize that relevance and deeper understanding won't help them as much as techniques will.

Some of the students become cynical; they bring themselves to learn the techniques and use the techniques, but they don't put their hearts in that work. Others convince themselves that what they are learning and doing is the best approach to mastering the subject. The students who are most able to convince themselves are those at schools like Chicago, where they are constantly reinforced in their belief that the technique is the science. At schools such as Harvard or Yale, where there are even a few faculty members conveying a sense of cynicism, that cynicism spreads and affects student after student. "Here's what we do to advance in the profession; forget what makes sense." Questioning by faculty opens up a Pandora's box of concerns.

Students differ in the degree to which they fit in. Some fit in quickly, others revolt—but it becomes clear to all at some point that to succeed, here is what they must do. And, ultimately, they do it—or they drop out.

We'll return to these themes and ideas in Part Three, where we try to make sense out of the mass of information as a whole and explain what is going on. But before we do, we present the conversations in which the students express their views directly.

Table 3.4
What makes a successful economist

MIT	Yale
• Respected by his or her colleagues; understands how theory reflects real world; has policy-making influence.	• A thorough knowledge of the economy.
• Someone who can look at [a] problem, formalize it, and put together a plausible solution.	• Analytic ability; knowledge of the theoretical underpinnings of economics.
• One who can make the society better off, studying what he likes at the same time.	• Ability to master some area and push outward to its present boundaries.
• Published a lot of articles, and someone whose opinion is valued by people both in and out of the profession.	• Includes economic policy in the general applied areas.
• One who digests the profession's theoretical and empirical work, and transmits it to the general public.	• Someone who has mastered the necessary tools and has broad enough knowledge about society and broad enough vision to analyze what makes real economies work well. He or she would not revel in the tools for their own sake but use them skillfully to make specific policy recommendations.
• One who makes the world a better place.	
• It's one who writes a lot of papers, and knows how to advertise them.	• I am not certain what you mean by "successful." I will answer in terms of what characteristics lead to good work: the ability to think in terms of formal logic while able to focus on the central aspects of a problem.
• Combination of theoretical soundness and good real-world instincts.	
• Doing original work in theory or econometrics and testing theory/methods on actual data.	
• Someone who is not only *skilled* in the techniques of analysis, but can *apply* that skill in an imaginative way to the real world.	• Someone who (1) makes a significant contribution to understanding the economy; and (2) still likes both her or himself and economics.
• Knows economics.	• I have very little idea except to note that the characteristics may be very different for academic vs. non-academic. For the former, at least, how about: an eye for the efficient assumption.
• One who can bring about his/her policy prescriptions. Otherwise, we're no different than boring academics or well-meaning clergy. "Those who don't do, teach."	
• Solid theoretical background with a sense of relevance to the real world.	• Interested in work, even in old age. People respect opinion even if not famous. Good life outside of economics. Well-rounded in the family life.
• Someone who can do rigorous work in theory, but has the ability to apply the theory to policy. Must not get sucked into the neoclassical trap, but remain aware of the power the economist has to do good.	• Combines an analytic power with understanding of the existing institutions and still manages to gain respect of the profession.
• A successful economist is one who has a "good idea," an original one, and writes a fair number of papers on it. A good economist is one who has his own general view of the economic system and is able to fit in it each economic problem. When this view is original you have an outstanding economist. *Examples*: Samuelson with the "maximum principle"; Lucas with the "rational expectations"; Leontieff with "input-output analysis."	• Can explain important economic phenomena with simple models.
	• Otto Eckstein—except that he is dead.
• One who applies economic tools to the analysis of real problems.	

(continues)

Table 3.4   What makes a successful economist (*continued*)

Chicago	Harvard
• Intuitive. • Able to assimilate several ideas and place [them] within a simple integrative framework. • Able to follow arguments and pick out assumptions which motivate and carry through [to] the conclusion. • A researcher who conveys his thoughts in understandable fashion, who applies his research to policy decisions. • Someone who understands the economy and can communicate it to others, especially non-economists. • Winning the Nobel Prize, making important discoveries, getting well-paid. • One who can recite the *Kama Sutra* forwards and backwards while sitting in the lotus position under a sacred fig tree. "Success" is too subjective a term for me to give a generalized response as you appear to want. I'll be a success if I'm happy—that's it. • Teaches at a good school; publishes a lot in good journals; research is respected by peers. • Someone who enjoys his work; tries to contribute to the overall good and enjoys his friendships and family. • Someone who is looking for the truth. • One who is frequently published in excellent journals or who is good at making policy and has responsibility to do so. • One who contributes to social improvement, armed with good common sense and solid theoretical background. • Someone who has mastered the existing techniques and developed new techniques. • The ability to formulate testable hypotheses. • One who is rigorous in his thinking—careful, thoughtful—and does empirical research and doesn't let politics blight his economics. • If an academic changes the way a profession thinks about some issue, if he accomplishes what he set out to accomplish. • Well-published and well-cited. • Publication in top journals; having the respect of colleagues; one who has a good deal of respect among his peers.	• Broad interest; well-read in a variety of subjects outside of and within economics; good analytical skills; a strong sense of perspective and appropriateness of technique and results; highly developed political consciousness (economics is only important because of its political and social implications). • [One] whose articles every grad student [has] to read. • One who doesn't just apply the methodology, but also formulates original and relevant research agendas. Also, an economist who doesn't sell him/herself to political interest; economics certainly isn't devoid of political content, but it is inappropriate to base one's work on one's political views. • Someone who can answer real-world problems. • One who studies *economy* and not a mathematical model, and applies skills to making the economy better (rather than pretending economists are value-free and responsibility-free). • Someone who can analyze, and propose solutions to, problems which actually have an impact on the welfare of society (and drives a Mercedes). • Empirical and original; policy-relevant; able to draw on institutional knowledge; adept at econometrics; open-minded (i.e., able to accept non-neoclassical results as valid). • Male, works 15 hours a day, reads *Econometrica* at intermission when his wife drags him out for an evening at the theatre, poor personal relationships, always negative about others' efforts. • Not a whore. • A good economist should either (1) come up with reasonable explanations of real-world phenomena; (2) come up with useful stylized facts; or (3) know how to apply economics to real-world situations. • Has written important papers in one or more fields; tenured at good school; big bucks consulting. • Understanding of real-world conditions; ability to deal with broad economic problems.

(*continues*)

Table 3.4 What makes a successful economist *(continued)*

Stanford	*Columbia*
• Tenure at U.C. Santa Barbara. • Poses relevant questions in the real world; tries to answer them. Interested in economy, not math. • One who does well what he's interested in and is recognized for it. • Careful, rigorous thinker about logical relationships; not bound to 'intuitive' results; able to reason outside of standard market model. • The ability to create theoretical and technical innovations [and] the ability to translate theory into political change. • "Successful" as "on the fast track"? "Gurus" like Bob Hall and professors and graduate students who follow them like groupies; this is an unhealthy trend with no good place in academia. "Ideal"? Honest and slightly irreverent people who can express their ideas in terms palatable to the general audience of economists. • Is creative; communicates to others; understanding; either makes a valuable contribution to theory or influences policy. • One who *cares* about a problem and works at understanding and finding solutions to it. *Conscience* is important. • Able to blend theoretical explanations with set of facts and use the former to illustrate connection with the latter. Good mix of intuitive and analytical arguments. A clear focus on the *economically* relevant questions. The biggest success: getting a sense of the "big" picture. • Respected by colleagues; active in the profession. Several good, well-known papers. Opinion is respected. • One whose ideas can be made accessible to ordinary intelligent people, whose theoretical perspective derives from a sense of reality rather than an idealist vision and who is modest in his/her claims. • One who does careful work on non-trivial concerns which help us understand human behavior and thus the structure of society. As icing on the cake I would add the ability to explain the results (and why they're valid) to those who don't speak economics.	• Should know the environment where he is working. Should have complete knowledge of socio-politic[al] and economic factors of the economy. Should know most of the economic tools to apply in the above environment. • Bright, good in using "mainstream" methodology to further his own economic/political insights. • Impacts on policy. • Ability to frame and answer questions which are relevant either theoretically or empirically; elegance of solutions; absence of excess technicality. • The opposite of those characteristics that typically place students on "the fast track." • One who is satisfied with his/her career and contribution to society, be it a tenured professorship or a private consultant. • Competent in his field and interested in relating to other fields; some type of concern for society. • One who is open-minded but grounded in a particular theory, who is unwilling to choose his orientation unless firmly convinced to. The ability to convey ideas to non-economists is also very important. • Unbiased, scholarly application of economic theory to problems of today. Extension of economic theory. • Someone who is able to combine a good intuitive grasp of the workings of the economy with a knowledge of the formal and econometric tools. • Good credentials in the academic world; i.e., access to the *non*-academic world. • Creates simple, useful models highlighting important connections. Teaches innovatively and effectively. Advice for government and for private sector. • Policy impact. • Good, relevant work. Social criteria: fame/renown in the field. • One who has challenged the minds of his peers and who has applied, or has done work towards applying, the discipline of economics in such a way as to improve the lot of humanity.

PART TWO

Conversations with Graduate Students

These conversations are with groups of students at four of the schools included in the survey. Each group represents a year of the graduate program. MIT and Chicago are represented by all four years, Harvard and Columbia by two years. In all cases participation was voluntary. We posted time and place for the sessions and left to the students the decision to attend. The groups, therefore, are not necessarily representative of their respective years. Foreigners, and especially Asian students, were underrepresented.

We decided to talk with groups instead of individuals because we were more interested in the social interaction among the students than in their individual opinions. We wanted to know how they encourage and restrain each other, which individual beliefs and opinions they would accept, and which ones they would oppose.

The editing of the conversations has been minimal. We have reorganized some of the conversations to make them easier for the reader to follow, smoothed sentences here and there to facilitate the reading, and eliminated extraneous and some repetitive passages. The names of the students have been altered, in accordance with our promise to them. Our apologies to those students whose comments may betray their identity.

We conducted the conversations during the spring of 1985, except for the Chicago conversations, which occurred in the fall of 1987. We both talked with the first- and third-year students of MIT; Colander talked with the Columbia students; Klamer talked with the Chicago, Harvard, and the remainder of the MIT students.

The conversations give one a much better sense of what the graduate students actually think. They put the results of the survey into perspective

57

and give one insight into graduate school economics programs. Because we wanted to provide as much context as possible, we have included somewhat lengthy conversations. Although readers can pick and choose among the conversations—no one conversation depends on any other—we believe that once you read one you will be enticed to read others, because the conversations do give a glimpse of graduate school that is seldom seen by noneconomists.

4

Ambivalence and Security: MIT Students

First-Year Students

Four students participated: Arnold, Tony, Carl, and Dave.

About the Questionnaire

What did you think of the questionnaire?

ARNOLD: It was good. I enjoyed doing it. I had difficulty with the question about what is important to be on the fast track. It lacked an idea of the fast track to where.

TONY: The fast track to tenure, maybe. *[They laugh.]*

ARNOLD: Yeah, but most of the guys here are not going to go into academic positions. I think about forty percent will. Or thirty percent.

CARL: Most of them do. Maybe seventy-five percent.

ARNOLD: I think it is less. Anyway, I feel that where you want to go influences the answer to that question a lot.

The other question that stuck in my mind was which economists I have respect for. I've never really had economists as hero figures that I admired. I had trouble finding something to answer to that.

TONY: That's the same question that really caused me to think. What people you admire the most. I've thought about it since.

ARNOLD: I think it would have been more helpful if you had asked what economists or articles or books had influenced our thinking, rather than use the word respect.

Any other reactions?

DAVE: I liked going through the questionnaire because it made me think about things that I thought about when I was deciding whether to go to graduate school. Once you get here, you forget about all that because you get lost in the little day-to-day details. They remind you of what you're doing and why you're supposed to be doing them.

Their Experience at Graduate School

How would you describe your experiences here as a first-year graduate student at MIT?

TONY: Difficult.

How about you?

CARL: Difficult—anxious.

For me it was really a whole new way of approaching economics because my undergraduate background is screwy. The courses I took were not nearly as rigorous. With so much reliance on mathematics and quantitative analysis, it is a whole new game.

How about you?

ARNOLD: I think the main thing that struck me was the pace. Things move here *very* quickly; the work load's quite a bit higher than what I ever had as an undergraduate. That created a lot of anxiety for me at first, but having gone through the Christmas exams, I feel much more comfortable with it now, and I feel more in control, even though I don't like the rate at which I'm doing things.

What is the work load? I mean, how many hours are we talking about?

ARNOLD: I think I'm an exception. I am trying to limit myself, for personal reasons, to spending no more than about forty-eight or fifty hours a week in front of books—absorbing material, doing problem sets, cutting out a lot of recommended readings, and so on and so forth.

You are married.

ARNOLD: Yes.

How about you?

CARL: I work many, many more hours, because I'm really very slow at problem sets and that sort of thing, so I probably put in close to seventy, including classes. There aren't many times when six or eight hours a week go by when I'm not studying. It's, I would say, a good seventy hours, plus.

TONY: It's really hard to say, because I don't really keep track of it. I have a family and two children; that takes a lot of time. But it's like every other waking moment, during each break of classes—during each vacation—I force myself to read one novel so that I can keep in touch with something fictional—choose something short. The work load wasn't as hard as the psychological adjustment.

You mean the math?

TONY: Well, you know, I didn't come from Harvard or Yale or something like that, and I was used to being a big fish in a small pond, so to speak. It's quite an adjustment to come here. As one of my classmates here said, as an undergraduate when he went in to take a test and looked around the room, he knew that there were problems that were going to be on that test that he could do that other people just wouldn't have a prayer of solving, so if he made a couple of slipups, it was no big deal because he had a sort of margin for error. Here, you look around the room and you ask yourself, "Is there *any* problem set that I can do that these guys can't do? No." Okay—so you don't have a margin for error. And it's tough. I think I made it pretty tough on myself, more than them making it tough on me. Until finally a great burden was lifted when I got my first B and now I feel much better.

DAVE: I think that's true of everybody. I know getting through the first set of exams, doing pretty well, and realizing that yes, in fact, it was just fine—I sort of breathed a sigh of relief.

Are you already able to pick out the future stars?

CARL: I think you can easily identify the people who are really technically endowed—people who get the best scores on the exams virtually every time—always have the cleanest solutions to the problem sets.

ARNOLD: I'm not so clear about that. I know that I associate some people with great expertise in certain things. There may be some people who are *extremely* good at the math, and there are some people who will put in *hours* on a problem set to crack a particular solution, and then there are other people who are very familiar with the current issues in macroeconomics, and there are people who are very good at political economics.

DAVE: But we don't cross much into that in the first year.

The impression we get from the survey and talking with people is that the first year consists of problem solving and learning math.

TONY: To a considerable extent. Well, the problem solving especially. I think maybe sometimes we exaggerate how much math there is. Maybe, now I am at MIT, I associate that with its mathematical orientation.

The (Policy) Relevance of What They Learn

Do you talk about economic issues?

ARNOLD: It's very limited. I've been quite disappointed with the amount of application to issues that's done in a lot of courses. They don't go out and discuss problems facing, say, the federal government. Let's say, well, we can look at this problem in these different ways, and we would come out with these different policy solutions. I've got a very strong interest in that kind of approach because I've worked with the federal government a few years before I came here, so I'm very interested in policy applications of economic theory. But we spent six weeks in the macroeconomics course doing a lot of algebra, taking a lot of derivatives, without ever really talking about how applicable these models were, how reasonable these assumptions were.

DAVE: I think there are two things going on. One is the first year we're getting equipped with the tools. I think it's very important to make sure that we cover an agenda of items. And then there's another feeling— I've seen this in a quote of Solow's—that policy is sort of for simpletons.[1] If you really know your theory, the policy implications are pretty straightforward. It's not the really challenging meat-and-potato stuff for a really sharp theorist. I think that's another reason why they don't spend much time on applications.

Do you agree with that?

ARNOLD: Not necessarily. I feel that the implementation of policy is a much trickier question than those people give it credit for. A guy like Michael Piore, for instance, on the faculty here, is very concerned with that sort of thing, and I get the impression that he's almost sneered at for caring about the institutional problems that come along with implementing theoretical results. And there are very few other people on the faculty whose work takes that sort of thing into consideration.

How about the rest of you? [They all agree.]

CARL: I was a little disappointed in the lack of discussion of application of these tools in any particular area. It's obviously important to be equipped with these sets of tools and to be able to understand the models. Sometimes I think it might help a little bit in generating an understanding of them if there would be some discussion of the strengths and weaknesses of these tools as applied to a particular situation. You know—"Here are its weaknesses and here are the reasons it can't be used and here are the reasons it can."

Would you feel that's generally shared by pretty much all the graduate students?

ARNOLD: I don't know. I haven't seen the signs that it's widely shared. I haven't heard it mentioned a lot. One time recently, I started to question the applicability of a particular micro model that was being demonstrated, and I said, "Who sets people up like that in the real world?" And someone was so overwhelmed by the fact that I had doubts about whether or not this was applicable that they suggested that I was ready to join a monastery and go into a state of meditation.

DAVE: That was a joke.

I have a different orientation on this. I think it's extremely important that you look at applicability and how well grounded the assumptions are—especially with things like rational expectations. We've been getting into this model in macro that takes the game theory approach to the macro economy and has the consumers acting as a group adopting a set of expectations with the purpose in mind of punishing the Federal Reserve, which is really *silly*, because you don't adopt an expectation to punish somebody—you adopt an expectation based on what you think is going to happen. I talked to Dornbusch about this and he did not seem to get that this was a problem.

It is kind of ironic, in a way—it can be ironic—that a lot of us get into economics because we're interested in social issues. It would be kind of ironic if I wound up just as a mathematical economist talking about stochastic dominance or something—after being interested in social issues. And that happens.

I do think that modeling helps one gain intuition as far as what is going on in the real world. So I adopt an in-between notion that modeling is very, very important.

ARNOLD: I don't think anybody would debate that. It's just a question of whether there's any time spent in training economists to argue about what the models are about.

TONY: It seems like about the only substantial prerequisite to success here is that you have a very strong mathematical aptitude. If you have good mathematical skills, you're good at problem solving, both of which are much the same thing. And I have doubts that that's what makes a valuable and productive economist.

ARNOLD: Intuition is awfully important as far as economic problems are concerned.

Do you think that intuition is actually improved through the modeling technique?

ARNOLD: I think they do fit in. I know in macro, for instance, I can convince myself of anything when I sit down and do the models. Similarly, in econometrics I tell myself a lot of tales.

It is true though—I think maybe it is true—that there's a little overemphasis on the models. People like Lester Thurow and John Kenneth Galbraith and Mike Piore are generally sneered at.

How do you people think about those people?

DAVE: Well, I'm a big Piore fan, but I'm not a fair example.

How about you guys?

ARNOLD: About the only thing I have time to read these days is Galbraith, which I read on the side and which I find very enlightening. I think he makes a big contribution. The two elective courses I've taken so far have been Piore's and Thurow's. I think they have problems with their approach—Thurow's especially is less rigorous than it should be. But I think they make a very valuable contribution, and one that tends to balance what we're getting from the bulk of the rest of the faculty.

Do you agree?

TONY: Yes. I haven't had their classes but I've read some of their stuff.

DAVE: One thing I find really enjoyable about Piore or Galbraith is the notion that to be a good economist you have to know something about the social sciences outside of pure economics. You really get zero social sciences here. After all, we're modeling behavior of human beings, and human beings behave for a variety of reasons. We never really get any introduction to Marxist explanations or sociology or what have you— we get really no good idea of what's motivating people's behavior—to get us started on our models.

Could somebody with no interest in economics whatsoever, but a superb mathematician, do extremely well?

TONY: I don't think so.

ARNOLD: I think he could beat the median.

CARL: I don't think they'd tend to do very well later, because it's really a question that the faculty's feelings about the students are based much more on what they're doing research on later and how they do in workshops and this sort of thing, and a pure mathematician is going to be able to point out errors in someone's proofs, but it's not clear that they're going to really be respected as economists.

TONY: There are certain areas that they can go into in economics.

CARL: I think in econometrics, if you were a pure mathematician, statistician, you could just fly through that to a degree.

TONY: But as far as mastering theory or macro or industrial organization or whatever—there's a great quote by Keynes in Heilbroner's book, *The Worldly Philosophers*,[2] about what it takes to be a good economist. He says you have to be something of a mathematician, something of a historian, something of a philosopher, and all these different things put together. And really, you have to have those things if you want to have valuable intuitions on anything besides the most mathematical proofs. Maybe we don't cultivate it enough.

About Economists

Who are the people here in this department you think are really good economists?

ARNOLD: Good technical economists, you mean?

A good economist.

ARNOLD: I think Dornbusch is a good economist. I think he's a really big player in international current macro policy. I think he makes really meaningful, real contributions. He is very technically adept.

TONY: Peter Diamond comes to mind, because he's done a lot of things in so many different areas. I mean, he just sort of changes areas every couple of years and goes off to write seminal papers.

Are there any other names you would like to have mentioned?

TONY: I'd say Martin Weitzman would be one name of someone who has some very good insights—*The Share Economy* and also a paper that I think we've hit in two or three different courses now.[3]

ARNOLD: I think Weitzman's work is an example that it's not so terribly important that you be terribly mathematical, although he's plenty good at mathematics—it's more important that you ask the right questions.

What Is a Good Approach to Economics?

Usually when we think about economics we think of setting up a model and testing it. Is that the way people still think about economics?

DAVE: I think we see plenty of people who don't do a lot of empirical tests. You see that with Blanchard in macro. . . . In some of Stan Fischer's papers there is none of that.

TONY: I don't know that it's really important all the time that you come up with some specification. Econometrics has only developed so far, and a lot of specifications are murdered to get some meaningful test out of them. Besides, they are sometimes wildly unrealistic because you focus on one thing to see how much action you can get out of just inventories or something like that.

ARNOLD: There's a really basic question: Do you want economics to be a science? Do you want this to be an empirically testable discipline? Or do you want it to be a branch of study like philosophy and math, where you're just trying to see what the interconnections between the assumptions and the results are?

TONY: There's a place for both.

What do you think?

ARNOLD: I very strongly feel it should be an empirical science. I started off interested in economics because I thought it was very pertinent to the issues that I read in the newspaper when I was in high school. I went to an extremely mathematical undergraduate school. I did well because I was good in math. Then I got a job with the government, as I said, and that turned me even more heavily toward the applicability of economics and economics as a means to an end.

Neoclassical Economics and the Rationality Assumption

How about neoclassical economics?

ARNOLD: I had a bellyful of alternative approaches as an undergraduate.

Did you find that useful?

ARNOLD: No, I think that Marxism on political and ideological grounds is pernicious rubbish, but nevertheless I know that this is an ideological orientation and an intuitive feeling of what works after having spent some time in communist countries. Yes, I think Marxist economists have contributed a lot. If I were going to add a name to that list of economists whom I most admire, it would be Karl Marx. He did give brilliant insight into economics, combining history and all different social sciences.

What do you think of the assumption of rationality in neoclassical economics?

TONY: I have real troubles with that assumption. Every time it crops up, and every time someone tries to force it on the real world, I can't help but feel that many times people are stupid. I find no way of being able to reconcile people's behavior with rationality. You throw in a lot of imperfect information and they just don't have any idea what they're doing.

Even in the modern formulation of rational expectations?

CARL: If you go to the roots of what economics is about, we're trying to study something about how people behave and how they act in groups. But when we make this sort of rationality assumption, we almost assume what we should actually be examining. That's an area where economists probably could benefit by a greater understanding of other social sciences, which are sneered at as not being scientific. In large part they're not scientific, quote-unquote, because they're trying to delve into all these various elements of human behavior which aren't easy to pin down.

TONY: I think there's one interesting example that's pertinent to this that came up in micro—I believe Frank Fisher's course. We were doing uncertainty, and he showed us the basic assumptions on expected utility maximization—how you could manipulate this to get a testable hypothesis. And he spent about ten minutes saying, "By the way, please note, all empirical tests show that people definitely do not behave in this manner." And then we continued using the assumption.

ARNOLD: If you don't assume rationality, you're left with ad hoc reasoning completely, I think.

CARL: Yes, but that might be a more useful assumption.

ARNOLD: Maybe in certain applictions.

CARL: It may not be more mathematically powerful.

ARNOLD: It is certainly true that certain people face a tighter mental budget constraint than others. But I think there's usually a reason for people doing what they're doing. I know I've behaved stupidly on many occasions.

DAVE: I think it's very important, because otherwise you have to have a subsidiary theory that eliminates choice. And very few people that I've seen want to get involved in trying to come up with something like that. It's sort of okay in the literature to say that people act rationally without going through a few paragraphs of saying why they might do that. But if you start saying that they don't act rationally, then you're really in the soup. So many of the assumptions we make are because they make the mathematics tractable. [Then it was time for their next class.]

Second-Year Students

This conversation occurred after the one with the third-year students. Four students participated: Chuck, Charles, Conny, and Cindy.

About Economists

What did you do with the question about which economists you respect most?

CHUCK: The only one I put down was Albert Hirschman. I like him. [Chuck mentioned before we began that one of his fields is development.]

Why?

CHUCK: He writes on a broad variety of topics. [Laughing apologetically.] I've just been reading a couple of his books—The *Passions and the Interests* and *Exit, Voice and Loyalty*.[4] He has a really good historical feel for history.

What did you do?

CHARLES: I put Keynes first. I think Keynes did revolutionize our way of thinking about the economy. He was also a great communicator in that he really did see *The General Theory* as much as a polemic as a theoretical work.[5] And I think he's managed to bridge the gap between being a high-powered academic—he was a second Wrangler in the Math Tripos or something—and being somebody who was able to talk with politicians and persuade them of his ideas. He managed to combine being a great intellectual with being politically important. I had Samuelson for number two because he sort of invented modern micro theory essentially. And Joe Stiglitz is number three.

Why?

CHARLES: Stiglitz is immensely prolific. Although a lot of things he throws out are quite similar to things he's already done, there are good ideas that come out, like the Grossman-Stiglitz optimal degree of disinformation in the market—that sort of thing.

What did you do?

CONNY: I put Keynes down.

Why?

CINDY: Essentially for similiar reasons. Samuelson for the breadth of work he has done as well.

The Mathematics in the Program

Would you say that this program is mathematical?

CHARLES: Not as much as the UCLA program. They say that is a pure math program. It's fairly mathematical here.

CHUCK: I would say so. Everything is formalized.

Is that all right?

CHARLES: Sure. People come here because they like to do technical models, usually. This program is known as a very technically oriented program, so that's why you apply here. If you are interested in Marxian economics, say, you might go to U.Mass-Amherst, maybe to Boston College, or maybe to Harvard to study with Murray Milgate.

CINDY: There is some self-selection. I certainly had heard that this is a great place for econometrics. And you'll see that many of us are majoring in econometrics.

CHARLES: Half of our class is, maybe even two-thirds.

The Relevance of What They Learned

Would you say that what you have learned so far is relevant for understanding the economy?

CHARLES: I think that what we have done has given us some insights into the micro economy, say the housing market, the labor markets. I found the macro courses kind of disjointed. I don't have that much understanding of the institutional nature of the American macro economy. I have a better understanding of the British one because we focus more on institutional stuff as undergraduates.[6]

I think the stuff we learn is useful, but it is not the whole story. You have to take account of the fact that this stuff is taking place in an environment that is conditioned by history, by social relations, and so on. We don't get that side in macro. It's largely optimizing and overlapping generations models.

Am I unfair? [*The others don't think he is.*]

It's maybe that that sort of stuff lends itself better to classroom teaching. I always thought that in class you learn tools—the rest you are supposed to learn on your own.

CHUCK: I think, though, that the emphasis on problem sets is kind of strange. I was used to teaching by essay.

MIT Versus Chicago

CHARLES: The approach here has not given any particular insight, but it has not pretended to . . . as opposed to maybe a Chicago approach. The style there is that not only do they teach you the tools, but they also make you believe that the tools explain the economy.

They don't believe that here?

CHARLES: No.

CHUCK: I haven't met anybody who does.

CHARLES: They tell you, "These are tools. They may help you to understand the economy, but here we don't believe that people really go out each morning and maximize their utility." The caricature of Chicago that is usually presented to us is that there people do believe that. Basically, Chicago gets a lot of stick around here.

CHUCK: Here we do set up intertemporal maximizing models. But several times Fisher in his course, I remember, said—after we had gone through some of those papers—"I think this is actually pushing the theory a little harder than it deserves to be pushed."

More on the Relevance

CHARLES: It's a set of strategic simplifications. You have to remember that that's what it is. It's not a description of reality. They do a pretty good job making you remember that, at least in the classes. Once people start writing their thesis, they may actually start believing it. *[He laughs.]* Then they forget that it's all just an approximation. That is actually dangerous.

Why?

CHARLES: It may lead to some pretty weird policy prescription. It can lead to the belief that thirteen percent of the British work force is unemployed because they are currently taking leisure and will work harder when the real wage is higher. But thirty percent of the British firms are not working anywhere near capacity. There is a heck of a lot of unused plants. The government is running an inflation-adjusted surplus. Essentially the country is suffering from a lack of aggregate demand. The same is true in some other European countries. But there are people like Patrick Minford at Liverpool[7] who are saying, "Hey, these people are all voluntarily unemployed; they're all taking leisure." It's ridiculous. You just can't believe that when you look at the way the world really is. Okay, you can start off by saying, "We'll work as if people are maximizing utility over some horizon," but this is a gross simplification. It's ignoring a lot of imperfections that characterize the real world. We may get something out of it, but you've got to be terribly careful in interpreting it. And you don't just rush up to the nearest politician and tell him, "Okay, the way to cure unemployment is to completely eliminate unemployment benefits. Then these people will find that the value of their leisure has declined somewhat." That's why I think it's dangerous.

Would it be right if I were to conclude that you are basically content with the tools you are learning? [They agree.]

CHUCK: I haven't seen any other tools that were more useful.

On Econometrics

Do you believe that econometrics is useful in the sense that it produces good or hard results?

CHARLES: Suggestive results. Econometrics does not give you the equivalent to Planck's constant. We don't have the experimental situation—we can't control for everything, which is why we put everything on the right-hand side of our equations. So you get results that are suggestive. You should not lose sight of the fact that these are not hard and fast results.

What do you think?

CINDY: Essentially the same. I would emphasize more the problems with the data. The data are just not perfect. They're not exactly what you're trying to measure, in most cases.

About Their Plans

Are you seeking academic jobs?

CHARLES: Primarily.

Universities, colleges?

CINDY: College. I want to teach.

Why college?

CINDY: They work awfully hard here.

CHARLES: That has to do with getting tenure. There are certain aspects of the MIT junior faculty lifestyle that do not appeal.

CINDY: Most people here will want to go to big schools.

Their Politics

Are there political debates among students?

CHARLES: Most people are liberals here, I think. It's pretty hard to find right-wingers around here, even by American standards. Most people are pretty liberal even by British standards.

You are not becoming more conservative in graduate school?

CINDY: No, I don't think so.

CHARLES: I don't know of anybody in our class, say, that would have voted for Reagan.

Are They Cynical?

I talked earlier with the first- and third-year students. One thing that came our of their conversations was that they were quite cynical about their experience here at MIT.

CHARLES: The first-year student already? Wow!

CHUCK: Cynical in what sense?

Cynical toward developments of the graduate training; cynical about the abundance of techniques; somewhat cynical about neoclassical economics—all thought it was a game that they are playing here, to get a job or to get tenure. I don't get that sense from you.

CHUCK: I like it here.

CHARLES: There must be something wrong with us.

CHUCK: I can see being cynical. I mean, it *is* a game—I mean, the tenure. You know what it is—you're an academic.

CHARLES: Getting all your publications done?

CHUCK: Yes. You know the joke—publishing the same article three or four times in different places with slight variations on the model you choose *[he mentions an MIT economist known for doing this]*. So there are aspects of the experience you could be cynical about. But since I'm not primarily concerned with getting tenure—I'm not concerned about getting a job at a top-ten university—I'm not really concerned about playing the game, so it leaves me much less to be cynical about.

Third-Year Students

Six students participated in this conversation: Paula, Josh, Laurel, Rob, Alex, and Harry.

Their Experience at Graduate School

This is your third year, so you have gone through quite a bit so far. How would you describe your experience? As positive? Inspiring? Frustrating? Difficult?

PAULA: All of the above. All of it. Parts of it are really enjoyable—other parts are utterly frustrating.

What is enjoyable?

PAULA: I enjoyed working on my thesis and doing research. The part that I found frustrating was some of the class work in the first two years, partly because I think I came in without the math background that one should have for a program like this.

JOSH: I'd say overall it's a pretty blah experience, a pretty mediocre experience. I had been exposed to doing research as an undergraduate, so I didn't feel some of the excitement of starting to do research, although I find that much more enjoyable than the course work. I probably feel pretty much the same way as Paula.

How about you?

LAUREL: I'll agree with Paula and Josh about course work. Undergraduate course work in the economics is sort of intellectually interesting. It seems like the first two years here are very much vocational—all of a sudden you're getting vocational training as opposed to intellectual training. Having done research as an undergraduate, it's frustrating to spend your time doing problem sets and learning techniques and not being intellectually stimulated all that much. Occasionally there's something interesting.

Can you say now that you are happy that you got this course work, and do you think that what you learned from that is important?

ROB: I would say that my understanding now of macroeconomics and econometrics—areas that I spent a lot of time working on in course work—is marginally better than before I entered the graduate program. I have no greater interest in those fields, and now I could probably pick up the literature and read it where I couldn't do that beforehand. I have no greater sense of what are, for me, important research issues in those fields.

LAUREL: I disagree, especially on econometrics, which also isn't my field. I think I can do a lot of things awfully useful, having learned what I did. The econometrics program here is very useful.

PAULA: There's a large body of stuff I remembered exactly as long as it took me to write it down and then just forgot. I always have to go back to scratch to pick it up again.

JOSH: I guess looking back on it, we paid our dues and it's really worthwhile that we've done all that. It's hard to know whether it would have been much more difficult to find a thesis topic if you weren't exposed to what you were exposed to. I certainly feel that the program here is too structured and that we should be writing papers instead—rather than two years of courses and vocational training preparing to write a dissertation.

Would you say that the emphasis in the first two years of graduate training is on mathematics and problem solving? [All except Laurel agree.]

LAUREL: Not necessarily. [He hesitates.] Problem sets are the mechanism that they use here to force people to go through the material, and the techniques that are required to solve the problems are often mathematical. But I think it's true that the economic concepts are usually there.

PAULA: How many problem sets have you written or graded—I have graded some of them too—where you get this problem, you get to the end and they ask you to interpret what you've just done. Ninety percent of the grade is put onto the math and they sort of blow off the interpretation part of it. Is that being unfair?

The first-year students complained that the courses are so mathematical that they had no chance to really talk about economics. Is that true? Do you recognize those complaints?

ALEX: I don't feel that if you do these models, you preclude talking about economic issues. It's more that not enough discussion went into what the assumptions mean. I remember trying to explain macro and wondering what *is* this? This is ridiculous. You know, having to learn how to do signal extraction problems, jumping to the saddle point—absolutely the most ridiculous thing I've ever seen. But you couldn't really discuss that.

ROB: It's not that it's divorced from the economics. It's not that the economics isn't discussed. But they very much take the modeling technique and the source of the models as given. They talk about the economics given the model, rather than about choosing the models or the assumptions.

LAUREL: Except for Solow.

ROB: Yes, you can talk with him a lot about whether these assumptions are reasonable, which is pretty much his approach to things. He worries a lot about different ways of doing things.

Their Theses

You are all in your third year and you are all searching for topics. Some of you might have found topics. How did you come to choose your topic?

HARRY: All of us are working on specific topics. Mine is about takeovers and disciplining management.

Because of the takeovers that are occurring in the economy?

HARRY: No, there was some other person that did a paper on takeovers and I started thinking about it through that. I thought it was interesting because it fits in with some other work I'd been doing.

JOSH: I had a topic I'd been thinking about for two years, and thought I wanted to work on it but couldn't make things come out the way I wanted them to do, so I did a little work and ended up with what I really wanted to do—found a way of fitting it into models that we'd seen.

LAUREL: I found what I am working on from sitting in a class, in a money class. I came in with a background of doing a lot of theory, kind of micro and game theory stuff. At any rate, I am now working on a game-theoretical model of price rigidity.

PAULA: I just stumbled into mine. For a labor class that I took second semester I had to write a three-page paper. The professor suggested a topic and I did that, and that topic grew into a topic for an econometrics paper that we write during our second year, and the issue that came out of that grew into my thesis topic. It is about union strike behavior and wage contours. I definitely used skills I picked up in econometrics, because it's an empirical thesis. But basically the course work I took was essentially irrelevant to what I'm writing my thesis on, except in the broadest of terms.

ROB: I got the idea for what I was working on from thinking a little bit about all these shakeouts in the personal computer industry. It seemed kind of puzzling that when these industries are young and growing, all these firms leave—very strange. So I started thinking about that, and I'm working on trying to model that kind of thing, as a sort of dynamic game.

About Economists

Which economists do work that you consider relevant?

JOSH: Can I pick a recently dead economist? Arthur Okun. Very relevant. And also academic.

Who else?

LAUREL: Larry Summers.

Why?

LAUREL: Partly because of the sheer variety of the stuff that he does. . . . It's also a kind of new approach to just about anything. He takes on policy issues and he takes on what's going on in the economy—he just goes right at it.

Since I'm a theorist, I'll mention theorists: Oliver Hart and Peter Diamond, both of whom take simple models and look at really relevant issues and try to understand what's going on—which forces may have large effects on the economy on a theoretical level.

ALEX: I guess Summers is doing the counterpart of that on the empirical side—taking a couple of facts which have obvious implications once they're recognized, but having the insight to recognize what the implications are.

What names do you come up with?

PAULA: Larry Bird, but I don't think he counts. If you want a kind of role model, in terms of the kind of work I do, I'd name my thesis adviser, who's Hank Farber. I admire his work because he's somebody who is able to look at complicated issues or relatively complicated issues, and see through to the essence of them, and he has a good sense of how much the data are able to tell you and with how many grains of salt you take the results that you get.

JOSH: I'll add another name—George Akerlof. He has the ability to sort of expand the horizons of what economics is about and come up with interesting new ideas.

Neoclassical Economics

Is it important for all of you to formulate your models in terms of rational behavior?

ROB: Just because I know how to do that.

LAUREL: I think most of us would like to have a theory of bounded rationality. It's the limitations of the theory that push us to this.

JOSH: It's also the chaos.

What do you mean?

JOSH: When you write a dissertation, you almost never take on some really risky thing. When you have a choice between a neoclassical framework and something else, you pick the neoclassical framework. You can get lots of help, you know it, plus the payoff is better.

That sounds rather cynical.

JOSH: I think there's an element of that in people. I wouldn't say that it totally drives our decisions, but it's a factor.

LAUREL: When you write your dissertation, you better show that you've learned all the appropriate stuff. It's not perhaps the best time to take on neoclassical economics.

ALEX: Not until you get tenure.

Would anyone like to take on neoclassical economics?

ALEX: Yes, if there's some reasonable replacement for the rationality postulate, some better behavioral assumption. In some cases it turns out that doing things rationally just is very messy, and maybe if you'd do it the other way, you'd get a better result, and it would also be more realistic. I don't know—I'm not about to spend lots of time right now finding this out—it would be a really bad investment.

Are there people who are committed to rational expectations?

ROB: I'd say there's definitely departmental ethos against that.

Is that so?

PAULA: If by "rational expectations" you mean the technique of how expectations in a model are formed, a lot of people use that. If you mean that there can't possibly ever be an effective government monetary policy because everybody sees everything and it's perfectly anticipated, I'd say there are very few people like that.

[Everyone talks at once. Someone comments, "But there are no Lucas types here." Another: "No one would insist on prices being flexible and unemployment voluntary."]

After Graduate School

*You're going to go out and get jobs pretty soon. Are you all going into teaching or consulting or . . . ? [Silence.] Anyone **not** going into teaching? [Only Paula is not.]*

PAULA: I haven't gotten very far in defining it, other than not teaching. I came into the program initially not wanting to go into teaching. I was working for a consulting firm and I enjoyed that work, although I don't know if that's what I'd want to do again. And then you get here and you definitely feel the peer pressure with everybody saying, "Oh, yes, I want to go on and teach." And when you declare you don't want to teach, they say, "What's the matter? You're good enough." But I haven't particularly enjoyed the lifestyle that graduate school has.

Why not?

PAULA: I guess I found my world concentrating only on people that I knew from the department, and I got sick of talking about economics after a little while—maybe that's just me. And I basically just didn't know anybody.

ROB: You'd kind of like to read a novel once in a while.

PAULA: Or watch television or go to a movie or basketball game.

Did any of you think when you came in that you would go into nonacademic jobs—and then changed your minds?

ROB: I've definitely thought about it as an option, depending on how things work out. It certainly is true that you can get away with a lower degree of dissertation work if you're not going into an academic job. So if your stuff doesn't work out, it's good psychologically to keep that open.

ALEX: That's an incredible put-down. *[People laugh.]*

ROB: Not at all. They don't care necessarily about the same things. They want to know if you know what you're doing and if you're intelligent and you know how to work the problems, but they don't necessarily care that you do this for your dissertation.

PAULA: They want to hire you if you can do well what *they* want you to do.

ALEX: Which may be different from solving, say, saddle point problems. *[They laugh.]*

How are academics' jobs ranked? Where do liberal arts schools fit in there?

LAUREL: Williams and Amherst are somewhere out of sight.

ROB: I know people who want to go to liberal arts colleges.

PAULA: They're the people who really want to teach more than they want to do research.

ALEX: That's true, but that's definitely not the thing to do—to walk into Stan Fischer's office and announce that you want to teach at Williams.

What would he say?

ALEX: Well, I haven't done it. *[We laugh.]*

LAUREL: You know, research really is the lifeblood of these kinds of organizations. And they're interested in the prestige of the program.

About This Group of Students and the Questionnaire

We discuss with them our concern that this group of only six would not be a fair representation of the third year at MIT. Paula mentions that no foreign students are present. She expects them to have a somewhat different outlook, partly because they are older. We ask about the technical students. Laurel does not think there are any such types in their year.

We continue talking about the economists they respect most. Paula mentions Adam Smith, adding that she has not read him. The others have not either. We then ask whether they have changed in the three years of graduate school.

ALEX: As economists?

In any way.

LAUREL: Frankly, I'm kind of worn out.

Intellectually?

LAUREL: Intellectually and physically.

JOSH: It's just a really grueling program.

ALEX: I'm more bored with economics. I don't like it as much.

PAULA: I go with Alex. I just feel like I cannot wait to get out of here. And part of the reason I don't want to go into teaching is I just want to get away from the academic environment. I don't know if that would be any different if I had gone to medical school or law school, but I find that my interest in doing something in economics that is not directly related to anything I'm doing has just dropped off completely. I don't even read the business section in the newspaper anymore.

ALEX: I don't think I have quite that strong a reaction. I guess I just am not worn down as much, maybe. I'm still curious about things, so I keep reading things that seem interesting.

JOSH: I don't feel like I've changed all that much. I feel slightly less optimistic about the ability of economics to improve the universe at large. You sit there and realize what a big mess the economy is, and you can't tell them what they should do to make it all better. It teaches you some of the limitations.

Fourth-Year Students

We were especially curious about the opinions of this group. After all, they are in the final stages of their studies, and with a Ph.D. from a top school, they are destined to be influential in the discourse of tomorrow. Their opinions could suggest the future of economics. How technically minded would they be, we wondered? What do they think of economics as it is currently practiced? And how did they change during graduate school?

Six students showed up—not a bad turnout. We talked first about the questions on the questionnaire. They generally repeated the comments that the students in the other years had made. Then we asked them whether they thought they had changed during graduate school. The discussion turned to the change in their career aspirations. (A few of these students have since the time of the conversation built up impressive reputations.) As promised, we have tried to conceal their identities; the students' new names are Claire, Larry, Wendy, Peter, Don, and Phil.

Their Plans

CLAIRE: I've been semisocialized into the profession. When I came here, I would have sworn that after my Ph.D. I would go straight into doing policy work. I was very skeptical of these hoity-toity articles for academic journals. Yet here *the* thing to do is to get an academic position and write papers for journals. Those who can't do economics do policy—

LARRY: Or teach in a liberal arts college.

CLAIRE: That's true, too. I was much more sympathetic toward liberal arts teaching when I came than I am now. So both teaching and policy I now value less, though I still feel quite strongly that some day in the not too distant future I want to use the tools I have to do policy. But it's more that the research side of things right now is much more valuable—or I just view it as what I'm supposed to be doing without necessarily understanding whether or not it's actually valuable.

LARRY: Someone said at the beginning, "Go and become an economist; then you're not limited in your options—you can always go and do policy." But actually it's very limited.

When a lot of your friends are judging you by how good a job you get and the faculty says, "Go and get tenure at a major university," it's very hard to say, "No, I'm going to chuck all this and be a failure." All of these people have been very important in the last four years. It's frustrating.

WENDY: I think you overstate that a little. For one thing, what people lose sight of is that we all have long lives ahead of us. George Shultz was an economics professor at MIT for many years, and he went on to do policy things. A lot of us at thirty-five or forty-five or fifty-five will probably be doing a lot of interesting nonacademic things.

PETER: You can argue about whether knowledge is advanced by young, imaginative people who really don't know too much history in their field and who can come up with clever things, and whether policy ought to be made by older, more experienced people. Being a little off-the-wall is not bad for an academic, but it would be terrible for policymaking.

DON: The discipline is advanced by young people with little knowledge of the world who have mainly their cleverness to back them up. We should not glorify people who spend a lifetime involved in the theoretical world, getting their hands dirty in minor pursuits, and in the latter part of their careers try to draw all those things together.

You are all seeking academic jobs?

CLAIRE: At least primarily.

WENDY: Most people would probably go to the big schools.

Are you optimistic?

CLAIRE: Yes. When you find out during your first year that four people went to Princeton, three to Harvard last year, and things like that, you feel reasonably good about your own chances.

The Techniques

They say that economics involves the learning of a lot of techniques. How do you evaluate that part of your experience?

LARRY: It's definitely what it was. MIT very much teaches you techniques. You don't learn much of the literature. In a typical money course, the articles are mainly from the last three to five years. There is no sense of going back to the old Friedman-Tobin debates or any of that. The lesson is, "You've got to learn to manage the equations."

PETER: I think it's overstated that all of us are such math jocks.

LARRY: Still, the point is the *technique.*

CLAIRE: None of us have really knocked ourselves out reading mathematics books in order to try to push the technique further. We've used most of the techniques that others have used—the things we were relatively comfortable with when we started our dissertations. They have been extended piecemeal here and there as we came upon particular problems, but none of us ever faced constraints coming from our lack of mathematics, and found what we were doing in writing our dissertations was learning more mathematics.

PHIL: I don't see the point in *not* having technical training—in not learning the trade.

DON: It's not a trade. It's an intellectual view of the world.

The Practicial Side of Economics

LARRY: Why should we study issues in graduate school for which there's no demand at the time? Like whether we should go to communism or something like that. Nobody in the country *wants* to go to communism. Why should we all be in graduate school deciding whether that's what we should do? I mean, does it make any sense?

DON: Shouldn't we be looking at different views of the world? The graduate students at Harvard talk about these things much more than we do here.

LARRY: It seems to me, you had four years to go to college and think about broad issues, and now it's time to—*[Everyone talks at once.]*

DON: You want to learn a trade. I think there's a lot to be said for that. You don't want to become so right that—

CLAIRE: You can even argue that economics is a field in which there isn't a lot of just thinking to be done. Philosophy of law might be interesting, but law school is mainly a training. Likewise economics is not meant to be one of the disciplines that you go into just to think. It's a trade school.

DON: That may describe the reality of what things are like here or in a lot of other departments, but I don't think that's what economics is.

What is the difference between economics and law school?

CLAIRE: We're going into a much better trade. There's a *lot* more that we can do. The kind of economic analysis that's going on in Washington is *terrible*, and the kind of policy that's going on is really misguided.

LARRY: But don't you want to teach? I mean, isn't that the way you're going to use your trade—in teaching?

CLAIRE: I'd like to suggest that we have the engineering school versus physics departments. In the physics department, people are academics—they push forward the frontier of knowledge. The engineering department uses that knowledge. The economics department combines the pushing out of the frontiers of knowledge with its application. So, some of us here are engineers, and some scientists.

WENDY: Michael Piore says that the tools we're learning don't very well equip you to do anything. To make a highly valuable contribution, neoclassical economics is unlikely to help point you in that direction. The tools limit the number of questions you ask and the way that you ask them.

PHIL: I like the kinds of questions that Piore asks. I really think of them as being more in sociology and things of that sort—you know, history—and—

PETER: Where do you draw the line?

PHIL: I don't care about the line. I don't care if there are sociologists in the economics department or whether they interact with the economists. But to my mind, it's kind of a different trade.

CLAIRE: The answers both get are in some sense the right answers, and all of our theory says that those answers are impossible.

What Is Good Economics?

What kind of work done in economics today do you consider to be good work?

CLAIRE: Well, if you go down the index of the *Journal of Political Economy*, what percentage of articles would most of us think are not stupid? It's pretty small. One problem is that we do not care about most issues discussed. Probably all of us would agree that many, many papers are just applications of some technique without really any ideas behind them—issues of formalism for formalism's sake.

That doesn't say much for the economics profession.

CLAIRE: We go to the money workshop. You'd think that for our edification the faculty would bring in the best young people throughout the country to give macro talks about their current research. All of us go, week after week, and come back and just laugh at their big reputations. What they do is usually very complicated and very implausible. The best analogy is . . . who's the guy who does the drawings, the funny drawings of the contraptions? *[Larry mentions a name.]*

Yes. When you talk to him, he seems a head-on-his-shoulders kind of guy, but he really has very little feel for the economy. It seems that his research strategy was to go to a senior colleague of his who's one of the builders of the macroeconomic models and really understands a lot of things, or to go to someone who does vector auto-regressions, get a fact, one fact, and then, while divorcing himself from all other knowledge and reality, come up with a very stylized model that explains that fact. It seemed clear to those of us who had attended the seminar that by not tying his model to reality in any other way, he just had gotten something that was completely ridiculous.

LARRY: I don't go to a lot of them, but one I did go to was about wages and strike activity. When I asked a couple of questions, it turned out that the guy had just gotten the data the day before and didn't know anything about it. He didn't even know things like that at least one of the strikes in the sample ended on an injunction. I mean, no contact whatsoever with reality—this has nothing to do with theory or with mathematics or anything else—just a level of abstraction from what they're working on.

WENDY: I can remember last year leaving the money workshop so depressed. I guess Lars Hansen had just given one. I remember walking home with a friend and saying, "What's the profession coming to? This person is one of the biggest people in the field, and it just seems like the worst thing we've ever seen, and worse yet, we didn't understand three-quarters of it."

DON: Do you want to spell your name? *[Laughter.]* I agree though. The people are very smart, and the work may show a lot of brilliance, but it seems that they're not dealing with the issues.

PHIL: I think people who have an intuitive grasp of real-world issues do a better job than the ones who do it on a mathematical basis.

What economists are doing good work? [Everyone talks at once.]

WENDY: I like Michael Piore.

DON: He accumulates a lot of very different observations that don't seem to fit together.

Who else?

LARRY: Would I get stoned if I said Bob Barro?

PHIL: No.

CLAIRE: Not that he's going about it the right way, but he is definitely asking big questions.

Why did you think you would get stoned?

LARRY: Oh—I hate Bob Barro's ideology, and so it's frustrating to have to say that he's asking interesting questions.

PETER: But unlike almost every other member of new classical macro-economics, he has no technique to speak of, and he just thinks hard about things and sort of looks at the data in an intelligent sort of way.

So far the only candidates have been Michael Piore and Bob Barro.

PHIL: I have to renominate my previously stated hero, George Akerlof, for thinking about why we have unemployment and why we have the business cycle.

PETER: I also like Robert Lucas.

Why is that?

PETER: Because he thinks about—

DON: He certainly has made a number of contributions that everyone here would think were very important.

[Everyone talks at once. They mention other names, among whom are Oliver Blanchard, Rudy Dornbusch (for his "very nice, pretty models and his engagement in worldly affairs"), and Jerry Hausman (for his tools). Thurow's name elicits the usual discussion. Don "would like him better if he was a little more rigorous—not in the mathematical sense, but in the sense of doing some good economic research." They wonder about his policies. According to Peter, "He's not pushing issues that are really important." The names of Martin Weitzman and Larry Summers come up. The students think Summers is the smartest economist around, even though his work has not made any breakthroughs. We ask them which economists at MIT they would like to emulate. Peter is quick to comment, "They all work too hard." Claire points out the positive side, "You know that between 8 a.m. and midnight, people— especially the junior faculty—will be in their offices so you can always get hold of them." In other words, she agrees with Peter. The discussion returns to the differences in the approaches of Summers and Hausman.]

Empirical Research

PETER: Do you ever really know what to make of Summers's empiricism?

DON: Except for certain cases, I want to defend the general empirical approach of Larry Summers over that of guys like Jerry Hausman. Jerry seems to be so careful—you've got to use multiple maxima, or whatever, and you come out with what look like precise estimates. I don't think I like that. When you do empirical work with Larry Summers, you're saying, "What are we really picking up here? What is the source of this correlation? What *might* this be a proxy of? Is it possible that we're overfitting the instrument from the first stage? Do we have a spurious correlation?" I put in a big plug for that general approach.

PETER: I don't think I'd accept your dismissal of Hausman.

DON: I assume this is supposed to be a frank discussion, so let me say that I'm really very, very suspicious of those things—and I'm not saying that I don't admire techniques. I'm *certainly* not saying that we shouldn't work on techniques. I've heard all kinds of horror stories, like Hausman imposing a constraint of the effect of nonhuman capital on the labor supply—you know, as you get wealthier you work less, even though in the cross-section we know that the wealthier people tend to work more. There could be something sophisticated in it that I'm not really understanding here. But as far as I can understand it, it seems suspicious.

MIT Versus Chicago and Harvard

It is my impression that here at MIT people take quite a strong anti-Chicago stance. Is that right?

DON: No. That's wrong. *[For quite some time everyone talks at once. Don's voice finally prevails.]* The truth is that Chicago macro really took over here when Stanley Fischer came here. MIT hasn't really had a contribution of its own for a number of years—maybe in the past couple of years.

WENDY: You understand that the rational expectations approach is really two hypotheses. We agree with rational expectations; we don't agree with the market-clearing theory. I think a lot of us believe that there are a lot of interesting techniques and a lot of interesting questions in the Chicago school, but we don't accept the basic premise that the economy is at all times in equilibrium.

PHIL: Dornbusch and Blanchard think in their hearts of hearts that if you want to understand what's going to happen, the IS/LM model will do pretty well, but if you want to do research or understand why the IS/LM model is a good model, you better have some equilibrium models lined up. They're very eclectic in their teaching. There's a certain orientation here—people should be doing what sells.

People have the impression that MIT students are much more uniform than Harvard students.

PHIL: I think we're very diverse.

WENDY: I agree.

In what sense are you diverse?

PETER: A lot of people have different types of training. Some people are math majors, some people are different types of majors, some have taken graduate courses in economics, some people have master's degrees in English.

LARRY: I think Harvard is more diverse.

CLAIRE: They are interested in art and we're not. They also seem to have diverse political beliefs and very different personalities.

DON: I think it's just that the papers that come out of here tend to be more homogeneous. There is an MIT research style—you are supposed to have a theoretical section and an empirical section, in which you say that the model is supported or rejected. That *is* kind of a style. Harvard has more highbrow theorist types on the one hand, and on the other hand, it has more people who don't really think about much and kind of agree with stuff.

PETER: The faculty here is extremely homogeneous, relative to almost any department except Chicago.

WENDY: I think we *do* end up more uniform. On the other hand, I think our training is, in general, better—that part of what you're giving up in your diversity you're getting back. The faculty won't leave you alone, and they tend to enforce a certain level of quality. They collect stars pretty early on.

Diversity and Skepticism: Harvard Students

First-Year Students

Six students showed up for the meeting, three women and three men: Brian (a British student), Janet, Albert, Vicky, Len, and Julie. They were lively, eager to talk about their experiences. The conversation became more reserved when a seventh student, Ed, walked in at the very moment they were talking about him.

About the Questionnaire

What did you think of the questionnaire?

JANET: Some things were hard to answer.

Such as? [They laugh.]

JANET: What I think economics is about. It reminded me that my impression of what economics is seems very different from what it probably really is. I think there is something wrong with what we are led to expect.

BRIAN: It's like stumbling to your death. All you can think of is getting through the math course, getting to the end of the semester. You forget why you are here, what you are doing. You never get the chance to do anything else or to sit down and think, "Oh why did I come here—is this really a useful exercise?"

Three years from now we may wake up and wonder, "Why am I here? What have I done?"

ALBERT: I agree with that. It's actually kind of embarrassing when you think about these things and you don't know.

Were there strange questions on the questionnaire?

VICKY: Which economists I respect most. I did not know what to say. I only know of people we have read in classes.

LEN: What about Barro? *[Loud laughter. Barro would join the Harvard department a year later.]*

Their Experience in the First Year

JULIE: We spent a lot of time this year learning stuff that is either not interesting or is not true. We start with one model and go through each conceivable permutation. It is a rather odd way to start.

Why odd?

JANET: I just don't think that that's what most people think of as economics when they are undergrads. They think more in terms of policy, taxation, and fiscal policy, especially on the macro side.

Maybe it is good because it signals that you are not undergraduates anymore. But the transition is very abrupt.

ALBERT: I agree. It was completely different. In macro we had done the Keynesian model, IS/LM. It made sense to me because everything was linked that way. But macroeconomics this year was a bunch of models. They were not put together.

JANET: I think that that is really bad here.

ALBERT: They wouldn't tell us why the models are so different.

VICKY: It is all very technical. You get all those equations and you are never sure what their signficance is. But perhaps it is good that the professors do not tie things together. In that way we have to make up our own minds.

Why do they do it this way?

VICKY: The way they explain it to us is that they sit down in the beginning of the year and decide what minimum of macro and micro the students are supposed to know, what are the issues in the fields, what models they need to read the literature. Then they put together a stack of papers.

ALBERT: Part of the problem is the disarray in macroeconomics. It is kind of funny. This semester we are learning model after model, but we learned so many things that don't work in reality. We didn't learn the right way to view things. Maybe that is a problem of the discipline.

LEN: It is not only that things don't work. In micro in the first semester we did consumer and producer theory. This material has a natural order. You might not agree with it, but at least you know what you are doing, where you are going. But in macro—

VICKY: Actually, I am taking an economic history course where you do start using macro models. It was good to know that some of those things are actually useful. That was reassuring.

JANET: By the way, what does that mean—natural order? So you look at microeconomics, see it has a natural order, and say, "Oh, that's nice." So what? *[They laugh.]*

ALBERT: As Len said, you may not agree with it, but at least you know what you are doing. Macro is not only not useful; it is also inconsistent.

JANET: I don't think they teach macro the right way here, but that is my personal bias. We had a discussion with some professors about this. Larry [Summers] tried to say that these models taught us how to think about things. Maybe. . . . To me, learning these things seems a lot of effort, and I am not convinced you end up with the insight.

I think it is worse here than at other schools. The department makes a big effort to enroll a lot of people with little background in economics. I think that's great, but for someone with a lot of economics, the disarray in macroeconomics would be less disturbing. Those who don't have such a background need to get many more hints as to why you need to learn all those models.

About Harvard Students

JULIE: One of the advantages here is the diversity of students. People at, say, MIT have a much more similar background, usually with lots of economics. More people here come from other disciplines. That is a big plus.

Why?

JULIE: One of the problems economics has now is that there is not enough time spent looking at the real world, at policy. There are too many people who spend their whole life looking at the models that are neat, work well, and can get published, so that they can get tenured. That's great.

But given that at Harvard there are so many people who don't have that type of background so that they already have started down that path, they have an opportunity to be more diverse. They may be less high-powered than the people at MIT, but they are probably better in terms of what we think economics should be. That would, for example, bring in more policy considerations. Some people who come here have valuable government experience. But instead of taking advantage of the diversity that they put there in the first place, the faculty here seems to totally eliminate it.

How about the politics of the students?

JULIE: That's hard to tell. Most of the people I talk to are pretty liberal in their politics. That may intimidate the people who are conservative. But I imagine that there is quite a diversity of opinions.

LEN: When you asked about the economists we admire most, I sensed a little bit of discomfort. I think it is because a person's choice indicates their views concerning the important issues. People are reluctant to reveal those. I know all the people in class, but I do not know all their political views.

JANET: There is also the problem that we do not have much time to talk with each other outside class. There is not much socializing. That is one of the drawbacks here. We could probably do something to change it.

BRIAN: This lack of discussion is quite weird to me. When I did my undergraduate work in London, everybody spent the whole time arguing furiously about politics. There would also be discussions between students and faculty. Everybody *knew* that economics is a social construct—that it is a battleground.

When I came here, it was as if I was deafened with this silence. I kept thinking, "Well, this is a foreign country, I better keep quiet. They may all think I am a psychopath." *[The others laugh.]* After a while, you realize that people do care, but it turns out that you can only talk about politics outside the department. Inside, the department is a place for work where you better not say anything.

JULIE: There are a lot of people with a liberal consciousness but who are also free-market oriented. Some people do not think through the connection between their economic and political thought. They keep them departmentalized.

LEN: Yeah, that is the typically technocratic approach.

ALBERT: Actually, before I came here I thought there would be more people like that. I wondered whether there would be others who would be skeptical of neoclassical economics like me. It turns out to be half the class, at least.

Alternative Approaches

JANET: The problem is that there is not enough time to discuss alternative approaches. Steve Marglin does some during two to three weeks. So it may end up that people get the idea, "Oh, I have seen all the other approaches. Wow, I am educated. I know all about them." It is actually worse than when you did not get them at all. You don't get anywhere near a fair perspective.

ALBERT: What Marglin did was not fair at all. He really only looked at the history. It was not systematic.

JANET: It wasn't. It was a joke.

Life After Graduate School

Before you came here, what did you think you would do after graduate school?

VICKY: Something in public policy.

ALBERT: Something in an international context.

LEN: I wanted to become the secretary of labor. *[They like that.]*

JULIE: I was pretty flipped between public policy and teaching.

JANET: I was interested in rural development.

Getting Socialized

Someone was mentioning (before I started the recording) the mold you get into here. How would you describe that?

JULIE: I think it is that they throw so much at you that you cannot do anything except turn out problem sets, go to the lectures, and figure out what the professor said. Maybe it is not so bad for me. I came in with one of the stronger backgrounds in economics. But for people who have less of a background, there is no time to think that this may be wrong, or this is a weird way of looking at things, or there may be some other way. You don't have time to do extra reading, so there is no use going to a professor and asking him for extra references.

VICKY: That is a real problem. You have to do what they tell you to do. I didn't, though. I did not take econometrics but took history of thought instead. That gave me some time to think.

LEN: I think the department would argue that it is not putting us through a mold, but that it tries to give us a basic common knowledge. However, if you do nothing but constrained optimization models for nine months, that socializes you not to think of problems that you cannot deal with through a constrained optimization approach.

BRIAN: The question of the mold is really interesting. You see, whatever was really neat in the literature five years ago is now the graduate curriculum. It seems to trickle on and on. You try to take on non-market-clearing economics around here. They say, "What? Sorry!"

JANET: Even though this is supposed to be the bastion of neoclassical thought, they are obviously very opposed to that sort of thing. But you get taught it anyway. We spent a good part of macro this semester learning Barro, Sargent, and Lucas.

VICKY: I don't think that is wrong.

JANET: Indeed, we need to see it. Ben [Friedman] actually does at the end say what is wrong with those models.

ALBERT: That is not clear either. One section is called "dubiousness of rational expectations" or something like that. Well, I agree. I don't agree with rational expectations. But he could have taken any of the models. Why does he criticize that? So he concludes that rational expectations do not explain business cycles. So?

JANET: Yeah, it was not quite fair. He did not give the counterarguments. He gave some simplistic ideas so that we could laugh at them.

BRIAN: The approach that I thought economics was about was that there would be these important aspects of the economy that you had to understand to figure out what was going on out there. These were your goals—how are you going to achieve them? Whereas here, it seems to be a kind of dual track. Larry [Summers] has said, "We really don't know what determines real wages and what determines productivity growth." But none of the courses are directed at achieving this. It has to be neat, mathematically neat, and fun.

LEN: But that is more particular to the discipline. This is what neoclassical economics is about, so that is what they present.

[We talk some about the articles and books they have read. They argue about whether an article on efficiency wages fitted in. They agree that it was fun and that it seemed to be relevant.]

JANET: My impression was that here you have economists who try to give some little twist to a theory. That seems to be exactly what we are learning. We learn what all the recent theories are, look for little holes in them, and write our Ph.D. theses on that. You don't really care what the framework is. And you don't really care if you come up with solutions to a real problem. It seems so strange.

BRIAN: It's disturbing. When you want to know why we are doing this, they tell you, "That is where the profession is at right now." That's no answer at all. Why is this where the profession is at? There is no response to that. You know, it's neat and trendy. So efficiency wages is now what everybody is talking about. Everything that went on before, they don't want us to know about at all. "Oh," they may say, "that is so Keynesian." But Keynes is alive and well in the rest of the world. *[One person laughs.]* I think it's disturbing that stuff in which many man- and woman-years of intellectual effort have been invested is considered to be wasted. Only what is published in the last few years is considered important.

On Economists

Who are the economists you like in particular?

JANET: Larry Summers, I guess. But that is because he is willing to talk to graduate students. He doesn't take his own work too seriously.

VICKY: He is pretty open.

BRIAN: He is aware of the limitations of what he is doing. Larry gets up, writes down this model—he is a pretty good teacher—and then says, "This doesn't apply to anything."

JULIE: But that is not necessarily a good thing. If you look for a role model, you don't want him to say that it does not matter all the time.

JANET: He gave some excellent lectures, though—for example, on unemployment statistics, on efficiency wages, and things like that. He gave us a sense of how weak the evidence often is.

JULIE: I think that at this stage it is very hard for people to say which economists they like. We do not know well what the economists here are doing professionally. We get an idea of their teaching abilities. Larry is an exception because he gives a reasonable amount of his own articles. But Ken Abel did not give us any of his articles.

BRIAN: I like Jeffrey Sachs.

Why?

BRIAN: Because he is concerned with what is actually going on out there. He is concerned with what economics is, or should be, about. He seemed to agree that this graduate education produces people who are technicians but who have no idea what to apply their techniques to.

LEN: I thought that graduate school was meant to inspire us, to get us to think about important issues. I like Freeman and Medoff because they have been very innovative. They have been criticized for not doing rigorous economics in some areas they went into. I also like Steve Marglin and Larry Summers.

More on Socialization

So far you have given me the impression that you are quite skeptical of what you are learning. What is the point, then, of being here? [They laugh.]

JANET: That is a good question.

VICKY: You need to know what is going on. You need also to protect yourself from being discredited.

ALBERT: That may be true, but when you learn these models, there is no way to understand why they are as good as suggested and why they are useful.

VICKY: But this is only the beginning.

ALBERT: When I was an undergrad and would question assumptions that seemed unrealistic, the teacher would say, "Oh, when you go further, you can relax them." But now I see that they are needed to make the models wash.

JULIE: You have to recognize that in this first year we have to go through a lot of theory in which not everybody is interested. But you have to start with the basics. You have to be exposed to those silly growth theories. You have to learn general equilibrium, things like that. You may not like them, but later you may see applications of them, and you may see how to change things. The latter is a very ambitious goal, but you can target yourself, especially when you become an academic. We are all very unhappy—or disgruntled at least—but I hope that things will change.

BRIAN: It seems to me that the first year is going to shape the rest of our professional career as economists to a great extent. I find it really disturbing. We are being socialized into something, but nobody in the faculty seems to know what that is, except they were socialized themselves five years ago. It's like being brainwashed. You may have heard stories of brainwashing during the Korean War. You are deprived of sleep, you are subjected to extreme stress, bombarded with contradictory convictions—you end up accepting anything. You end up in the middle of the semester completely malleable. You write down whatever you can and try to understand it. If you get your head above water, you survive. But you won't know where you are—all the intellectual landmarks have been leveled. The way I feel now is that I try to float with the current. I am not particularly happy about it. I have no idea where I am going. Before I came here, I had very clear ideas—now I don't have a clue.

I think it's true for a lot of people that after their undergraduate studies they knew better how the economy worked. But now I cannot even remember. In my first year I feel I made negative progress.

LEN: You forget all the institutional knowledge that you had.

JANET: I don't feel that I have learned any economics. I spent the entire first term thinking, "Is this economics?" This has no relationship with anything in economics. I feel as if I am learning engineering skills. I now understand dynamic optimization. You know, when I read the inflation rate is going up and the exchange rate down, I have no idea why that is.

LEN: An interesting thing about Harvard is, of course, that a lot of interesting people come through. Talking to Amartya Sen and Alfred Chandler is fascinating, or Phil Mirowski.[1]

JANET: And the students are interesting.

BRIAN: The motivation to come to grad school is probably pretty much the same as everybody else's motivation with things like status, money, and intellectual satisfaction. I was surprised when I came here to find the high status of economists in American society. And it was quite clear that people with a Harvard Ph.D. are on the fast road toward something. Back in England economists are sneered at, so people study economics for the satisfaction part. It is therefore rather odd to see people consider grad school as they would law school or business school and think of economics as a profession.

JULIE: That is certainly true. You have the Harvard name, and if you go into the real world, that makes a difference to people. Two students here came up to me and said that they wanted to rule the world. They were serious, and they saw a Harvard Ph.D. as the first step to achieve that goal.

JANET: That promises to be a serious conflict between these two. *[They clearly appreciate the comment.]*

BRIAN: They don't do badly. I can think of the prime minister of Greece and three to four members of Reagan's cabinet who were Ph.D.'s in economics. The status is really pressed on you. When you say here that you are an economist, people think it is a big deal. When you say that you are a Harvard economist, it is kind of eerie, because they think that you are a tremendously important and wise person. Well, I am not.

JULIE: But that may be a typically American reaction. It doesn't necessarily mean much. But there is something to it. For everybody who does not want to go into academics, the Harvard name gives a definite edge.

Harvard Versus MIT

How does Harvard grad school compare to MIT grad school?

ALBERT: I am sorry to say this, but I sense, especially among second-year students, an inferiority complex. Smart people really.

JULIE: Among the faculty too. There is a huge one. The econometrics sequence is a good example. They try to push us through the high-level econometrics because people told them that Harvard graduates don't have as good a training in econometrics as MIT graduates. I think that Stanford is more MIT-oriented too.

What does that mean, being MIT-oriented?

JULIE: Lots of math, being rigorous—you know, testing all the time. Everybody is a very good technician when they come out. I think that is really silly. Harvard is very different from MIT and they should exploit those differences. And then, you can cross-register.

ALBERT: The thing with that cross-registration is that a lot of people here go to MIT, but very few MIT students come here.

Do you know of any person who chose to come to Harvard even though he or she was admitted to MIT? [They can think of one person who did.]

JULIE: The MIT faculty pays more attention to individual students than the Harvard faculty does. When you first get here, you see that all the professors have office hours. Then you find out, "Oh, at Harvard you don't drop in during office hours. You make an appointment a week in advance to see someone during their office hours." That is very off-putting.

The Nature of Economics

BRIAN: There is this constant argument about whether economics should be like physics. A lot of people take for granted that it should; others say it is impossible.

JULIE: It's ridiculous—economics can never be like physics. You can't do controlled experiments, first of all. There is no way you can cut California off from the rest of the United States, or cut the minimum wage to see what that does to employment. You can't do that.

ALBERT: Minimum wages do change, though.

JULIE: Yes, but then the institutional factors are all different, and you can't control the people. You can't do it, and I see no reason why you would even try.

VICKY: Economics is about *people.*

JANET: No, it is about maximizing agents! *[They laugh.]* I thought that economics had a more coherent framework than psychology and sociology and that it had a nice way to generalize in a formal way. I thought that was what economics was!

LEN: A couple of times Ken Abel talked about efficiency wages and some of Akerlof's arguments, more or less putting them down as being sociological.

JULIE: That is a dirty word.

BRIAN: I feel that I have been socialized in that if you can't formulate a problem as a mathematical problem which is solvable, then you are not interested in it.

Do others feel the same way?

VICKY: It's scary if you would deviate from that line.

LEN: You can forget about your degree!

JULIE: Even if you see a problem that you could at least discuss in words. My word! If you don't have equations, you would not get it published—so you would have to forget becoming an academic. People like Arrow or Solow or Samuelson might be able to do weird things like history of thought or journalistic stuff because they have a reputation already. I think that's frightening.

LEN: I came here to learn neoclassical economics so that when I end up in the public sector I can deal with neoclassical arguments.

BRIAN: That was my idea too—to learn this thing, the neoclassical tool kit everybody talks about. A lot of British economists have been to America, and anytime anybody argues with them, they say, "It's transparent that your argument conflicts with the substitution matrix." The poor guy has no comeback. I came here with the belief, "I'm going to learn this stuff but ain't going to do it." But after four years doing this, you are incapable of thinking about problems in a journalistic way. It is not that there aren't other ways of doing economics.

ALBERT: What are those other ways?

BRIAN: Keynes did it differently.

JANET: I am not sure what economists are doing or why they are doing what they are doing except that they are getting paid for it.

JULIE: They have fun!

JANET: They created a discipline. But what is the social value of it? Unless you study economics because it helps you to understand reality and policymaking. You say we do it to get some knowledge about the world. But that's not what economics is directed to.

JULIE: But look at a particle physicist or an abstract mathematician.

JANET: Economists have their nice, neat little models. And they say, "Oh it's an abstraction from reality, but maybe we get to see something interesting."

JULIE: I don't think that people are so cynical that they make up a neat, little model so that they get it published. Economists can make so much more money outside academia. If all you care about is job security, why don't you work for a bank?

BRIAN: It's a serious problem, all these economists recreating the world—the Barros and Lucases. Economists should know better—you can't re-create the world in your own image. What is worrisome is that technical whiz kids like Lucas, Sargent, and Barro don't seem to care about what happens to their re-creations.

JANET: That's where the discipline is at. There is not much attention for issues such as structural unemployment or deindustrialization. Look at the articles in the top journals. They all make some technical point.

Another Student's Opinion

They talk about a student who seems to be very promising. Ed is described as "very mathematical, he has wanted to be an economist since he was fifteen; he is willing to play the academic game." Someone suggests he is a technocrat, but someone else mentions his interest in history of thought. At this point Ed enters the room, prompting people to laugh and tell him they were talking about him; Brian jokes that he just finished describing Ed as an all-American economist. Because we have talked for a while, I suggest that people should feel free to leave. Only Vicky leaves. We talk about the possibility that this group may not be representative of the first-year class. Brian thinks they represent 75 percent of the class. Julie doubts that. I ask Ed, the new arrival, for his reaction to the first-year training.

ED: That is a very difficult question to answer. In some ways it is extremely important because I want to go on in academics, and I feel it is very important to know the discipline. That's why they call it a discipline. *[People laugh.]* There are a lot of hoops to go through. But in another way I don't think that I will be using much of it in whatever I do—hopefully I will not be forced to crank out first-order conditions all the time.

> *I have already asked what economists people like. Do you have some economists you would like to emulate?*

ED: People like Gary Becker. He has done some really interesting things.

JANET: *[Softly.]* Oh God! No. *[Someone laughs a little.]*

ED: But he's brilliant in what he's done in applying economics to all different areas. I also think that the stuff by Kydland and Prescott is one of the most important things that has come along. *[Janet is now joined by Albert and Brian in making sounds of disbelief. It is as if they are gasping for air. Ed continues.]* Becker, although I don't agree with anything that he's done, is probably one of the most creative economists. Lucas is creative, too.

JULIE: Okay, I agree about Becker that he is very interesting to read. But his results are bizarre.

ED: I agree with that. But his approach—it is not that high-powered, it requires less expertise. There is some value to that.

What about Kydland and Prescott?

ED: As I said, their stuff is one the most important things that has been done in economics in the last ten years. It relates to problems in philosophy, such as backward causality, which I think are very interesting. I should say that my interests are not in economics per se. I like other fields, too.

Such as?

ED: Philosophy, social sciences, philosophy of science. I think that economics can be very important, not just in technical ways but in a broader context.

What is your attitude about the role of mathematics in economics?

ED: I have a very ambivalent attitude toward it. In certain ways you could not have gotten a lot of results, like the Kydland-Prescott results, without mathematics. But I don't think it is a necessary requirement. My preference is more toward literary types of things, lowbrow theory.

Theorem proving, the stuff that Greg Mankiw does—sometimes there is some real insight to that, but there is too much emphasis on the rigor of theorem proving.

I ask the others their reactions to Ed's comments, pointing out that his remarks give a different, much less cynical impression.

JULIE: Much of what he is talking about does not come out in the first year.

ED: No, yes—in some sense I didn't learn anything from coming here. I got a lot of technical confidence, but in some general way I knew of the topics.

How? College?

ED: By reading on my own, mostly.

JULIE: You are probably the most well read of the people in our class. *[They continue talking on a variety of subjects. At one point Julie remarks on her admiration for Solow, whom she had met at some informal occasion.]* He's great. I told him that I really did not know what I am doing here, taking all those first derivatives all the time. I realized by talking to him that there is more to academic economists. He is funny, interesting.

He worries about the mathematics in the profession and how that dictates what problems are interesting—to make problems tractable so that you can get tenure.

LEN: But he did that himself with his growth models.

JULIE: Yes, but now he says he can afford to be cynical.

LEN: But that's how he made his career, by being extremely narrow. He was just blown to bits in the Cambridge controversy. No one pays any attention to that stuff anymore.[2]

[They continue talking about the quality of teaching at Harvard. One instructor is singled out as a good one, but they note he probably will not get tenure. Ed believes the MIT faculty cares much more about teaching.]

ED: When I came to Harvard, I knew that the teaching would be abominable. I did not care because I presumed that would mean they would leave you alone more to work on things that are more interesting to you. After the first year, that is.

[They continue to discuss the efforts of other teachers. It is generally the usual graduate student talk, intended mainly to vent frustration.]

Third-Year Students

Harvard students were not very forthcoming. The number of second- and fourth-year students was too small for our purposes. One factor in the small showing may have been the separate conversation we had with the political economy club. About seventeen students and two faculty members took part in that discussion. The presence of the faculty members and its informal structure made this conversation unsuitable for inclusion here.

Three students came to the meeting of the third year students. Bill's specialization is mathematical economics, Carlos does macro and labor, and Gary did his orals in econometrics and economic history, though he now does a lot of macro.

About Graduate School

How would you describe your experience at graduate school?

CARLOS: I think it is very unpleasant. I haven't enjoyed it here very much at all. I don't think the place is a very friendly place. The faculty is not very supportive and interested in us at all. Overall I have not been very happy here.

BILL: I am very different, I guess. I am fairly happy. When you say it is not friendly here, that is very much true for the faculty. The atmosphere among the students is actually quite nice.

CARLOS: I agree with that.

BILL: There is a diverse group of people. You learn a lot of economics from the students. That may contrast sharply with the University of Chicago, where they flunk out so many students. There the environment is so competitive, at least in the first year.

CARLOS: I agree that the students are a big resource.

BILL: It is not uniformly true that every professor is an asshole. It depends very much on what field you are in.

You have to make an elaborate effort to meet the faculty. But although it is true that they are hard to catch, it is also true that I haven't found one who is not quite friendly and approachable when I got him at the proper moment. But that moment is something quite different from their standard office hours.

GARY: I am very happy here. The graduate students are wonderful, and lots of professors are excellent too. The total intellectual experience has been quite amazing.

CARLOS: I don't think that any of the professors are vicious. They are into their publishing and getting tenure. That's the way they are. The pressure for them is intense. So they are interested in what they can get out of the students.

BILL: Dean Michael Spence once said if he had absolute power, he would shut down the NBER because it siphons off a good deal of the professor's time as a place to hang out, and it also siphons a lot of time of graduate students.[3] There they have superior office space, so that further divides the department. There are two centers of intellectual activity, neither of which is large enough.

GARY: A lot of real education seems to get done through apprenticeship, through research assistantships. I myself worked for Larry Summers for a while.

How do you look back at what you learned in the first two years? Was it useful?

BILL: I am not sure. To give an example, Mankiw's class on general equilibrium will unlikely be useful for me. He presented it very clearly, so I came to understand a piece of received economics. That is important, I guess, but that is not necessarily useful.

CARLOS: A lot of that stuff is essential for understanding journal articles. You have to have it.

Life After Graduate School

What were your plans for after graduate school before you started?

GARY: I was thinking of doing some academic/public-policy career track.

Do you still think that?

GARY: I am more academic.

Why?

GARY: I suspect that I have been ruined for working hours in a real job. I like having control over my own time and not showing up for the nine-to-five schedule.

CARLOS: I thought that I would probably be seeking an academic position. My view has changed somewhat. I would like to do some type of economics that I believe can be useful. I am not sure. Also the rat race for tenure. . . . Quite possibly I will still do it, but I am not sure.

BILL: I have always been interested in a university position. When I first came in, I was very interested in mathematical economics. Then I sort of got bored with that. It was a slow process. In the beginning of this year I was losing interest more and more. So I don't know what to do. Maybe I'll do something in Soviet economics. Probably I'll do some mathematical approach to a particular topic in Soviet economics.

Their Theses

How about your theses?

GARY: I am thinking of writing a thesis on a comparison of Britain's and France's return to the gold standard.

What is unclear to me at this point is whether we are expected to write theses in the way economic historians write them. They write relatively large pieces. But more and more people write three pieces, stapling them together. They do it at MIT, and here at Harvard that is more and more true. They can't say what their thesis is.

How is the process of choosing a thesis topic?

CARLOS: Thinking about the thesis generates a tremendous amount of anxiety. You need to get support for it—faculty people must like what you want to do.

GARY: In general it takes a year to find a topic.

Economists

Who are the most important economists for you?

GARY: Here I probably would pick Jeffrey Williams and Larry Summers, chiefly because they do applied stuff on the level on which it ought to be done.

CARLOS: Summers gives a lot of insight, at least into the economists here. He gives you the data; his theory is not as technical as it probably has to be, but just enough to show the point. Of the ones here he is the best.

How about people outside Harvard?

CARLOS: One point that Medoff made about Lucas is true. Even though their views are night and day apart, he acknowledges that Lucas comes up with interesting new ideas. Even if their papers are wrong, they stimulate research. A lot of other economists don't have much insight or—I don't know. [A brief discussion on Lucas ensues, in which Gary objects to the technical nature of Lucas's work.] It's true the profession has become too technical and too mathematical, and he is on that route, but at least he has some insight into how the economy works. He presented a challenge to existing ideas and stirred things up. Of course, he has drawbacks, but when you judge his overall influence—

GARY: I have not seen much come out of that work that advances my understanding of how industrial economies work. I have seen a lot come out of the work from people like Michael Piore that advances my understanding. I don't see why the criterion for being a good economist should be that of generating excitement.

BILL: The economist that comes to mind is Kornai. [Kornai was visiting that year, with a chance he would stay on the faculty.]

What is good about him?

BILL: First of all, the inspiration for his work was going around Hungary and talking to managers. So it appears that the basis for his work is solidly grounded and earthy. He makes sincere attempts to get a realistic picture of an economy. Rather than just collecting hundreds and hundreds of facts, he tries to make general statements and develop a general theory. He is well versed in neoclassical economics and somewhat influenced by it, but it doesn't act as a sort of straightjacket on him. He doesn't get stuck determining consistency properties or figuring out a maximizing model.

Economics in the Public Sphere

What about people like Thurow and Galbraith?

CARLOS: I have read some of Thurow's books, but I do not remember much. I think that we get indoctrinated to think in neoclassical terms and to look down on something that is more qualitative. I have that prejudice built in me, but as for now I don't really—

BILL: I have not read Thurow and have no strong opinions about him. A lot of Galbraith's stuff is very interesting. One reason to respect both of them is that they are willing to talk to an audience outside the profession. There are strong barriers against doing that. People immediately say that you are selling out or that you are not doing serious work anymore. Martin Weitzman is a good example. He probably has very wide respect in the profession. He came up with this *Share Economy* book, which was hailed in the *New York Times.*[4]

GARY: Negative reactions come to people who do it too soon. Once you have paid your dues, it's okay to consult and to give policy advice. Then it's okay to write for *Newsweek.*

The Conditions for Success

What makes a successful economist?

GARY: What do you mean by successful?

In the sense of success in the profession—reputation.

CARLOS: Technical skill, I think, is a lot of it. Being good at theoretical models as well, but I think high-tech—or high-powered as it is called—theory and econometrics sell very well. It is applied math. I think that is not completely true, but all things being equal, that stuff is clearly respected. If two papers get the same results, the more technical one will do better.

GARY: What about Dunlop? He is essentially a major institutionalist who has spent his entire career managing in some way or another America's labor relations.

BILL: I speculate that if you put Dunlop in a twenty-five-year-old-body, he would unlikely get tenure.

ED: He might have a better chance here than at lots of other places.

The Role of Mathematics

BILL: Mathematical prowess does not say everything. Lucas's technical skills are not the best. There are much more striking examples in mathematical economics. Definitely, some of the more terrifying are at Indiana State University. USC, which is not high prestige, has about six of those, people who do functional analysis.

GARY: Lucas and Sargent even recognize as much, as they did in your book.[5] They refer to people like Townsend as being much better at it. But his papers are really very strange.

BILL: Or Jerry Green. My advisers at Northwestern, who were mathematical economists, would say of him, "A great technician, but I can't remember anything interesting he has ever done."

GARY: The results have to be interesting.

BILL: It's not clear what makes results interesting. You know, extending existence-of-equilibrium proofs to more general spaces is not considered interesting, although it is really hard to do. Sanford Grossman is definitely less proficient than David Kreps but has more status. He has addressed issues like, if you have efficient markets, it seems to be paradoxical that anyone should gather information. It's strange to see all those stockbrokers who make a living off that. So Grossman shows that some information is used efficiently and that markets play a very nice information aggregation role, and yet it makes sense for people to talk to their stockbrokers. That is a puzzle widely recognized by the profession as such. So they will recognize that he has an interesting solution to the puzzle.

CARLOS: He has something that is of slightly more general interest.

BILL: Jerry Green believes that his work is very general and has all sorts of implications.

GARY: Sometimes they are hard to see.

BILL: But there is an important role for applied economists who will take his stuff.

Neoclassical Economics

Would you take offense if I labeled you as neoclassical economists?

CARLOS: I wouldn't, because it is the truth. I am educated in it. I would like to know other approaches better, but that takes a big investment. And right now I don't know whether other approaches might be useful.

Neoclassical economics has problems, but it has a lot of good things to say. The problem is that it should not be the only approach.

GARY: But what an approach—that can't even explain something like the design of a typewriter.

Are you a neoclassical economist?

GARY: Yes, but the typewriter example is just the smallest of a huge variety of situations that are stuck for institutional reasons, and of arrangements that in any viewpoint of rational organizations are absurd.

BILL: I find the question hard to answer. I am probably very neoclassical, but I feel uncomfortable admitting that.

GARY: If we draw the line between neoclassicals and nonneoclassicals as it is usually drawn, we are all neoclassicals, but we may not think that is where the line ought to be drawn. It may seem that I have more in common with Sargent than, say, Steve Marglin or an institutional historian. And that is not the case. So I am not sure of the meaning of the label "neoclassical."

CARLOS: I think that most of us have more to say to Sargent.

In the macro fields you tend to identify schools. Do you associate yourself with any particular school?

CARLOS: All schools have something to say. I don't know.

How about rational expectations?

CARLOS: Their views are different but so is their approach. I like Ben Friedman's approach better.

GARY: Lucas, Sargent, and Barro should be kept within the economics profession. The arguments and the models they use do not make any concession except to the formal tradition of post–world war American macro, and can only be understood within that tradition. Generally, they are not very good in translating what they say in forms of discourse that are accessible to those outside that tradition. They should not appear on the pages of *Fortune* magazine. No one who does not have formal graduate training is capable of understanding them.

Theoretical Versus Applied Economics

GARY: The economics profession has theoreticians, econometricians, and applied types. The theorists exist to fight among themselves and tell applied types what to do, what theoretical considerations should affect the practical work. Econometricians tell the applied types whether the information they are using is sound and whether the tests they are using are statistically sound. Applied economists like Alan Blinder and Ben Friedman take the influences of the other two and combine that with their knowledge of institutions and history to understand the functioning of industrial capitalism. So the question who is more important—Lucas and Sargent on one side and Blinder on the other—is hard to answer. Certainly, if you attempt to understand anything about the history of industrial economies, you may prefer to listen to someone like Blinder. But there is also a feeling that people who do sky-high theoretical research are also necessary. If you have no one like Lucas and Sargent around, the discipline would eventually dry out.

BILL: A lot of people would say that's the situation now. The problem now is that theorists don't care what the needs of the applied people are. So the people are operating on islands.

GARY: People did argue that the best thing to happen to economics during the seventies was the emergence of people like Spence and David Kreps, or people who took high-tech, imperfect information theory and said, "Okay, we are going to transport this knowledge to the study of I.O. [industrial organization]." People thought that was a tremendous improvement.

BILL: The one thing that struck me in David's methods course is that he seems to have this view that on one hand everything is presented in class as extremely far removed, and on the other hand he talks constantly about the imperfection of the tools. He suggests that as soon as the tools are flowing in, the theory will be more relevant.

Do you think that is a reasonable expectation? [The question draws a chorus of "No's."]

BILL: That's why I have my doubts about the division of labor. You know, it's easy to see Mike Spence having lots of conversations with Jerry Green as well as business professors, and Jerry Green saying, "I'm toiling away on those tools, and I am sending them your way," but he would not know what they need. Ultimately he is not interested in that.

Economics and Other Disciplines

BILL: People also have that idea of a division of labor between economics and other disciplines. They think, "Those people over there may do wonderful work, but we do not have to pay any attention to it. Other people may have a lot to say about how preferences are formed, but we assume them to be given." Some people may think that the integration with, say, sociology will come at a higher stage.

GARY: That's what Gary Becker is already doing.

BILL: But he takes the view that sociologists basically don't know anything. Economics is an island. It would be interesting to figure out what the boundaries of the discipline are.

Tom Schelling has this notion of the fictitious scholar. People imagine that there are colleagues to whom they address themselves.

CARLOS: The incentive is to specialize. To get the most done, that is simply the best thing to do. Take one guy here who teaches macro. I am sure that he knows his specialization well, but he repeatedly makes elementary mistakes in his teaching of material that is outside the area of his expertise. Another guy, an econometrician, is great when he's doing the equations, but as soon as a question on applications comes up, he seems out of it.

GARY: Students in sociology I know have asked me how you can possibly learn enough of our discipline in four years to become a professor. I think that we can. In most other social sciences, you spend six years reading widely to get a knowledge of the field, as well as writing the dissertation. For economics, the degree program is shortened because the departments feel they have to compete with the private sector. An assistant professor masters only a small area. You learn later.

[We end our discussion talking some about the other students in their class. One student believes that Hayek is the best economist around. They mention a student with whom I had talked before they came in. They consider him high-tech, one of the very bright people in the class. In our conversation this student had told me he came in with a background in engineering. He likes rational expectations and does not mind the label of a technocrat, but he confesses to having serious interest in politics and the history of economic thought.]

6

Eclecticism and Concern: Columbia Students

First-Year Students

Two students participated. Bob was outgoing and extremely interested in our project and our opinions of Columbia and other graduate economics programs. Zhao was an Asian student; he had been talked into coming by Bob.

On Their Choice of Schools

How did you decide on Columbia?

BOB: I came here because according to the rankings, it was the best school I got into.

ZHAO: I thought it satisfied my basic requirements. I think now that you have mentioned it, that Harvard might be a little bit better than here—I mean as the basis for anything in economic theory. Some branches, some fields here are good. But now we are experiencing basic training in economic theory, I think the training in this department is not so tight. It isn't quite as rigorous as it is at MIT or Harvard.

We have some classmates from Harvard and some other schools who can make comparisons. If you are taking micro courses there, you are graded on exercises. But here, we don't have such a requirement.

BOB: There are problem sets in micro, but they aren't graded. You don't hand them in, you do them on your own. There's no incentive to do them—the T.A. will do them. And in macro they don't even give out voluntary problems.

What other courses do you take in the first year?

BOB: Micro, macro, econometrics, and usually economic history in the first semester. Then an elective replaces history in the second.

ZHAO: In our second semester here, they deal with recent developments. From my information, that is not dealt with equally at other schools. They have three or four courses in micro and advanced micro, whereas we have two. So that's our advantage here. It's one of the things I like about Columbia.

But the lack of problem sets in the first year is a disadvantage. If you have done a lot of problems, you have some feeling, some experience, which is relevant for what we are getting into. I think the requirements should be focused on basic micro and macro theory, not so much on econometrics.

In my view, econometrics takes too much time here. One of my friends who is at Chicago takes just micro/macro, and that occupies all his time. He didn't mention anything about statistics or econometrics. I think that's a good strategy for basic training. Nonetheless, I have confidence in the training here.

BOB: I agree. We spent a lot of time on econometrics.

Was graduate school what you expected? Did you feel trained enough to handle the math?

BOB: I went to the University of New Hampshire in political science, and the first few months here were shocking because it's entirely different from undergraduate. It's very mathematical—it's a different outlook. But I adjusted very rapidly.

ZHAO: I'm a foreign student and had some problems with speaking. Listening is not a problem.

BOB: One of the things that worried me when I first came here is that a lot of people have master's degrees already. Their background is stronger. They've seen this type of material—they're used to it—and they're coming in and competing with people who are still wet behind the ears. We have someone with a master's degree from Oxford; someone else has a master's from the London School of Economics—you know, really top-grade schools. And so it's a bit different competing against these guys.

How much math have you used in the various courses like macro?

BOB: Not too much. And you can pick it up as you go along. We often use differential equations, which I didn't know beforehand. And in international finance and advanced macro we used optimal control theory. But I'd still like a pure course in mathematical economics that would fill in all these gaps. In the first year, at least, you can pass the final without really knowing what's going on in optimal control theory, but it's really useful—almost necessary—to pass the advanced macro.

Do you feel that after the first year you're competent to read anything in the **AER?**

BOB: Pretty much. And that's one of the things I really enjoy about graduate school. As an undergraduate, you're intimidated by the economic journals because they're very mathematical and other things. But the first year you overcome that. First of all, you aren't afraid of reading the journals. Second, you learn some of the tools and some of the ways of reading. You know, what they're trying to say and things like that.

How many people do you expect will make it through to the next year? How many did you start with in your class?

BOB: We started with about thirty-five, and one guy dropped out shortly after that. He was an older guy, about fifty. *[Addressing Zhao.]* Probably most people will come back, don't you think?

ZHAO: I'm pretty sure that only one-half will come back.

BOB: *[Incredulously.]* One-half! I had no idea it would be so low.

Views on Economic Theory

What do you think of the rational expectations assumption and new classical economics?

BOB: I've enjoyed rational expectations. I think it's neat. I'd *heard* of rational expectations as an undergraduate, but I hadn't really been introduced to it. Here we cover it in macro a bit, and I bought a book and did some side reading on my own. Some of the articles are interesting, although they're a bit difficult to understand at times.

ZHAO: We have a lot of discussion about policy assignments in our classes. I think the major contribution of the rational expectations school is its policy implications. Those implications are really important. The idea comes from the functioning of financial markets in the sixties. Then in the eighties you come to the macro aspect, and I think that the basic message is that the government cannot just cheat people by increasing aggregate demand. The basic message is quite clear, and it's useful for the management of the U.S. economy. If we evaluate the school, we can see that the basic assumption is good and very helpful for the policymaking situation.

BOB: Some of the articles we've read for our classes have been relevant to this—articles on the vertical Phillips curve and things like that. And what's really neat is, the recent recession we've had, from eighty to eighty-five—the recession and the recovery are explained perfectly by Milton Friedman's Nobel lecture where you had seven percent unemployment with Carter and fifteen percent inflation—with the recession you brought that down. Friedman explains how there's a short-run Phillips curve, but in the long run, we're back to seven percent unemployment and four percent inflation. These issues aren't discussed in the macro courses, but we get articles on them assigned to us.

On Succeeding in Economics

Is it fairly clear from the beginning who's going to be on the fast track—who's going to be the top person?

BOB: Math helps.

ZHAO: The top people are quick at judging or arriving at a way of looking at problems. I mean they are sensitive, or inquisitive.

How important to being on the fast track, to succeeding, is a knowledge of the economy?

BOB: I don't think it's too important. I think to be on the fast track you need to publish, and to publish you don't need articles on what Fed policy is right now—it's mainly theoretical articles that get published. For example, Joe Stiglitz turns out papers, but there's nothing institutional in them.

ZHAO: I agree that institutions aren't important, because I found out that some people base their formulations on intuitive reasoning—on assumptions one, two, three, four, five—and then set up an optimization scheme that explains everything. Of course, the problem comes up from a lot of assumptions made before. So instead of some sort of logical, we have intuitive, reasoning.

Do you feel you're getting a good background in economic literature?

BOB: We don't get enough to satisfy me. But, you know, we all have our different interests. I personally am interested in the historical perspective, and if we don't get enough of that in class, I'll do it on my own. So I'm not worried about it in that respect.

First- and Third-Year Students

Five students participated. Jane and Allen were first-year students; Margo, David, and Mark were in their third year. We included both first- and third-year students in this interview because we thought it would be interesting to see the interaction among classes. Before we began taping, we talked for a while off the record about why we were doing the project, about graduate school, and about their Columbia experiences in general. We started the formal interview by asking the students to describe their backgrounds.

The Students' Backgrounds

Can you give me just a little bit of background on each of you?

JANE: I'm a first-year student. I got into economics because I began to think that that was the most valid approach to the study of the Soviet Union. I worked in the field of Soviet studies for several years after college before I came to graduate school. I have little background in economics. I did not major in economics. I'm finding that an enormous obstacle in terms of not having an appropriate math background, and I don't know economics as well as my colleagues do—I don't have the basic economic jargon down. It's taking me a long time to get used to.

ALLEN: I'm also a first-year student. I originally was interested in law, and I was working as a legal research assistant in a law firm, although my undergraduate major was economics. The firm hired an economist, and since I was the only research assistant with an economics background, I began working with him. Eventually, my law school applications were torn up in favor of economics applications.

MARGO: I'm a third-year student. When I finished high school, I thought I was interested in physics, but I also had a lot of interest in politics. These two didn't go together really well. I was in a very demanding physics program as an undergraduate. Then I switched to history, but that didn't work out. And finally, although I'd only taken one economics course, I decided as a junior that economics seemed a good midway discipline between the hard-core sciences like physics and politics/history/sociology.

DAVID: It's basically the same with me. I was interested in politics, journalism, and the way society works. I started at an engineering school and was good at cranking through numbers, but found it dissatisfying. I started doing political science—found that a little bit too talkative and boring *[the other students laugh]*, not analytical enough. Economics seemed a perfect match between technical-type work and social relevance.

MARK: I was an English major as an undergraduate, and I wanted to be a novelist. But then I had a Shakespeare course that I didn't like and I had to make a decision between English and economics. I decided I was more interested in economics courses than in discussing how Macbeth's wife not having children affected her. *[Laughter from the others.]*

Relevance of Economics

Are your courses relevant?

JANE: As a first-year student, I'd have to say I don't have an answer to that. Perhaps in three years when I've done more work.

MARGO: Are my courses relevant? No, definitely not. If I wanted to do policy, I wouldn't do it through economics. If I was interested in changing society, I would not do it through economics, although I might use economics as a legitimization.

MARK: I think much of what we do is overkill. You get very, very sophisticated kinds of analysis, when in fact a basic, almost undergraduate, analysis is all one needs to understand everything that's ever written in articles or in the texts. We can criticize it, but once you're in graduate school it's hard to say if one could analyze issues in college as well as one can now.

It's possible that you really have to go beyond the simple theory and start getting into its core to understand what the simple theory is about. I think it's hard to say that, well, no, it's not relevant. Certainly a lot of what we read I don't think is necessarily modeled on the real world, but on the other hand, the theory we learn helps us to understand things.

DAVID: I worked for two years doing modeling and forecasting for a large economic forecasting firm. I did not really know the theory behind it, but I think the models which I built, which were in the energy field, had relevance and had policy uses where it actually gave valid insights to the people using the models as long as they didn't believe in them. Unfortunately, for marketing reasons, the models were often presented as all-powerful and as providing answers. That they didn't do, but I think they did help show what was going on.

As for the theoretical stuff that I'm learning now, I think that the important thing is going to be to synthesize the pure theory that I've been learning with my political intuitions and economic insights. That hasn't taken place yet, but I hope it will later.

How about your class work? Do you feel you get policy there or theory—or a combination?

ALLEN: I think it's all theory. One of the questions on your survey was what puts students on the fast track, and if I remember correctly, one of the choices was "general knowledge about the economy." You can walk in off the street and take the courses and not know what the Fortune 500 is and blaze through with flying colors. You can also come in and know the difference between subordinated debentures and junk bonds and fail miserably. So knowing all the jargon—and in fact about the economy—I don't think really means a heck of a lot in the first year.

How about later years?

MARGO: No, I don't think we get policy at all in our courses. Well, there's theory of commercial policy, but we don't really get policy in that. We get questions like what's the optimum tariff, but that's still pretty theoretical.

MARK: I disagree with that. When you're an undergraduate, you go in and the professor tells you his view and you think it's wonderful and you adopt it as your own. That's not what a graduate teacher should do. A graduate teacher should teach you enough so that you can read the paper and start thinking about things in a more sophisticated way.

MARGO: But the tools might be biased. You're becoming an expert on one set of tools and you might never realize that they're biased.

MARK: But they're tools nevertheless.

MARGO: Yes, but they define the way you think.

MARK: Any tool does that—nothing is pure.

MARGO: Right. But if we're only getting one type of tool, then we're coming in with a certain bias toward what we read in the newspapers.

MARK: But the question was, Is policy involved in courses? And this year I found that in several courses that was true. It becomes more and more true as you get away from the first year. The first year is a period where you try to bring everybody up to a certain level of theory.

JANE: I haven't really formulated a lot of opinions on these things yet— or I have opinions, but I don't know that I trust how well formed they are. That's one of the things I'm beginning to learn—that I can't just accept my own opinions like I accept someone else's opinions. I have to look at both sides. And I think that's a good thing to learn—I think that's a positive thing to learn. Whether I'm learning it because of my professors here at Columbia is another matter.

Policy and Politics

Have any of you changed your political persuasion as a result of graduate study in economics?

MARGO: I've changed my political views a lot since I was in college, but most of it is not because I've studied economics. It's for a variety of other reasons.

ALLEN: Same here. Being out in the work force, I've learned certain things about the real world. I mean, that's it, you better believe it. That's shaped my views, and graduate work really hasn't changed that—yet.

DAVID: When I started studying economics, I put aside my political views for a while. I put them aside because I was going to have to learn all these methods and technologies and all these methodologies. Now that I'm a third-year student, I've started to get involved again in politics. Partially it's because of my dissertation. I guess, if anything, I've learned to take some of the economic knowledge I had and modify my political beliefs a little bit—but that also has to do with current economic trends in which people are forming a consensus that welfare payments may not be the best way to redistribute income, for example. You try to work such new information into your views.

MARK: I agree with Margo. I was thinking of it in another way. I've become less of a knee-jerk liberal and more sophisticated about things. Some of it has to do with the prevailing views in the country—you can't help but be affected by it. On the other hand, this is a pretty conservative department, I think. In many ways you get that from other people. You're sort of buffeted, and when you start thinking about these things deeply, you start hearing a lot of different views. You start realizing that maybe what you always just took on faith maybe isn't something you should just take on faith.

What makes a good economist is the ability to take his own political biases and use current methodology and become so fancy that he can convince someone else that his underlying bias is true. *[A couple of students disagree.]*

What do you mean, "become so fancy"?

MARK: What I mean by that is when an economist is writing a paper, his biases are hidden. You have to read a lot of papers by an author to infer what his political bias or ideology is. That ideology is well hidden in the math and the techniques. It would probably be more helpful if an economist were to come out and write a couple of political science papers first. Then you'd know what he was trying to do when he's working in economics.

DAVID: I don't think that's fair. "Being fancy" has a certain flourish to it, and it gets published—sometimes things are fancy and they're boring. I think things that are done most elegantly are done very simply, and I have a much higher appreciation for papers like that. I think a lot of people do. I don't think math for math's sake is often advocated. *[The discussion turns to politics again and Mark continues.]*

MARK: Everybody that I know, and myself too, believes that there has to be a wedding between their political beliefs and economics. I came to economics out of political reasons. And yet I wonder if people in political theory feel like they have to be justifying their own political views through their work—do they have to do their work on Locke or Hume or somebody, and does it have to be giving some relevance to the political debate that we read about in the *New York Times* last week? I'm not completely convinced that is what I'm doing.

I think you can understand a lot about the world—like ninety percent of what's going on—sort of intellectually in terms of economics by having a really good undergraduate background, and a lot of it is clear then. A dissertation goes beyond that. It has to be the upper three percent of expanding knowledge or something. And to be able to say, "The real exchange rate moves this way"—you know, it doesn't add to your political views or it's not going to add a lot to political debate.

MARGO: You go around asking yourself if what I'm learning here is going to add to my political views, or how can I put my political views into it. I know one of us has a special interest in politics, but I don't think most people are *that* interested in politics. What they *are* bothered about is, "Hey, how does this fit into reality?" When I go to a cocktail party, I can't answer the questions, "What's going to happen? What should I invest in?"

MARK: But they're bad questions.

MARGO: Oh, they're bad questions. But we can't answer others either— questions such as, "What should we do about unemployment? What should be done about welfare?" That's not politics. We should be able to answer those questions. Or maybe we shouldn't.

MARK: I don't think there are easy answers.

ALLEN: My response to questions like that is, "Oh, I have no idea." And then I go on a tirade of half an hour!

MARGO: But in two minutes the people aren't going to know what you're talking about and have absolutely no concept of what you're trying to explain, and finally they say, "Oh, thank you very much," and they run away.

DAVID: Speaking of politics, in my dissertation I just wrote a proposal for a grant, and one of my things was to try to understand how do economists feed back on the policymaking process. How much—in, let's say, the early sixties—how much of the military buildup was due to the fact that some of the advisers said, "Well, go ahead, it's good for the economy. You have guns *and* butter—you have the space program. It's good for the economy." Was that well thought out? And it might be true that if that's thought out better, the policymaking process won't make the mistakes that it has. And so in that sense I think that's an important feedback to look at.

Teaching

What can you say about the faculty here? What are the traits of the ones you most admire? And what are the traits of the ones you least admire?

JANE: For me, if he's a good teacher, I admire him. If he's not a good teacher, I don't admire him.

MARK: I think I know who Jane is trying to talk about, and he's the one that I admire most. It takes about a year after he's said something to recognize all of a sudden what it was that he meant. He has a lot of trouble conveying his ideas, but at least he *has* a lot of ideas. Some of the other professors can teach you exactly what they're thinking, and they can sit the whole hour and write equations on the board, but there is a lot less economic thought behind it than there is behind the "poor teacher's."

Theory and Reputation

What about the theory?

JANE: If you ask me, that's [the absence of a high-level theoretical economist] one of the weaknesses of Columbia when we go into the job market. We don't have a high-level theorist here.

ALLEN: What do you mean—like pure money theory?

JANE: In micro. Micro theorists, topology—we don't have anyone like that here. We don't touch it.

Does that bother you?

MARGO: Yes, it worries me greatly because I'm interested in micro theory. That's what I want to do.

JANE: It's a liability not to understand foundations.

ALLEN: I kind of think that math for math's sake is nice—just to learn the math—and then it's a good way of thinking. And then maybe some of it might be relevant to economic ideas. You look on the course schedule for next fall and there's no advanced micro course.

JANE: Which means that we have to do it all in the same semester, which is a liability.

Some first-year students told me that you don't have many problem sets here. Do you find that a disadvantage?

JANE: I do.

DAVID: Yes.

Why do you think they don't?

DAVID: They don't want to grade them. They don't want to write them. *[General agreement.]*

ALLEN: It hindered me terribly because in the first semester in macro, you'd go into the lecture twice a week and learn something. Then we would go to the lab. And we wouldn't learn further about what we had learned in class—we would learn an entirely new topic. Then after the fourteen weeks, you sit down and take your final, and you're asked to examine the increase of the money supply in a certain model, and you've never done that. And you're stuck.

How do you feel relative to the other graduate schools out there? What's the feeling here at Columbia?

MARK: I'd say we don't have much contact.

MARGO: I don't have *any* contact.

JANE: I have friends at Harvard, and you certainly do feel a difffference in terms of how much pushing you get toward going on the job market, toward sending your papers out to be published. All those things matter a lot. The amount of attention you get here is far, far less.

MARK: I don't know. I heard stories when I was applying to graduate schools. My adviser used to teach at Harvard, and she told me that when you're fed up enough, just go to the dean's office and say you're mad as hell and you're not going to take it any more. I don't think this is terribly different than other places.

JANE: When I was applying to graduate schools, my adviser told me, "You should consider Columbia for international, but you should be aware that you're going to have to do it on your own."

ALLEN: That's what they told me, too.

DAVID: My adviser told me before I came to Columbia, "Don't go to Columbia."

ALLEN: That's the same with me. They said, "Don't go to Columbia— you'll take forever doing your dissertation." But this person also told me, "Don't go to Harvard—they're second-rate."

JANE: Everyone said that Harvard's overrated—don't go there.

ALLEN: I'd been through here as an undergraduate. So I knew what was what. I knew who was who and what went on. I think the problem is that if you don't speak out, nothing gets done. I had a first-semester econometrics course. The professor said, "We're not having a lab in this course." This shocked me, and I went to the department and said, "He just canceled the lab in this course." The department said, "Well, we'll reinstate the lab." If I hadn't gone and said something, there would have been blind acceptance, which would have gone on and on until the final, when everyone fails the course.

MARK: I think that's true. I think a lot of people in graduate school come from colleges where they hold your hand a lot. It's expected that they'll show you exactly what to do. That doesn't happen in graduate school. It's a lot healthier if you work for a while. When you work, nobody's going to hold your hand or nobody's going to tell you what to do. You realize if you ever want to do anything interesting, you have to take a lot of the initiative. So if you come to graduate school with some experience outside, I think it helps.

DAVID: My first year I worked with two or three other students, and we went through problems on our own, saying, "Okay, here's this model. Which questions can they ask us?" And we'd go through five different possibilities.

MARGO: But I don't think the outlook on this question is like Reagan saying, "Well, if it's not done for you, you should go out and do it yourself." All of us are paying tuition of eight thousand dollars. They're providing you a service—they should provide you with problem sets.

JANE: We should have more problem sets. We should have them in all of our theory classes as well.

Are there any other general complaints about the program—that you can say on tape?

MARK: I don't see any attempt to promote any kind of class consciousness. They really don't foster a sense of community among graduate students. It's partly true because we're in New York and don't live on campus—that's one problem. Then, there's no meeting place.

Time Spent Studying Economics

How many hours a week do you work on economics?

ALLEN: Including course work, I'd say about fifteen to twenty hours a week. *[The others express amazement at the small amount of time, but say that Allen already has a strong background. He agrees this makes a difference.]* When I came in, I had basically all the courses I had to take here in my first year. That was the first year. Basically, all the courses I had to take I'd seen quite a bit of before. And also, fifteen to twenty hours is an average. That isn't true the last week of the term, in which I work 168 hours.

MARGO: He's an exception.

MARK: The first year I worked. I remember doing nothing but doing economics. I worked about sixty or seventy hours a week easily—and I lived in Brooklyn.

MARGO: I work nine to eleven o'clock at night.

DAVID: But the second year was a lot, too.

JANE: I'm more along Allen's lines. I have to commute four hours a day, and I have a job in addition to graduate school, so I don't work anywhere near sixty hours a week. It shows, though. I think what you're seeing is a great disparity in the background of first-year students.

Their Employment Hopes

What kind of a job do you expect to get?

MARK: I'd like to get either an academic job or a job at the Fed. I'm constrained to be around Boston, but I don't expect to get a job at MIT or Harvard. I don't figure to get a job at a top school—rather at a midlevel school.

DAVID: I probably won't take an academic job if the school is really low on the list. [The others concur.]

If I'm going to do an academic job, I want to be surrounded by innovative and creative and intellectual people. So a major university— one of the top ten or fifteen—is what I'm looking for.

And if you don't get that?

DAVID: If I don't get that—I'm pretty much a computer hacker, so I'll get myself a modeling, high-paying foreign banking job.

JANE: I really want to teach. But I agree that I want to teach good students.

MARK: The top ten or fifteen is pretty restrictive.

JANE: Yes. It's not that I have to be at a major university. I think there are very attractive aspects of teaching at a small liberal arts college, a good one. But at the same time, I'd like to do research.

ALLEN: I'm one of the rare few leaning toward the private business/ government sector. I'd really like to go into consulting work, in either litigation support or working for the International Trade Commission— something in policy. But I wouldn't mind splitting my time, as many people do, with an academic job. The academic life is certainly appealing— four months off. You can't beat it. But it's not my main thrust, and the problem as I perceive it is that if you're in the graduate program and you make it known that you're not headed toward academia as your main job, they look down their nose at you. "You're going to make a whore of yourself making money." You get into the problem of it's very nice to have people to work on theory, but if there's no one to apply the theory, then what the hell is the purpose of it?

MARGO: You really have close contact with the faculty only when you do your dissertation. And I don't think you really have to have a Ph.D. to do a lot of business.

MARK: I agree with you. I've found that, in economics at least, there is a vast wasteland between the B.A. and the Ph.D. If you get a master's degree and try to go into the business world, in my experience it doesn't mean a heck of a lot.

The nature of a Ph.D. is more that of a union card—or is its value in what you learn?

ALLEN: I think it's more like a union card. Personally, I learned more in my one-year work experience between college and graduate school, in terms of applied economics, than I did in the first-year program. I would love to use my work experience. Unfortunately, you need a union card to go anywhere. The ranking is like this: B.A.—you stay in a research position. M.A.—doesn't get you anywhere. So you've got to get the Ph.D.

JANE: I would love to go into academia. And I would have the same ambition.

Are your ambitions realistic?

JANE: We don't get very much reality about the job market. Somehow it filters in. You might have a friend who's an upper-year student, and they might hear about the job market—and they went to Texas and then you start getting worried. But otherwise you don't hear enough about the competition and pressure out there. Little information works its way down to us.

MARGO: I think a lot of people come in here and they have huge egos. They come in and they think, "As soon as I finish here, within three months I'll have full tenure at MIT." I think a lot of people are unrealistic that way. I remember thinking my first year I just wanted to tend my garden and maybe get married and raise a family and teach at a place where I wouldn't be bothered. Since then, I think my ambitions have become larger, but still I'm not going to fight for a position at Harvard. I'd be very happy at a place like Brandeis or B.U.

DAVID: I'm not really thinking about the job market until later. I'm really going to choose a topic that I'm interested in doing my dissertation on. However, the constraint that I want to go to a top graduate school to teach basically means that I have to write a very good dissertation. So in a way that's the thing that's motivating, that's pushing, me—that I better get something damn good.

MARGO: Especially coming from Columbia. You really have to get something that's tops.

Views on Economic Theory

How do you react to the new classical economics and the rational expectations assumptions?

DAVID: We got drilled with a lot of rational expectations business for at least four to five weeks. I find it interesting, but I also find it hard to believe that my mother is sitting home trying to figure out what the Fed is going to do next year.

MARK: You know, that's interesting. People in Argentina are very sophisticated about a lot of these things because it costs a lot more for them if they're not.

MARGO: Inflation is much more institutionalized there. People know what the real interest rate means because it means something to them.

ALLEN: Here the vice-president tells you that the real interest rate is what you pay when you buy a car.

MARK: If you think about rational expectations as an intellectual process, you can see a real continuum from Cagan's early work through Friedman and Phelps and then to rational expectations—and then sort of throwing screws into the machinery so it doesn't work so perfectly, thereby avoiding super neutrality problems.

MARGO: I don't think rational expectations is going much of any place right now. That's my own personal belief. But I don't think that's quite dealing with your question.

The problem I have in the macro field is that we get very little homogeneity in what we learn. We do get a course in which we get discussions of inflation and unemployment, and then we spend tons of time with busywork issues such as the neutrality of money and rational expectations.

Plans for Dissertation Topics

What kinds of dissertations are you planning to do?

DAVID: Money and international finance. I'm working on a model and empirically testing the model.

MARGO: I'm writing three papers for my dissertation. I decided not to do a long dissertation. One reason that I decided not to do it was that

I put my politics aside when I came here. And I don't find that there's anything that matters enough to me in economics that I want to spend two years writing about. Not any topic. And any topic I really do care about—I don't think sophisticated economics is the way to approach it. So I'd rather do three papers, learn three different areas, write somewhat interesting papers and learn something, but not put my heart into something.

ALLEN: I'm going to follow the other track. I'm going to go whole hog and take a lot of political economy courses next year. I want to study thoroughly the effects of defense spending, the different methods of financing defense spending, and their effects on the economy—whether it's monetization of defense spending or debt financing. So it's somewhat technical and somewhat political economy using this new Directly Unproductive Activities analysis. In my view, that is what the federal spending is.

Alternative Viewpoints in Economics

MARGO: I want to ask one question. I thought you were interested in knowing how general beliefs about what was true in economics get formed. One thing I want to say is that we don't get many alternative viewpoints in economics. Take the Cambridge controversy—we never see that in micro. I learned about it when I was an undergraduate, but you don't see it here. I think most things are not really fleshed out here. One of the reasons may be that they can't be posed—or when they are, like the Cambridge controversy, they get too complicated.

DAVID: There's only one professor I've had this year who does go into work other than his own work. Most of the teachers here just give you their own papers and those papers related to their papers, and you get their point of view. And they never spend time discussing the differences between different views. There's only one exception—a professor this year who digs like a lawyer deeply into controversies and tries to find out where exactly are the differences. He asks questions like, "What's the assumption made here that leads to this result? And how does that differ from this?" I think that's a much better approach to learning economics.

MARK: That's related to the idea that teachers in graduate school aren't teachers—they're researchers, which is a real problem. They show you what their research is, what papers they'll cite—but it's rare that you'll see somebody that has a broad view.

Do you think that's different from any other graduate areas, say, political science, history, philosophy?

MARGO: They have much more important traditions than economics does. I mean, if you want, you can ignore reading Adam Smith. You really can't ignore reading Aristotle.

Can you really ignore reading Adam Smith? Can you ignore reading economic literature?

MARGO: Yes.

JANE. "Can we" or "Should we"? "Can you"—of course.

Is that a loss? [All agree that it is.]

DAVID: I've been doing reading on my own on the side.

MARGO: I was going to say probably everyone does. Maybe I'm wrong.

JANE: I don't think that's true—that almost everybody does.

MARK: On the other hand, it's a little bit like physics. I bet not many physicists read nineteenth-century physics.

ALLEN: But that's different, because in physics the knowledge has changed.

MARK: So has economics. The world has changed. It's not a mercantile world. There are things that occur now that didn't occur thirty years ago, or twenty years ago, that are very important in the change—things like capital mobility.

MARGO: That may be so, but do you think we're getting better economics courses? We're not saying we're giving up the economics of mercantilist times because now we're living in a much more capitalistic world. The capital mobility—we're not being taught that. I don't think that's the reason why we shift. I don't think that the reason we shift is that we say, "Adam Smith was the product of his times and Lucas is the product of his times, and we're living in Lucas's time and so therefore let's study Lucas and not Adam Smith."

MARK: I think political theory is of more lasting value. Sociological theory has more lasting value. I think economic theory becomes outmoded or outdated or supplanted.

ALLEN: Except for the very good ones.

What are the very good ones?

JANE: Adam Smith's theory is one of the good ones. Ricardo's is one of the good ones. Marx's is one of the good ones. Mill's is one of the good ones. We don't read the good ones.

DAVID: Okay, but you can look at this century, too.

How about this century? Who would be the good ones?

ALLEN: Schumpeter is, but we never deal with him, whereas in Europe people are really concerned with him.

MARGO: We dealt with that in a history course.

DAVID: I wouldn't look that far back. Not because they aren't good, but just because it isn't what I would want to read, given the limited amount of time that I would have. I would maybe read Schumpeter, but I wouldn't go back and start reading a lot of Ricardo or a lot of Malthus or something like that because given limited time, I wouldn't want to do that. I would read Keynes or Tobin. We don't read those.

JANE: I was surprised when I came here that we didn't have to read more basic works.

MARK: But also, I think they become distilled, in a way. People know a lot about Keynesian economics who've never read Keynes. I think in graduate school you should be reading the original, because things become lost.

JANE: You should see my reading list for this summer—and it should have been my reading list last summer, before I began this program.

Commitment and Loyalty: Chicago Students

The following conversations took place in the fall of 1987, shortly after the stock market crash and little more than a year after the survey had been distributed. Because several students had not been part of the survey (and because memories for these matters tend to be short anyway), we asked all participants to complete a shortened version of the questionnaire before the discussion. The responses were not significantly different from those for Chicago in the original survey.

First-Year Students

Four students participated: Rick, Andrew, John, and Dong (who arrived shortly after the meeting began).

Why Chicago?

How is it at Chicago?

RICK: I am excited about studying here. Sometimes I feel really frustrated. You probably have heard that about a third of the first-year class does not pass the comprehensive examinations. That is in the back of our minds. I am always thinking about that. But I am very glad to be here.

Why did you come here?

RICK: For a number of reasons. It is an outstanding economics program. I do tend to agree with the ideological direction that the University of Chicago supposedly has.

What about you [to Andrew]?

ANDREW: One of the things that struck me is that the teaching is better than what I've experienced before. When I was doing my M.A. at Warwick [in England] last year, someone would come in and discuss a really complex paper. Nobody would understand what was going on. Here you are in a way more "students." It is much more efficient. You are told what you have to know. You have to listen very carefully at lectures and make notes. You just learn so much. It is nicely laid out so you don't waste much time. There is a lot to do, but my rate of learning is so far higher than it has ever been before.

Why Chicago?

ANDREW: I applied to six schools in the U.S. Chicago was the only school I could afford. Yale gave me an offer, but the money was not as good. As it happens, I think that I am better suited to Chicago.

JOHN: I have a slightly different background. I was working for a consulting firm and decided to make a career change. As an undergraduate, I went to MIT. When I came here, I experienced what you would call a culture shock. I saw your survey—this is certainly a different kind of place. People here have a very fixed view about the world.

RICK: Are they more fixed here than at other places, or are they just different from what you are used to?

JOHN: I thought that MIT was much more open-minded, but maybe I am a little bit biased.

Did you know that when you came here?

JOHN: Yes. In fact, during recruitment I had asked several professors whether they really had such a strong ideological view here. Everyone sort of cocked their head this way and said, "No, that is not true. What are you talking about?" Once I came here, I found that it is true. They have a strong ideology.

RICK: It's true. Very often—although only a couple of times in macro—derisive remarks have been made about the Ivy League institutions.

JOHN: It is also more pervasive in the terminology people use. All of a sudden, nasty adjectives are used to describe something, such as "Keynesian." Someone even used "Galbraithian." *[They laugh.]*

Are you talking about professors or students?

JOHN: This was in conversations among students. I guess they were using "Galbraithian" as a sort of symbol for fuzziness and something not well thought out. I was amazed that they use such adjectives.

RICK: I haven't heard it, but maybe I will use it from now on. I like it.

You say that there is a sense of excitement about being here. Do you all share that view?

ALL: Yeah *[in chorus]*.

Is it the teaching or is it something else?

ANDREW: It is very different from anything that I have ever experienced before. Everybody here is so enthusiastic and eager to learn, whereas I am used to being among people who are not very interested in the material or in learning economics. The enthusiasm of the people here gets my motivation going as well.

RICK: I came from a good liberal arts college. Maybe it is being at a quality university which makes it enjoyable for me.

I remember the first day when we had our orientation. Lucas's very first words were, "I think that the University of Chicago is the best place in the world to do economics." He went on to say, "We here at Chicago believe that what we do matters and is more important than events in Washington." *[They laugh.]* That may be a little bit of an exaggeration, but, boy, was it good to hear that.

[To John] Were you excited about that?

JOHN: Actually, I was upset about that. I always viewed politics as applied economics and that economics without political ramifications was not all that valuable by itself. I was upset.

RICK: I think he was suggesting that what they do here now will one day have ramifications.

ANDREW: Yes. It is nice to have people who have a lot of confidence in what they are doing. I am used to people coming up to me and saying that all these models are just an intellectual exercise. I did not have much of an answer. Then I come here and people really do believe they are doing something really important.

What is your answer now?

ANDREW: I have a lot more confidence that economists, especially those here, are actually doing something constructive.

In what sense are economists constructive?

ANDREW: Gary Becker's theory of the consumer seems to me really relevant. In his lectures he applies it to all kinds of areas. You begin to realize that it is useful.

Chicago has the image of being difficult.

ANDREW: I guess it depends on how you feel relative to other people. I feel reasonably well prepared. I got some of the stuff before when I did my master's. I don't feel the pressure as much as some of the American students do. International students have a better background. But yes, it is somewhat of a shock when someone tells you that only thirty percent of the people get through the first year.

JOHN: There is a lot of pressure here. It is true, the Americans have to catch up with the foreign students.

What Makes an Economist Successful?

The questionnaire contained a question on what makes an economist successful. How did you deal with that question?

JOHN: I thought that you meant what brings success here. I think mathematical skills are the most important asset. However, I have been here only seven weeks, so I could be wrong.

How about knowledge of the economy?

RICK: What does knowledge of the economy entail? You mean knowing something about the statistics that the government puts out all the time?

ANDREW: I guess knowing what is happening with the inflation rate, unemployment, and so on.

JOHN: I took it much more literally. Before I went to graduate school, I wanted to know what the economy is like. I took a year's leave of absence from the company for which I was working and drove all over America and visited all kinds of little towns to see what was going on in Marion, Indiana. What happens when GM closes its plant in a small town? I think that if you are going to be a good economist, you know what the economy is really like. There are people behind those statistics. Unemployment has very tangible effects on individuals in towns and communities. In that sense, I view a general sense of the economy as very important. But I am not sure that that's really going to help me at Chicago.

Why not?

JOHN: Because here it's mathematical models and techniques that get a greater weight.

RICK: That is true for all graduate schools these days.

JOHN: I don't know. Compared to MIT . . .

RICK: MIT is the most mathematical, theoretical school in the country.

JOHN: Maybe they are just more open-minded.

On Assumptions and Disagreements

How do you respond to the assertion that the basic assumptions in economics are unrealistic?

RICK: I haven't read Friedman's essay on "Positive Economics" *[they laugh]*, but even if they are not totally realistic, they can help derive conclusions which are generally correct or more correct than the alternatives.

ANDREW: You have to have something. You have to specify some assumption because otherwise you can't have any theory—you can't have any predictions. And then the economists have no role to play. So you've got to start somewhere. Given a particular set of assumptions, you can construct models and see how closely related they are to the data. If they fit well and explain well, that's fine. For example, the maximization assumption imposes restrictions. As it happens, it is fairly consistent with the data for a lot of countries. As far as I am concerned, that is a pretty reasonable thing to assume.

If these assumptions are so reasonable, why are the disagreements among economists about them so persistent? Why do you have a Chicago school that is so distinct?

RICK: That is a tough question, and I don't quite know how to answer it. I haven't been part of a discussion where those fundamental assumptions have been discussed.

ANDREW: I am not sure that there are such massive disagreements between, say, MIT and Chicago. *[They laugh.]* I guess that at MIT they, too, believe strongly in microeconomics and adopt rationality as the basic assumption—maybe not as strongly as here—and the policy conclusions are not so wildly different.

JOHN: I disagree. *[They also laugh about that.]* I'd say that macroeconomics there is entirely different. It is nothing like what we are being taught. It is much more Keynesian—much more the economy as a whole—whereas here you make a very strong assumption about individuals. The rationality assumption is extremely strong here. The big problem is that people, especially when they are deciding where to spend their money and in what to invest, are not always rational. They can also be irrational. This throws curves into theories. That's why it seems that the stock market crash of a few weeks ago is unexplainable here because if everyone is perfectly rational, it should not have happened. But I don't think that anyone at MIT would have trouble explaining it, saying that the economy went out of whack, that people were not acting rational in the first place.

RICK: Speculative behavior does not have to be nonrational.

JOHN: In many cases, speculative behavior leads to nonrational results. I think that my biggest objection to Chicago so far is that you seem to be making assumptions about people's behavior and macroeconomics. If you try to model an individual consumption or investment function by aggregate equations and you cannot do that for any individual, then you get very skewed results when you do it for a couple of hundred million. That is what I am most uncomfortable with.

DONG: *[He had just arrived.]* I object to your statement. A good theory may not exactly predict a society's behavior—as long as it is the best theory, it provides a good starting point. So a good theory does not necessarily capture what is really happening in the world.

So you would say that the theory you are learning here is the best one available?

DONG: I used to study at UCLA and George Washington University. I think that the Chicago approach is better.

Why is that?

DONG: It seems to have a more rational basis.

What makes you uncomfortable about the Keynesian theories?

DONG: I don't know. I don't have a deep understanding of all that, but my intuition is that the theory taught here has a more solid basis. It starts from the rationality hypothesis.

On Mathematics and Economics

Do I understand that you are excited about the possibility of being precise, of being mathematical? That you think the mathematics is important for you as economists?

DONG: Yes, I think so.

RICK: I guess it is a necessary evil. To do a good job, you have to use mathematics. Mathematics is a tool. I'd rather learn it now than later on.

ANDREW: It is also vital for actually testing theories. That is a very important part, specifying what you believe in mathematical models and then checking those models with the data.

JOHN: Yes, the mathematics ensures that you can compare your models with the data. It also ensures that your theories are rigorous and consistent and that you haven't made assumptions which violate one another. However, I think that the mathematics only takes you so far—there are psychological aspects to economics, but our society wants to see theory proved as much as possible through mathematics. If you want to have people believe in an economic theory, you need the mathematics behind it.

RICK: Maybe I will change my mind in a few years, but I now think that the profession in general is too mathematical. When I look at the journals, I get sick sometimes.

ANDREW: But maybe that is because you are not used to the math. It used to put me off. If you do have a set of ideas, the best way to check is to write them all down and then solve your model. Maybe you neglected some indirect effects in your mind.

DONG: When you develop your theories in a science, you need math. Math is a very powerful tool. At the same time, we should be aware that the world is not as rigorous as the mathematics. You do need your intuition.

RICK: I am surprised by how often I have heard the word intuition during the last three months. In class, when we are going through a bunch of math, the professor will say, "Let us think of the intuition." I did not know that economics would be this way, but then again I had never had so much math thrown at me. We were doing intuition all the time.

What is surprising about the use of intuition?

RICK: Intuition is kind of a shortcut to where you are going. Sometimes it is probably too vague. Now I am arguing for mathematics.

JOHN: I agree that mathematics is important, but I agree with Rick that it is too prominent. I think that when we are discussing human behavior, intuition is very important. But one reason to come to Chicago is to get a firm mathematical basis because I know if I want to have any effect on governmental policy, it is the mathematics that will convince people—even if they don't understand it. If you go to a congressional committee and you can wave a report with lots of statistics, it will be more convincing than a report that just makes good intuitive sense. That is just the way the world is right now. So it is really important to know the mathematics.

The Economy

Do you talk about the economy?

ALL: No! A little. *[They speak at the same time and laugh.]*

Did the stock market crash bring about a discussion?

JOHN: Not in class so much, but over lunch tables with other grad students or professors one certainly does.

DONG: But Becker mentioned it.

ANDREW: Yes, he was good. He was teaching us all this analysis, the stock market crashed, and the next day he came along and showed how all the stuff we were doing fitted nicely.

JOHN: But did he give any reasons for the crash?

ANDREW: No, he didn't.

RICK: Well, he said something to the effect that this would decrease consumption.

DONG: There was an article in the student newspaper in which some reporter asked the professors about the stock market.

RICK: They all say, "We don't know what happens, so the government shouldn't do anything."

On Policy and Economics

What role do you expect you will play as an economist? What do you expect you will contribute?

JOHN: I would like to go back to Washington and work maybe for the Congress or the CBO [Congressional Budget Office] and help them to assess actual policy.

RICK: I am kind of unusual around here. I do not have the goal of getting a spot at a major research university. I want to teach at a small liberal arts institution. I have to devote myself entirely to economics while I am here, but I do not want to be a research economist.

ANDREW: I would like to go back to England and take the ideas that I have learned around here with me and maybe spread them around in England.

Do you get the sense here that the role of economists is to contribute to the formulation and assessment of economic policy?

RICK: Even before I came here, I thought that microeconomic analysis was a great way of looking at problems, all kinds of policy problems. I'd like to be able to make students say one day, "Wow, I guess that I have been looking at this all wrong. If you take these few assumptions of microeconomics, then I have to change my opinion totally." I'd like to help, or at least give students an opportunity, to take those views.

[To John] You intend to go into policy, but isn't the message of Chicago to stay away from policy?

RICK: To stay away from policy?

Well, to stay away from Washington.

RICK: Maybe stay away, but when I think of Chicago, I think of Friedman and the effect he has had on policy.

JOHN: I perceive there's an underlying attitude here that the government doesn't matter—or that if it does matter, it only messes things up. So you should keep away from it.

Chicago economists don't go to Washington.

JOHN: Yes, I do agree with that. And that's why when you *[turning to Rick]* first mentioned Robert Lucas's opening comment that "we feel that what we do is more important than what goes on in Washington or Tokyo," it seemed to confirm to me the belief that politics doesn't matter.

RICK: I saw Friedman in Washington four years ago. At that time, of course, he was not a member of the faculty of this institution. He came and spoke for an hour to congressional staff. It was exciting—I loved it. Why? I had read *Free to Choose* and his articles in *Newsweek*.[1] Then I actually saw him during the middle of his lecture take his tie and say, "As Adam Smith said more than two hundred years ago . . ." about the market place and so on and so forth. It was exciting.

On Economists

Do you have heroes among economists? Are there some economists you respect more than others?

RICK: Adam Smith.

ANDREW: Friedman for me.

RICK: And Buchanan. I have not really gotten into public choice.

Then why Buchanan?

RICK: The idea of using economics to analyze how policy is coming to be and how rules can influence the outcome of political systems.

[To Andrew] **Why Friedman?**

ANDREW: Just because he has done so much. I also admire in him that he was prepared to stick himself out on a limb and come up with all these ideas when everyone else was saying the opposite. He was going against the tide. Almost everybody was regarding his ideas as crazy, but he stuck to them because he believed firmly in them. And he managed to persuade people, and other people slowly edged toward his position. Not many people are willing to do that—they do not want to appear extreme. And then, he developed monetarism almost single-handedly.

How about you?

JOHN: That's difficult. I do not particularly care for Milton Friedman, especially after I once saw him on "Nightline." He was criticizing corporate contributions to charity. I cannot imagine a Nobel Prize winner going on national TV criticizing any kind of contributions to charity.

ANDREW: But you see, he puts himself up. The typical reaction is, "What a nasty man!"

JOHN: He has guts, but that doesn't mean he is right. *[Some confusion.]* I don't think that such a statement on "Nightline" has a beneficial effect on the economy as a whole.

In terms of who my heroes are, I *[hesitates]* have the feeling that I better say Adam Smith. *[They laugh.]*

[To Dong] **How about you?**

DONG: Keynes. *[Cries of surprise.]* That is a special story. I come from China. I read Keynes a little while I was still in China. I think that Keynesian theory is a useful tool for policy. It is very important for the situation China is in.

But Keynes does not have a privileged position in this environment.

DONG: Yes, but I came here to hear the other side—the pure capitalist side of economics.

But you still like Keynes better?

DONG: It is hard to say at this point. Keynesian policy can have a very effective influence in China. On the other hand, monetarism gives a good perspective. I think that China needs a mixture of both. It is a central planning economy going toward a market economy. It will gradually reduce the influence of the government.

JOHN: Now that someone else has said it, I also agree that Keynes is *[drowned out by laughter]*. I did not want to be branded as a token Keynesian.

[To Dong] **Are you the exception here with your preference for Keynes?**

DONG: I think so.

Miscellaneous Topics

Do you discuss IS/LM?

ALL: *[In chorus.]* No. We have yet to see an IS/LM diagram. No, you saw one: he [the professor teaching macro] drew one with his right hand and had an eraser in his left hand. That was it.

What do you have against IS/LM?

JOHN: It involves this overall assumption of aggregate demand in the economy, an aggregate demand for money, which is frowned upon here. The macroeconomics here is very much like microeconomics. We work on individual levels and sum it up.

ANDREW: It maybe also has something to do with the stress on intertemporal decisionmaking. IS/LM is initially a comparative static model. That does not work when you consider intertemporal decisions.

JOHN: I think that is why I feel uncomfortable here. In Keynesian theory, if the aggregate demand curve shifts, one doesn't actually know why it shifted. If it shifts in, you get a recession and it tells you what to do.

Here, with the intertemporal models, you actually model individual behavior. You try to give reasons for individual choices—but everyone is not always rational. *[We talk about things in general. Dong lets us know that he is planning to go back to China. John mentions the role of economists and how they may convince a politician or a layperson.]* You do not go use your jargon with Joe Six-Pack when you want to convince him about monetary policy. Buzzwords become important.

ANDREW: I don't agree that economic theory is necessarily hard to portray to the public. Like the question whether minimum wage causes unemployment—that is an easy idea to get across to almost anyone.

But a significant number of Harvard graduate students disagree.

RICK: Yes, that blew my mind.

ANDREW: All I am saying is that it is an easy idea to put across to the public. The idea is easy enough to understand.

Second-Year Students

Five students participated. We called them Rod, Lee, Susan, Daniel, and David. As in the previous conversation, we began talking about their reasons for coming to Chicago. Lee had had the option to go to MIT, but the financial constraint forced him to Chicago. Daniel chose Chicago over Harvard because of the challenge he expected to get. Politics was not a consideration for him. For Susan, a libertarian, politics was decisive. They all give a moderately positive description of their experience in the first year.

The Problem-Solving Aspect

ROD: One thing that comes out of all the problem solving is that it is hard to take any of it very seriously. Some of the models are extremely good, but a lot of them are not. At times people seem to make certain assumptions to get the results they want.

DANIEL: One thing to remember is that the results are conditioned on the assumptions.

ROD: I realize that. But what if all the assumptions are kind of strange? Then it is hard to take the conclusions seriously.

LEE: But the idea is, I think, to show you how you could model. The results are not necessarily what the models are about.

ROD: That is why it is a little unsatisfying. When you take a physics course, you feel that what you study is quite well connected with reality.

SUSAN: People are much more complicated than that. You cannot expect that much.

Chicago Versus Other Schools

Do you think the approach you are learning here is different from others? How would you describe it? [Little response.] There is the impression that Chicago is different from MIT.

DANIEL: Here you only learn about Chicago. I don't know what is going on at MIT. On the reading lists here, they give you their own papers, not the papers of MIT people.

Is that so?

SUSAN: Yes.

DANIEL: Apart from some classic papers you cannot avoid. The macro sequence is very extreme.

SUSAN: The macro classes are certainly very different. We spent one introductory class on Keynesianism and that was it. You never got to see it again. You also are not getting any economists from MIT here. *[We briefly discuss the role of mathematics in economics. They seem to think that math is useful, but they also stress intuition.]* Math is also useful because in that way the assumptions are spelled out. One of the problems when you read old economists like Ricardo is that you cannot figure out what they are saying. So there has to be some sort of mean.

About Economists

What is it that makes an economist successful nowadays?

SUSAN: It is hard to say what you have to do. Good economists are very bright people. Becker is very much like an intuitive economist.

DANIEL: Lucas gets more of his results intuitively and then uses the math to justify them. To be a good economist, therefore, you need first of all the intuition. If you don't have the intuition, then you won't be one of the leading economists. But, again, there are some complements. If you don't have intuition as Becker does, then you better study math.

How important is Milton Friedman nowadays? Does he feature in your courses?

SUSAN: No. It has all been rational expectations and differential equations. We do not talk about his stuff.

Who are the important economists for you?

DANIEL: Again, I only know Chicago economists. I don't know enough about economists in other places. Here I am only exposed to the literature that these people wrote. From things that I had to read during the first year, Lucas seems full of intuition, and it is easy to understand that it is meaningful.

SUSAN: If you look at his nonmathematical articles, you will see that he writes very well. In order to be memorable as an economist, you have to know how to write.

ROD: The economists I respect most are Becker and Lucas.

Why is that?

ROD: Probably because of their lectures. Lucas, as a matter of fact, gives very interesting lectures.

LEE: He works in interesting areas. He is intellectually very honest. He is rigorous in his approach. He gives you a good and interesting way of looking at the world and tells you what the limitations of that way are.

DAVID: For me it is Becker.

Why?

DAVID: I really am intrigued by his application of economic principles, of optimizing principles to all sorts of interesting types of behavior that historically were not studied by economists. I think it is interesting and immensely valuable. It's really *the* thing that kept me interested in economics.

It surprises me that you don't mention someone like Hansen.

DANIEL: That's because we don't understand what he's doing. *[They laugh.]*

You have no desire to do what he does?

DANIEL: No. I would like people to understand what I am doing.

LEE: What he is doing is very, very abstract.

SUSAN: It is a matter of wading through the notations.

LEE: Lucas gives you the intuition before he gives you this paper in which he proves these things like the existence of equilibrium. Then if you want to be convinced that the equilibrium exists, he tells you to go to the math. Hansen gives you only the math.

ROD: You are talking about what Hansen taught last year. In a course this year, I got a very different impression. He is actually an excellent mathematician and statistician. There is no question about that. His classes are all about how you make these arcane, abstract models comply with the data.

SUSAN: Hansen is still pretty young, so you can't say that much about him.

DAVID: The problem is that his stuff is very hard.

DANIEL: I think part of the problem is also specialization. Modern economics is very specialized, *very* specialized, so that people from other fields do not really know what he is doing. Lucas and Becker speak about things everybody can understand even outside their fields. So it is easy for students to be happy with that.

ROD: Coming back to the economists we respect. We talked thus far only about economists who are here, but you have to respect Solow— and Samuelson too—even though they are kind of old and out of the way.

Chicago Economics

What is the key in the economics that you are learning?

SUSAN: I think it is very strongly neoclassical.

What do you think neoclassical means?

SUSAN: I think the assumption of rational behavior is very important.

Many people have reservations about the assumption.

SUSAN: I do not think it is so much an assumption—it is what you can do with it. That was Milton Friedman's point.

DANIEL: I agree with that. If you don't assume rationality, then there isn't anything to say.

SUSAN: Yes, then you can do what you want.

LEE: *[He has just joined us.]* Here they take economics very seriously.

What does that mean, taking economics seriously? Do other people not take economics seriously?

LEE: First of all, there is the analytical rigor with which most of the people here do economics. They have a very strong belief that their way of looking at the world is the good way of looking at the world. They do not shrink back from defending their points of view. And even though they are not actually involved in policy formation as such, I think that there is a very strong underlying current in their work that they are trying to understand how we can make the world better and how economic insights can improve things.

Improve how, what?

LEE: I think that is a question of efficiency. It is a question of making existing institutions more efficient or of coming up with institutions that are better.

ROD: You have never seen any of that during the first year.

LEE: In the first year you certainly don't.

ROD: That is imposing value judgments.

LEE: True.

ROD: They have taught us so far without imposing value judgments. You could not really tell, unless you have read their papers, what their dig is.

LEE: But you always get the feeling that they are looking for improvements, even though the improvements really are not a matter of facts. You get the feeling that they do not create all these models in a vacuum.

ROD: I agree.

Economics and Policy

> *What is the relationship between economics and policy as you get to see that here at Chicago?*

DAVID: My personal impression is that they do not give it much attention. I came here knowing that and expecting that. I really wanted to learn economics. Policy would come later.

I think a lot of schools have a problem in that they get the policy before they study economics. I wish that the department was bigger so that there would be people doing policy. But I respect the way the program is organized.

LEE: The problem is that economists often end up talking in terms policymakers don't understand. They end up not having much of a voice when it comes to policymaking.

ROD: I wonder whether that is right. It is really pointless to try to change the world if you do not know the way it works. I think that most people here are preoccupied with how things are.

> *How come Chicago has a conservative reputation?*

ROD: The TV series. *[They laugh. The reference is to Milton Friedman's series on public television.]*

> *That series did not have much to do with what you are learning?*

ROD: Some of the older professors are extremely conservative, but the younger ones seem to be more Democrats. But this is not something that comes out.

SUSAN: You cannot get policy implications out of the more technical stuff, such as the Lucas type of stuff. If you do I.O., you get quite a bit.

LEE: Yes, I think that the young economists tend to become much more eclectic.

DAVID: I think that is a reason to stay away from policy. Certain professors in the department, like Stigler, are classic conservatives. But then the younger people, like Hansen—it would take a million years to figure out his policy. *[They laugh.]* You couldn't find one even if you wanted to. Maybe that's why that sort of stuff is so encouraged here.

Is it?

DAVID: In macro that is certainly the direction they have gone.

The Objective of Economics

What is the point of economics?

DAVID: It's a *tool*. Why study econometrics? I guess the point is that seventy years down the line, the equations will work right and we will be able to predict things. At this point it is developmental.

ROD: That underlies the Lucas position. In order to understand the implications of government intervention, you have to have a certain model. The models we have now are simply not good enough yet.

DANIEL: You cannot really separate policy from economics. Economic policy is coming straight from economic theory. As you said, in order to know what policy to take, you should first understand the economic environment. The problem here is that the tendency is to understand the economic environment in the long run, and most policymakers are interested in the short run.

The current models have implications, but not for the things with which policymakers are currently concerned. Nobody cares about the money supply in the long run. Most people are far removed from what we should be doing in the real world.

SUSAN: But the world is too complicated.

DAVID: Yes, relative to the models. Certainly we are talking about macro right now. I am no expert in that. But my impression is that these models are very simple. You can add complexities to them, and each step should describe the system better. But I don't even know if there is this fundamental belief that somewhere out there is the ideal model.

LEE: What I understand is that right now we do not know enough to make solid policy predictions. Some people make predictions anyway, but that is a matter of belief. The tools are not sufficiently developed yet.

I am now slightly confused. On one hand, people here are very confident.

LEE: Confident in their models, whatever limited purposes they serve. With the current models you can answer only small questions. But there is definitely the hope that someday we will have a richer class of models which explain a lot more things a lot better.

Do the others share this conviction?

SUSAN: To a certain extent, yes. We have learned to be suspicious with respect to large models with one hundred fifty variables or so. I am not sure they are very useful. I think there are advantages with simple models from which we can draw some broad implications.

DANIEL: It is a matter of belief. If you believe that these models will develop into something that could explain the world, then it would be the biggest invention of the twentieth century!

DAVID: *[Laughing.]* Twenty-first century?

LEE: There is the feeling that somewhere down the line we will be able to explain the world a little better than right now.

ROD: The idea is that we try to explain what little we can, and try to build from that.

DANIEL: I accept that. This is just an academic discussion.

ROD: We are now talking in the context of macroeconomic theory. If we would talk about the other areas, it would be different. It is not that there aren't people in the department who are heavily involved in policy. There are things you can say, which can make the economy better off.

DANIEL: Impose a lump-sum tax?

ROD: Putting in value-added tax, no longer raising prices to farmers— things like that. Doing things to make the labor market more efficient. About interventions like that, economists can say something.

DANIEL: So let's agree that all we said applies to macroeconomics only.

SUSAN: Macroeconomics is in disarray anyway.

DAVID: One thing about macro, though. I am not sure we should impute this belief that there is some great model. You are not sure that anything is coming out of it. Maybe it will be better. I don't know what their beliefs are—they don't come up in class. Hansen may well think, "You never will be able to get any policy from this."

ROD: I think that is not true. Lucas is always saying, "This is a good model that shows what we are trying to do." You want a model that explains policy interventions. Probably there is not a good model. Whether there will be—that is the big, fascinating question. For policy you want a model that accounts for business cycles. Well, the Kydland-Prescott model . . . *[One student gasps, another chuckles.]*

What about it?

DANIEL: No names, right?

Well?

LEE: We haven't seen too much of it.

Why do you react the way you do?

LEE: It has raised a lot of controversy.

ROD: This model accounts for the business cycle without either a government or a money supply. There is this great irritation that you would do that. It shows that everything is wide open. Any reasonable model should be considered.

[We briefly talk about IS/LM ("That was treated mainly tongue in cheek"); rational expectations ("Should be in the models"); history of thought ("If you want to do a favor to a developing country, you should give it a copy of The Wealth of Nations*"); and their politics (Susan is an outspoken libertarian; the others either refuse a label or are liberal).[2] I ask them what they think of the idea that graduate training is like brainwashing. Susan does not accept that.]*

SUSAN: They are not trying to brainwash you. They are trying to convince you. This is an intellectual experience.

DAVID: It is pretty hard to be brainwashed when the person who is telling you it is telling you it in a way that is so exaggerated—so much so that he is making an argument—that you don't sit there and say, "Yes, I believe this." You sit there and say, "That is an argument." That is the attitude that is clearly projected here. These are arguments, not a religion.

ROD: Maybe the brainwashing is in the assumptions. You are not supposed to quibble with the assumptions.

DAVID: If there is any brainwashing at all, it is not in terms of policy implications but in terms of what economics is. I think all of us would agree that economists better have a model. Right? I am not sure that is true everywhere. And we almost all agree that in a good model taste is not changing.

SUSAN: It is true that we follow one line, but if you do have to, the Chicago line is the best one to follow.

Third-Year Students

Four students—Nick, Mike, Herbert, and Paul—are present from the beginning. John and Edward join us later. We begin talking about their experience at Chicago. They quickly get onto the topic of the Chicago core exams. For these students, the exams obviously lived up to their notorious reputation. If it was not the exams themselves, it was the hype that preceded them. They also talk about their reasons for coming to Chicago. Nick came for the challenge: "The choice was between UCLA and here. I came here for the prospective student thing, and what I got from that was the challenge, 'Are you man enough to make it?' So I decided right then 'I go!'" Herbert transferred from another school. Even though he does not consider himself a Chicago type, he was attracted by Gary Becker's work. Herbert's interest in psychology makes him the maverick in the group.

Chicago Economics

Do you think there is a distinctive Chicago line in economics?

NICK: There is a piece by Milton Friedman hanging in the department where he says there is.

MIKE: I don't know whether there is a Chicago line, but there probably is a Chicago attitude. It doesn't seem to bother people. Maybe it is Friedman's influence. Anyway, the realism of assumptions is not terribly important to people here. The models they are making are built on intuitively obvious concepts. I have a friend at Berkeley and I can tell that we have had a very different education in terms of macroeconomics. I asked him what he had done. He said, "Oh, the usual thing. A quarter on the investment function—you know, I equals I(r)." *[They laugh.]*

HERBERT: It's really true. Having gone to another program where you saw IS/LMs all over the place, I have yet to see an IS/LM diagram here.

NICK: Cochrane did that.

HERBERT: Oh, I was not there that day.

NICK: You miss the first day and you miss IS/LM.

MIKE: And unemployment!

PAUL: I have a friend who did his undergraduate work at Harvard, probably in policy. I saw him last year—he is now doing graduate studies in political science—and he asked me, "Do they still do neoclassical economics at Chicago?" *[He chuckles.]* He seemed quite astounded that people here still take neoclassical economics very seriously. That phrase Professor Lucas apparently repeats to every entering class—we heard it our first day. He gets up and gives this little speech and says, "We take economics seriously, and that makes Chicago different from every-where else." Maybe that is the thing that defines it.

What does that mean—"taking economics seriously"? Don't people at other places do that?

MIKE: Gary Becker is an extreme example of that. You write down the model, work out the results, and that is the answer.

NICK: You can work at the economics of anything.

PAUL: Yes, economics is viewed as a very powerful tool that will explain nearly everything. It is kind of painted here that people at Cambridge treat economics as a sort of mathematical exercise. It is all very pristine and wonderful, but it has no application to the real world. I get the feeling sometimes that at other schools—not so much Harvard and MIT, but the lower-ranked schools—it is policy-driven. Someone wants to write a book about why the government should do X and throws some economics together. That's not taking economics seriously.

Why not?

PAUL: It's letting your policy prescription drive the economics. I hope that no one around here does that.

MIKE: The stuff people do here is irrelevant in terms of policy. You don't see Bob Lucas jetting up to Washington every week.

PAUL: I would say, though, that what they do is relevant in the longer run. In the sense that, as Keynes said, we are all slaves of some defunct economist. These people are not defunct yet, so nobody is their slave yet. But some years down the road they will have a big influence on policy, I think. In the same way that Milton Friedman's influence peaked long after his main intellectual work was done. He was near retirement when monetarism finally emerged as a legitimate policy.

HERBERT: In a certain sense, Chicago is defined by a real commitment to certain kinds of methodological principles which we strictly adhere to. Our commitment to rational expectations as opposed to adaptive expectations arises from a belief that it would be more parsimonious to postulate. In some sense, people here would be unhappy when their expectations are rational in some models and adaptive in others. Here there is a commitment to being very parsimonious in fundamental assumptions, whereas people at MIT are maybe a little looser about that. They have the attitude, "Let's not make the theory work as hard as possible to fit the data. Let's be less parsimonious about that."

[To the others] Do you agree with that?

MIKE: I think it is correct.

PAUL: Joe Stiglitz or George Akerlof would say about the disarray in macroeconomics, "Let's draw in some psychology or throw in something of this or that." Whereas around here, it is kind of, "Let's put our nose harder to the grindstone and find a maximizing model, a traditional economic model, to explain things."

MIKE: That stuff is less disciplined. That's why we say that we take economics more seriously.

HERBERT: Exactly. I think students at MIT and students here share what the cultural idea of science is. The reason you find them saying that economics is less scientific is that they are not committed to that rock-bottom theoretical program.

Mathematics and Economics

What about the role of math? Is it very important?

PAUL: Why don't we have John start on that? *[John entered a short while ago. They laugh.]*

JOHN: I just came in, so I am out of context here.

NICK: A week ago at Jimmy's *[a place where they hang out]*, we touched upon the possibility that math is not a description of things.

JOHN: When we were talking about the expected utility stuff?

NICK: Yes, we were talking about whether you can create instances— and even if they are there only under extreme assumptions, we can still say, "Well, in general this holds." Theories are basically what happens in general, not all the time.

PAUL: I am not sure whether that will be clear. Herbert is studying for a behavioral science prelim at the business school, for which he has been reading lots of articles by these psychologists who don't care for the expected utility of the economists.

HERBERT: To put it mildly.

PAUL: To put it mildly. They have done a lot of experiments which purport to show that under certain circumstances people behave with intransitive preferences, or that there are context effects, or all kinds of other things—all of which violate expected utility. We had a lot of discussion in the department about that. We got going about that at Jimmy's. It is a thought-provoking issue for us. Expected utility is what you are taught here—and then you are confronted with a whole discipline that says it is garbage. So you worry about your intellectual capital a little bit.

I liked the perspective that was offered to me by David Friedman in a conversation I had with him. He said he felt that the really interesting part of economics was the coming up with ideas and then writing them down in words. He felt that doing the math was a sort of cleanup job. Formalize the idea, find out under what circumstances it really is true. I wouldn't go quite as far as he did, making that sound like a dull and boring thing to do. It's not trivial and can be interesting. But the thing that really attracted me to economics initially was the neat ideas, the neat way of looking at the world, the tremendous explanatory power of the model. That's not really dependent on the mathematics.

HERBERT: As a matter of fact, the mathematics will gradually reveal to you the circumstances where certain ideas break down.

Is there a big emphasis on the mathematics here?

MIKE: I don't know what to compare it to. Compared to my undergraduate education, yes.

JOHN: Compared to the literature, I would say no. If you pick up a journal like *AER, JPE,* or *Econometrica,* the level of mathematics which they are using is noticeably higher than what you get from an average course here, unless you take a specifically mathematical economics course. I don't have the impression that this is that mathematical a school.

NICK: That is the kind of mathematical cleanup job those people in the journals do.

PAUL: I think sometimes that professors use mathematics if they can't lecture. *[They find that pretty funny.]*

NICK: So that's why this is not a very mathematical school!

HERBERT: We have one professor who shall remain nameless *[laughter].* I remember when I was a first-year student, I would go out in the hall after class with a couple of other people and try to figure out an intuitive explanation of what this guy had been talking about. So we'd sit down and say things like, "How about car batteries and cars? Yeah, that's what it is. You drive around with your car battery all day and it gets run down, and you sell it back to the garage and they charge it up. Yeah, that's what it is." You had capital that had three different things going on. It got worn out and sold back to people who made it into new capital. We said to the professor sometimes, "I don't understand what you are talking about." This particular professor would rephrase it with another type of mathematics. *[They laugh.]*

EDWARD: *[He recently arrived.]* You cannot say that he has no intuition. That *is* his intuition.

What do you think of that?

EDWARD: Whatever turns you on. *[They laugh.]*

JOHN: Wait, not all courses here are mathematical. Becker is not extremely mathematical, Lucas is not, and even Townsend is not. *[Now they all talk at the same time.]*

HERBERT: Think about Prescott's class. The first thing he said on the first day of class was, "Everybody knows what a compact set is, right?"

Well, most of us knew at that time what a compact set is—it was not on the tip of my tongue, though. But only a few people raised their hands. He said, "That is one of the first things we teach our students at Minnesota." That's not one of the first things we learn here!

[They talk about a few courses in which subjects such as compact sets are taught. Edward mentions the more practical approach Milton Friedman took in his classes. He apparently brought up examples that he picked from the newspaper and analyzed. They regret that this is not done anymore. John thinks that Becker does some of it.]

Chicago Economics and Ideology

What is Chicago's reputation?

JOHN: *[Softly.]* Extreme.

MIKE: That's a parody, but there is probably a lot of truth to it. What I can tell from the questions people ask me is that the University of Chicago seems extremely ideological and extremely free-market oriented. Most of the people still seem to think that Milton Friedman dictates every aspect of life here.

PAUL: When he is not in Chile. *[Some chuckle.]*

MIKE: I think also—and this goes back to the question about mathematics—a few economists I talked with were very surprised when they heard what I was reading the first year. They expected that I would be reading Friedman's *Price Theory* book.[3] They thought that was the way economics was taught here—in a very intuitive, policy-oriented way. They were amazed that I was reading Debreu and Varian.

What do you think of this image that Chicago has?

MIKE: It's kind of fun.

PAUL: There is more to it than that. It is the image of the loyal opposition in economics, in a way. Someone at Harvard or MIT trots out some proposal for a new market failure. Then Demsetz fires up, or somebody else, and says, "Wait a minute!"

MIKE: That's a definite role for you to play in life. Someone will say, "We need some price controls," and look over to you. *[They like that a great deal.]* "So what are we going to do?" This is a game. The few times I have talked with people who do economics—that doesn't happen too much—they like to say these things. They wait for your response, and I give it to them. I get into it—it is fun.

JOHN: That's true for most people here. I think it closes them off from thinking seriously about economic problems.

EDWARD: I never once felt that I was being indoctrinated.

MIKE: You don't need to.

EDWARD: There is self-selection going on.

MIKE: Not only self-selection. It's also the other students. Nobody has to say, "This is bad—government sucks." Everybody knows that it is expected that you should know government sucks. You don't need anybody to tell you that.

Do you ever discuss wage and price controls?

JOHN: No, never.

Efficiency wages?

[One says "Yes," another "Hardly, no." They have a discussion about a professor who apparently presented a paper about efficiency wages. John does not think that the argument is actually an efficiency-wage argument; he can't believe that professor would teach the topic.]

PAUL: I worry that the wrong impression is getting across here. I have talked before about coming here because of the shared value thing, but since I have been here, I really have the feeling that for most of the faculty it is not so much that values are driving their choices as it is the other way around in a lot of cases. A lot of these people come with these feelings about government from studying government from an economic perspective.

It's my feeling that a lot of other schools, despite all the pooh-poohing that went on when James Buchanan got the Nobel Prize—"Oh everybody knows that, da-da-da"—treat the government as a black box. The economist types in "do X," the policy comes out, and, miraculously, the government does X. Isn't that wonderful—we have made the world better off.

So I don't think necessarily that there is an ideological predilection against government. It seems to me that you read paper after paper about "Gee, isn't it amazing how this kind of cynical interest-group type of explanation seems to explain the observed policy effects a lot better than a sort of public-interest type of model?" After a while that leads you to a presumption against government intervention.

I know several people who came in as kind of new liberals, who sat through some of the classes where you read a lot of these papers. They changed.

JOHN: Why do you think that would not operate at another school, say like Harvard?

PAUL: I don't think they study that kind of stuff. I don't think that those people are worried about these issues. Maybe people who study government because they have an initial dislike of the government say, "Well, let's apply economic analysis to this."

HERBERT: There is also this methodological commitment I was talking about earlier. If there are arbitrage opportunities, we would assume people will exploit them. If there are externalities and the appropriate information requirement is satisfied, people take steps to eliminate those. If you're committed to those, which are really behavioral postulates, not ideological postulates, you really are committed to trying to make them work. And then you more frequently get situations in which government policy is irrelevant. It's not always clear what is driving what, whether it is ideology driving the behavioral propositions or the other way around.

You people don't talk much about distribution issues?

JOHN: God, no! *[They laugh.]*

HERBERT: We do, though, but . . .

EDWARD: Yeah, there are lambdas in some equations.

JOHN: We never talk about it in a policy sense.

PAUL: It seems that is what the Friedman-Stigler-Becker approach is all about.

JOHN: Okay, that is in a positive rather than a normative sense.

PAUL: That is true. We don't talk about it in a normative sense.

EDWARD: I think there is a sort of bias here that it is not a reasonable economic argument [to say], "There are people suffering! We should feed them!" It might be true that there are poor people out there and that we should feed them.

HERBERT: If Mario Cuomo is going to run for president, I am going to vote for him, but I'll keep doing economics the way I do.

There is no inconsistency?

HERBERT: Not at all. In economics I try to understand behavior. That does not prevent me from believing that poor people need help. I happen to have that belief.

About Economists

Who are your ideal economists, your models? [Silence.]

EDWARD: I am a big Lucas fan.

Why is that?

MIKE: He is so cool. *[They laugh.]*

EDWARD: If I had to rank economists, I would rank Lucas first. I really like these rational expectations people. I like people who knock down the status quo and change the argument. And that's what Lucas did— he changed the conversation. And he changed it probably in a good direction. He began to be more formal about expectations and all that. It is not just that rational individuals have rational expectations, but it is especially the formal dynamic modeling in macroeconomics. I also like Friedman.

But he is not very formal.

EDWARD: I liked his '68 presidential address. That was one of the few times somebody said, "This is going to happen—the Phillips curve is going to shift out, and we are going to get inflation and unemployment at the same time." And then it happened. He was right from the very beginning. That was good work.

HERBERT: Yes, but he was wrong about OPEC.

EDWARD: He was wrong about a lot of things. Everybody is. But that does not matter. *[Laughter.]*

Why are other people so hesitant in saying who their favorite economists are?

NICK: You can knock down any modern economist on some issue.

PAUL: Friedman and Stigler both come to my mind. I admire both of them for the fact that they stuck to their guns during a time they were really outnumbered. A lot of people thought they were cranks. History proved that at the very least their opponents were as wrong as they were. I admire Friedman's ability, doing about the best one can, combining being a scholar but also being a popularizing ideologue. That is hard to do. I admire Stigler for the fact that he is still so intellectually active at his age. I hope that I can do that. But Stigler is kind of quasi–Chicago school Marxist history. *[They like that.]* According to him, the function of economists is to sit back and laugh at the world. That bothers me a little bit.

Why?

PAUL: I am kind of an idealist. I had vague ideas of changing the world a little bit. It seems to me that economists have had some effect in matters of regulation and things like that. So I don't like to be told, "The technology in industrial organization and interest groups out there determine everything, and you are valueless."

HERBERT: Yes, whatever happens, happens. That is the feeling you get. Everything is endogenous. There is nothing you can push on.

PAUL: Stigler is very Marxist in that sense. You know, Chicago gets a lot of money from corporations because it defends their ideology. Liberal economists will always be around because people have an interest in socializing the economy. This calls into question your desire to be an objective scholar.

What about the preferences of others?

JOHN: I like Debreu. *[They laugh.]*

Why?

JOHN: I respect the stuff he has done. It is very thorough and very deep.

EDWARD: When people ask you, "Why are prices what they are?" you walk to your bookshelf, grab *Theory of Value*, and throw it at them.[4]

JOHN: A lot of microeconomics is packed in that little book. *[They break into laughter, and someone yells, "Come on!" and another, "Yeah, I know the world is a compact set!"]* Listen, Varian is just an expansion of Debreu.

HERBERT: For me it is hard to say who my model is. Because of my interest in risk, I like Frank Knight quite a lot. Time has shown, not necessarily in economics, that his emphasis on uncertainty is very pertinent. I think Marshak is great too.

EDWARD: I also have a lot of respect for Solow, from what I have read of him. I didn't like his comments in your book. He seemed to be antirational. But he deserved the Nobel Prize for his work on growth theory. That was an excellent contribution.

MIKE: I get a lot of utility out of people who do something different. I think for that reason Akerlof is interesting.

PAUL: He enlivens titles.

MIKE: I am a little embarrassed saying this. I do not want to take him as a model, though. I don't think he is the greatest living economist, but he may be onto something.

How about people like Summers?

PAUL: Summers takes a fair amount of abuse around here.

NICK: I haven't read anything by him.

HERBERT: Is this a macro person?

[They laugh. We finish talking about the history of economics (Paul is especially interested in the Chicago tradition) and life after graduate school (they all seem to aspire to academic jobs).]

My final question: If I go away with the impression that the third-year students of Chicago are pretty content with their experience here, would that be right?

NICK: We made it thus far. *[They agree with that.]*

Fourth-Year Students

This is a well-attended session. Of the twelve students that show up, ten of them (Harold, Brad, Carlos, Mason, Edward, Bill, Ralph, Chiang, Kareem, and Marcello) actively participate in what becomes a relatively long conversation.

About the Experience in Graduate School

How do you look back at your four years here? Was it a good or bad experience?

HAROLD: I had fun! *[They laugh.]*

BRAD: Chicago is a good school, you learn some stuff that is interesting. Chicago is a great city. What else is there?

HAROLD: Certainly better than working for a living. *[They talk about being intimidated the first year. For Carlos, a student from Latin America, it was a "humbling experience." And Harold had fun.]* I was not laughing the entire first year. It was hard. When I say it was fun, I mean it was more enjoyable than whatever else I could have been doing. It was work.

CARLOS: At times they'd give you problems and you knew there was no way. You'd sit down, look at it, and realize that there was nothing you could do. No inkling, no clue.

MASON: *[To Carlos]* But you were not in the study groups. They discuss the problems in much more detail than the professor. He just hands them out and has a T.A. [teaching assistant] work them out at a problem session once a week.

HAROLD: And we know how bad they are!

[When I asked them why they came to Chicago, they told about professors at their colleges who tried to dissuade them. One was told, "They treat you like dirt over there." Carlos expresses his appreciation for the fact that Chicago is willing to take chances with people, accepting candidates other good schools would not even consider.]

About Economics at Chicago

What has this place done to you, to the way you think about the world? Have you changed your mind in these last few years?

HAROLD: I did. I went to a school which had a neo-Keynesian approach to macroeconomics. Macro and micro economists were on opposite tracks and never talked to each other. I was not of a critical mind, so I took it and believed it. When I decided to go to Chicago, they all warned me, saying, "Remember, they will try to brainwash you for four years." So I came here and decided that all the brainwashing done is done in the other schools. If you want a program where micro and macro are consistent with each other, I have no qualms with how I changed my position. You can have different views. You see, there is this nonclearing approach that is going on at MIT and Harvard. We don't do that—it does not fit in the equilibrium paradigm. It's a whole different structure of looking at the economy.

BILL: The thing that is different here, different from where I went as an undergraduate, is that they believe in what they study. They believe in the neoclassical system of economics. They believe in the paradigm, in that way of looking at the world. They teach you to look at the world in a consistent manner, all based on the assumptions of the neoclassical paradigm. You look at all aspects of life from birth to death in a neoclassical framework. They teach you to adopt this framework, to use it consistently and not haphazardly.

HAROLD: You assume rational behavior, maximizing behavior, which everybody does in price theory at any school. The Chicago view is, "Why would you want to get rid of the assumption when you do something else? When would you not want to assume that people are rational?"

EDWARD: Yes, and that also when you are analyzing questions that are outside economics as well—

HAROLD: Right, exactly.

EDWARD: —sociological questions, like questions on marriage and divorce. Why can't you apply something systematically? Other people have doubts about that—I had them when I came here. But you really develop economics by unrelentingly focusing on questions, systematically analyzing them. You do not want to come up with exceptions such as structural changes or different preferences.

HAROLD: For me, whenever I see something weird, the first thing I always wonder is, "How can this be rational?" People aren't stupid! They are not consistently doing dumb things. For anything that is going on in the world we ask, "What is going on? Why do people behave in that way?" I think that is really good. It broadens the way you look at things and sharpens your mind.

MASON: It is interesting to talk to people who go to other grad schools. Some from my college ended up at Princeton, and one at Stanford. They ask questions about the stuff we do. They ask, "How do you do this?" And I say, "You don't understand. We start every problem with max utility, micro or macro."

EDWARD: You know, I am not convinced about that. The whole approach still has a lot of problems. I do not think that it's necessarily bad if some model has some ad hoc assumptions. *[Some jumbled protests.]*

EDWARD: I do think that it's important. I don't resist it. It is interesting to ground macroeconomics in microeconomics. That's the thing to do. But that does not exclude the possibility of doing other things. It can't explain everything.

How about the students at the other places? Don't they do this?

MASON: They don't do it at all. Or they do very little of it. It's strange. We went through the same college and we had the same ideas on economics. After a year or so of doing macro—or whatever we do here *[he laughs]*—we would never get the same results. We exchanged problem sets once *[now the others laugh too]*—it was not going anywhere. We thought we would have an advantage, having the syllabus of other classes. I couldn't even find some of the books they were using. *[They laugh.]* It was kind of interesting. I thought they were exaggerating when they were talking of a Chicago school versus others.

One of the questions on your survey was, "Do you think that economists agree?" When you go to a neo-Keynesian school, they tell you that everybody agrees about everything. Here at Chicago you find out that is not really true. We don't agree about very much with the other economists.

So you have a sense that this place is different from all the others?

RALPH: Yes. I have been at Eastern schools. Here we view the world differently, even in economics. They are much more willing to make working assumptions than we are. In their classes they are much more interested in policy issues. Here they are much more interested in the theory, in whether it is consistent.

HAROLD: It is really interesting about this place. They come up with ideas, and people at other schools say, "Look how ridiculous these ideas are!"—and then years later they do it also. That happened with rational expectations, that happened with the economics of the family, that happened with the quantity theory of money and with the shifting Phillips curve.

EDWARD: I read your book, *Conversations.* There is one quote of Solow that sticks in my mind. It is an answer to a question about whether they talk to each other. He said he couldn't talk to Lucas and take him seriously. He never feels like talking with someone who claims that he is Napoleon. *[The others begin to laugh.]* I thought that was kind of an insulting comment. From what I understand of macroeconomics—I am not a macroeconomist myself—that kind of attitude is appalling—to dismiss someone who proposes rational expectations as a raving lunatic. That's insulting.

BILL: I think that's confined to Solow. Tobin and Modigliani are totally different. That's Solow's personality.

RALPH: I don't know how much it changes your view of the world, but—and now I am talking about my friends at those Eastern schools—they start by assuming disequilibrium.

BILL: Fixed prices!

RALPH: Fixed prices, government intervention, monopolistic competition, or oligopolies. I think that is not what we would call useful analysis. We might agree on some problem that has to be explained, but we start from different assumptions.

CHIANG: They also consider that institutions are wrong. We don't care about institutions.

Why is that? [They laugh.]

CHIANG: I don't know.

BILL: They used to. When Barro was here and when Friedman was here, they worried about the Fed and the banking system.

CARLOS: But that was not the whole time!

BILL: I know. But then Lucas came. The first time he wrote our money and banking prelim, he looked at Barro's and Friedman's questions and could not answer them. About the banking system he had no clue. So it has changed. We haven't ever had institutions.

Mathematics and Economics

We talk about the role of mathematics in economics. Like the students of the second year, they emphasize the combination of mathematics and intuition. Harold, for example, says, "The math is useless if there is not an intuition behind it." He thinks little of papers that push the math to the limit: "If a majority of the people can't read the paper, what good did you do?" Edward comments on the changes since he has been in graduate school.

EDWARD: This is my sixth year—I can't pass the core exams anymore, the ones they are giving now. I don't know what is going on, but the story I like to tell about the current state of math at the University of Chicago is that last year I saw the solutions for the exam of the first macro course that were posted. One page had not a single word of

English—it was all differential equations. That was the final exam. I am sure that these people know what they are doing, but I took macro from Robert Barro. I thought I learned a lot from that. It wasn't all mathematics.

BILL: I took Hansen's macro course the first year he was teaching it. I was scared. We spent five weeks going through all these models, learning all these techniques, doing all that math. After those weeks I sat there and I said, "What is this actually saying?" All this math of five weeks was saying was that the price of an asset is the discounted value of the future dividend. That was what had been said in five weeks. You learned a lot of techniques to get to that, a lot of models. But it was not saying anything interesting. It was an example of playing around with math for math's sake. *[They laugh. They continue with a discussion of Hansen's work. Harold appreciates Hansen as an econometrician. Others agree. They bring up the Minnesota approach.]*

MASON: There is a difference between being formal and neoclassical and being mathematical. In Minnesota the macro sequence is much more technical than ours.

KAREEM: The math is not what makes things interesting. You have to be saying something interesting. Formalizing is something that just about anyone can do.

HAROLD: To reinforce what everybody is saying—I took the math-econ prelim here. They have this little book that lists the prelims of a lot of other schools. I looked at Minnesota's true/false/uncertain questions. They were like, "If Rm is mapped on Rn, n is bigger than m, the mapping cannot be onto." *[They laugh.]* This has nothing to do with economics! I went through twenty of these questions—there is nothing that has anything to do with economics. All math, and then I went to two of the long questions. One was, "Use Debreu to prove that a general equilibrium exists." And another was to prove a hyperplane theorem. This is total crap! And then I looked at the Chicago prelim. It is an odd kind of prelim, because it is basically what the theoretical people are working on. When I was taking it, one was talking about taxicabs. There are these odd-looking problems—that's what they are working on and you use the math to solve it. I assume MIT's and Harvard's are much more technical.

MASON: But they teach you math at Chicago.

HAROLD: Yes, but at Minnesota you learn everything about the Hilbert space. Fifteen questions have to do with that. This is math for math's sake. That is not done around here. It is not valued here. It is not what the school is about. It tries to explain real-world problems.

Economics and the Real World

I ask what they think the point of economics is for them. Bill jokes, "To get a job." Marcello simply wants to understand the world, but Edward wants to change the world. Carlos expresses the Chicago line, saying that the models are not good enough to say how to improve the world. Bill elaborates.

BILL: The standard policy of Chicago is, "Leave everything the hell alone *[they laugh]* and the best possible solutions come about." When I was taking Becker, he made the same comments about three times in class. He would be talking about something, showing that everything is Pareto optimal, sufficient, and then there would be this pause and he would say, "If you want to change the distribution of this income allocation, that is a normative issue and is totally separate from what we are doing."

I think a lot of policy is just disguised as an attempt to change efficiency, when it really is a redistribution of income to different groups in the economy. When we're talking about tariffs or voluntary quotas on Japanese cars—

HAROLD: Or the minimum wage.

BILL: We argue that all these things are not playing fair, that this can't beat other efficient outcomes. A lot of these things are just rents for some people. This has strong policy implications, but a lot of these implications are like, "Let's not interfere with what is going on."

RALPH: Now you are talking more about macro. When I was an undergraduate, I was led to believe that we could do stabilization policy. Now I don't believe that's true.

KAREEM: But these normative issues can be the more interesting ones.

RALPH: It is not that I believe that nothing should be done. There is not enough understanding.

KAREEM: But we have more understanding than the politicians, for example, on what the consequences of a tariff are.

BILL: And you have a better understanding of why politicians support tariffs.

KAREEM: Yes.

HAROLD: Or why the AFL/CIO comes out and says, "Raise the minimum wage to five dollars an hour."

BILL: And why all the Democratic politicians follow along.

MASON: Before I read the results of your survey [See Chapter 2], I thought if there is anything that the economics profession believes, it is that minimum wages are just stupid. Now I have seen the results.

But the standard view in the profession has been that minimum wages are a bad idea. You wonder what's been the economic impact on the government of the United States. Maybe you can argue that without us the minimum wage would have been twenty dollars an hour. I don't know. Once in five years there is enough momentum of people who want to raise the minimum wage. "All these black youths are unemployed. I don't understand—there must be discrimination!" That's ridiculous.

EDWARD: It's amazing. There is an article in the newspaper by a professor at Harvard advocating an increase in the minimum wage for the most pathetic reasons. I handed it out to my undergraduate class, and said, "Find the fourteen mistakes here." I said this is proof that Harvard does not deserve its image. [Laughter.]

HAROLD: One thing Chicago really made an impression on me with is the idea, "Let the market work!" If someone wants to work for three cents an hour—well, as long as no one holds a gun to anyone's head! I mean, voluntary exchange is an incredible engine that seems to work. When I was at college, they never emphasized the point of voluntary exchange in macroeconomics.

On Economists

In the discussion about which economists they respect most, the names of Becker, Stigler, and Lucas come up. Mason admires Becker for pushing economics as far as possible. I ask why the students choose only people in the older generation.

HAROLD: We can identify with Becker. [They laugh.]

RALPH: Technicians—they are a dime a dozen. Anyone can be a technician. They are not ever going to answer anything interesting. I know somebody who is a technical wizard, but he only uses it when he has to. He is not going to jump in from hyper space!

HAROLD: Hilbert!

EDWARD: That's what's so exceptional about Chicago. People are not wedded to the technical apparatus. I think the Chicago approach is intuitive.

What Are the Topics?

Do you talk about topics such as efficiency wages? [A general "No."]

HAROLD: That's totally flushed down the toilet. [They laugh.]

BILL: Stiglitz was here presenting a paper the other day. He had an efficiency-wage paper. He got laughed at.

HAROLD: It's not clear that you can get out of here with a dissertation on efficiency wages.

But what about being open to new ideas?

BILL: But you have to be open to new ideas that you can back up. It's not clear that you can logically pull efficiency wages out of a maximization model.

KAREEM: The problem with efficiency-wage models is that you do not know why people do not contract these things away. That's the type of objection you get here. A lot of other people may find it interesting, but here people think that it is not grounded. Why do people do this rather than this? There has to be a reason for it.

BILL: You cannot have hundred-dollar bills lying on the sidewalk.

KAREEM: It's just not clear. I do believe that there is involuntary unemployment. *[A few gasps, followed by some "No's," and loud laughter. They leave the subject for what it is and return to efficiency wages.]*

BILL: Listen, Stiglitz is a bright guy. I just don't believe that he believes in efficiency wages, that he looks at it and comes to a logical conclusion that efficiency wages matter. In the paper he presented the other day, he started pulling what I would call ad hoc assumptions out of the air to come up with a model for why the demand is jumping around. By slapping efficiency wages on it, he gets movements in demand without movements in wages. He's piling things onto his theory just to explain the data. I would rather see him develop a consistent theory without things slapped on here and there.

HAROLD: But the way he presented it, efficiency wages were not that important.

BILL: No, no, efficiency wages were the only way you got movements in demand without movements in wages.

HAROLD: He did not go through that. *[A brief back-and-forth ensues that is drowned out in laughter.]*

What are the important topics here at the moment?

MASON: Labor is a very big field at Chicago.

What about business cycles?

RALPH: The theory of growth is quite hot now.

What about money? [They repeat the word a couple of times as if they are wondering what to do with it.]

RALPH: They are trying to explain why money exists, period. They are not trying to explain its effect on the economy. Why would you expect something called money in a system?

On History

I point out that they have not yet referred to Milton Friedman.

CARLOS: That is one of the biggest misconceptions about this place. You go home and you say you are going to Chicago and people say, "Oh, Friedman!"

MASON: I think he is old. *[Laughter.]*

BILL: He doesn't believe in rational expectations.

EDWARD: I think Friedman is rather eclectic. I am biased—my father was a supporter of his. But I think we are too ahistorical. I am not just talking about going back to Friedman, but also about going back to Smith. I don't think that people know much history.

KAREEM: People do not look to Friedman's models and try to solve them or work with them. That's not the thing to do. That does not mean that he is somebody without an influence.

RALPH: Nobody here is doing a lot about business cycles or Friedman's type of stuff.

What do you think of the lack of historical background that Edward just mentioned?

MASON: That's probably true everywhere.

BILL: In a workshop a guy from Michigan State made the comment that no grad student reads things that were written before he went to graduate school. Rosen was sitting at the table, Becker was. These guys did not argue with that.

What happens is that the past is embodied in what we are learning now. So we are looking forward, not backward. That's not necessarily a bad thing. There is a direct progression from Smith to Ricardo and from Marshall to Knight, which we already have picked up. It's not necessary that we read what came before.

CARLOS: Schumpeter made the point in his book. He claims that without a perspective you are at a loss. Even though I studied history of thought, I do not agree with that. It is useful, it's interesting to read. It's useful to find out that even the great ones screw up. But if you pick up any current microeconomic textbook, anything that was relevant in the past is probably contained in there. I regret that Adam Smith is now made into a caricature as the prophet of laissez-faire. But I don't think that going on without having read him is a critical loss. It's nice if you did it.

HAROLD: Yes, we learned what Marshall knew.

KAREEM: I don't think you can be that categorical. I think it is a good idea to learn some old things.

BILL: But given scarce resources, I am not sure it is the optimal thing to read. *[Someone argues that they had done some economic history, but it is pointed out to him that the history of economic thought is something different.]*

HAROLD: History of economic thought has never been a requirement, whereas economic history was. I took economic history and found it pretty boring. I think it would be much better to have a history of economic thought. Stigler teaches that, but I have never tried to sit in on it. It would be a more useful requirement.

Their Future

Where do you picture yourselves to be when you are going to look for jobs? [It is the fall term, a time when many will begin exploring the job market. They will have their first interviews after Christmas. Some uneasy laughter. "The six-thousand-dollar question," someone remarks. A few jokes. Edward hopes to go to a liberal arts college.] Why is that?

EDWARD: I like teaching. I have a comparative advantage in teaching. I don't like to go to a place where I will not be compensated for teaching. "Publish or perish" is not very appealing to me.

HAROLD: I agree with that, especially the perish part. *[Laughter.]* Seriously, teaching is fun and academics is fun. But a lot of junior faculty here work their tails off. That has not been a major goal of my life.

So you do not expect to be at a major university?

EDWARD: That's correct. *[Others concur. I express my surprise about their modest aspirations.]*

BILL: It is not clear that Bob Lucas, if he were sitting here as a graduate student, would have known that he would make a major impact.

CARLOS: Some of us may.

KAREEM: I don't think anybody can sit down and say, "I am going to have a major impact."

RALPH: That does not do away with the fact that our placement is not very good. We do not get into places like Harvard, Princeton, and MIT.

So where do people from here end up? [They mention, among others, Rochester, Carnegie Mellon, Minnesota, Stanford, and Northwestern.]

BILL: It is easily possible for any of us to be at a major university.

CARLOS: It is kind of exciting that someone in the four continuous classes may end up winning the Nobel Prize forty years down the road.

Why do you think that?

CARLOS: Well, look at the track record. It is amusing that someone you are going to class with may end up a Nobel Prize winner.

Is there a sense that there are stars among you? [A general "Oh, yeah!"] How do you figure out who the stars are?

BILL: When the mean on an exam is a thirty-five and the highest is a one-ten [110] out of one-twenty [120], you sort of know.

HAROLD: Or when you are in class and a guy has something to say about an article that was mentioned in a footnote, you sort of get the feeling that he is hard-core.

CARLOS: There is a guy in the second year who was asked by Becker to do a dissertation with him. That is a good indication that the guy is on the right track. He has never said that to me.

Anyone here who belongs to the stars? [Embarrassed laughter. One student gets singled out.]

On Being an Economist

In the survey, students suggested that in order to be successful, problem-solving ability is very important and knowledge of the economy very unimportant. What does that say?

BILL: When you say "understanding the economy," I was thinking of the people who work for DRI [Data Resources Incorporated]. They understand the economy, but they are not going to be famous economists. They can take their models and tell you what the interest rate is going to do. You ask me what the interest rate in the next period will be, and I tell you what it is in this period. *[They laugh.]* They have a more thorough understanding of the workings of the economy, of the inflation rate, of the debt, and any of those things. I can care less about any of those things—I am totally uninterested in that.

MARCELLO: You have to know the facts, the data, but you do not have to be up-to-date.

EDWARD: You can characterize this as a lack of interest in institutional knowledge.

CARLOS: You go home and everybody knows you are studying for a Ph.D. in economics, and their first question is invariably, "What is the economy going to do?" If I knew that, I would not be in grad school. I would be out investing somebody's money to make money for myself.

MASON: In that case, you would say, "I know, but I can't tell you. Give me your money and I'll show you."

HAROLD: Knowing the literature is important, but it is not the most important thing. You can't go anywhere if you don't know the literature. But knowing how to solve problems is much more important, of course. People may know the whole literature, but when they sit down they have no ideas, no original ideas. And if they do, they do not know how to set it up. So if you don't know how to solve problems and only know the literature, you cannot do anything else but teach what other people have done. *[This they find humorous.]*

Are some of you planning to go into policy—or policy-related institutions?

MARCELLO: I am, but that was the idea from the very beginning.

BILL: Working at policy you lose your ability. If you are going to do theory, you better do it when you are young, because after five years in policy type of work you are out of theory—it's gone.

HAROLD: Policy is boring.

Theory is interesting? [Some agree. Someone says, "It's hard."]

MASON: Come on. It's fun to figure things out.

Is theory important?

KAREEM: How can you do policy without theory?

SOMEONE: Often they do.

KAREEM: But they should not.

But you also say that the current theory cannot tell you how to do things.

BILL: The theory that we are working on now is important for influencing policies ten years down the road when they finally figure out what we are doing now. I mean, you have a lot of theory going on. You want to take what is applicable and throw out the rest of the garbage. That doesn't mean that what you are doing now isn't important. But for what is occurring today—no, I don't think it is that important.

[After talking about economists who try to engage in policy issues, we discuss the students' politics. They have problems with the label "conservative." The sense is that most would not object to the label when it comes to economic issues. We return to the, for them, obviously pleasant topic of what makes Chicago different. They talk about the curiosity of the faculty and their liberal scholarship. Edward brings up Becker as an example.]

EDWARD: Take Becker—he can get into anything. When I took my girlfriend to a party, I told her not to make any casual remark about medical school to Becker because he would ask, "Why is that?" *[They laugh about his imitation of Becker's voice.]* It's invigorating.

BILL: Yes, we continue asking why. As long as you keep asking why, you are never at a loss. Becker's textbook is a pain because every other page you get a "Why?"

[During the discussion that continued a few more minutes, they once more let me know that the Chicago approach is superior to those approaches that bring in psychology and sociology.]

MASON: Sociologists seem to have explanations for anything in the damned world. But all they explain is what they observe—they cannot tell you the implications of some change.

HAROLD: It's like history and political science.

EDWARD: Any competing model has a chance. There are plenty. A priori, if you have an alternative way of answering a question—say, a Marxian or a feminist or whatever way you want to cut it—you have a claim to be listened to.

HAROLD: So to speak. *[And then it was time for their lunch.]*

PART THREE

Interpretations

The survey questionnaires and the conversations paint a picture of graduate education, but they are subject to many interpretations. In this section, each of us provides some interpretative comments on the survey results and the conversations.

8

A Case of
Mistaken Identities

Arjo Klamer

Economists talk endlessly. They teach; they give seminars; they brain-storm, argue, and chat with each other in the office, on the phone, and in the hotel lobby during their incessant conferences. All this talk is not "just talk." If everything could be said in writing, economists would not need to waste time with seminars or spend money for trips to conferences. Students could take graduate courses by correspondence in the comfort of their homes. But if one assumes that economists and their students are rational, they apparently gain from talking with each other face to face.

That they do gain in this way makes sense. Writing in general is constraining, and scientific writing more so. In their talk, economists are more likely than in their writing to reveal what they really mean. They talk, and usually do not write, about their doubts, their values, and their beliefs. In conversation, economists give their frank opinions of other work, tell stories and anecdotes that clarify the formal argument, and communicate to their students where to look for the road to success. Accordingly, in the spoken dimension of their discourse, economists conduct crucial negotiations on where to go in economics—and what theories, ideas, tests, and even economists to discard.[1]

The conversations in Part Two are "sound bites" from all this talking. They convey an impression of how graduate students come to form their opinions and beliefs about economics and economists.

Colander and I did not merely listen—we asked the questions and tried to steer the conversations into areas of our interest. Going through each conversation was like walking through a maze. The graduate students showed us when we began with mistaken notions and sent us in new directions. During the conversations, we found out, for example, that our image of students as technocrats was an unwarranted prejudice, and that diversity among the schools was more marked than we had expected. The conversations also showed us that there is more to the thesis that students are socialized into the profession than the survey numbers indicate. Above all, the conversations revealed that graduate students are experiencing an identity crisis—a conflict between their idea of what an economist is and the identity that their graduate training imposes.

Are They Technocrats?

Colander and I began our inquiry because we wanted to understand what happens to those who enter the economics profession. With Leijonhufvud's tribal metaphor in mind, we were curious to find out to what extent the intitiation rituals of graduate school transform students. We were especially interested to know whether graduate training molds open-minded first years into technocratic fourth years.

This was, I now realize, a question of identity. We expected to find that graduate students become like engineers in the sense that they become preoccupied with techniques and forget the economy and policy. (Howard Becker, a sociologist, studied graduate students in various disciplines. An engineer, he found, identifies himself as someone "who has learned to reason so rationally and effectively that, even though this has been learned only with reference to technical problems, it operates in any line of endeavor, so that the engineer is equipped to solve any kind of problem in any area quickly and efficiently."[2])

The survey confirmed our expectations. The students considered problem-solving abilities and mathematical excellence far more important to success than knowledge of the economy and the ability to do empirical research. But do they agree with the situation?

The students tell us they do not. They resist the identification with engineers and do not like the preoccupation with techniques in graduate school and in the literature. They want more ideas, more policy relevance, more discussion of the fundamental assumptions, and more serious consideration of alternative approaches.

The resistance appears when the topic of mathematics comes up. Janet(1) of Harvard (the number behind each name represents the student's year in graduate school) complains, "I feel like I am learning engineering skills." Ed(1) of Harvard, who is described by his fellow students as a technocrat, belies that label when he talks about his interest in philosophy and history of thought. Chicago students are nearly all of the opinion that the intuition behind an argument is what ultimately counts. The mathematics is secondary. Rick(1) acknowledges that "to do a good job, you have to use mathematics," but to him the math is a "necessary evil." He believes that the profession has become too mathematical. To clarify his own view, Paul(3) cites a well-known economist who believes that math is a mere cleanup job. Ralph(4) disparages the technicians among economists, saying that "[they] are a dime a dozen." He and the other fourth-year students make fun of the heavy mathematics in the Minnesota program.

Talking with the MIT students was particularly revealing. According to others, they are in a technically oriented program, but the third-year MIT students do not think that anyone in their year can be called a "technical" economist or a "highbrow" theorist. The fourth-year students could appreciate the tools they got, but, in the words of Claire(4), "None of us have really knocked ourselves out reading mathematics books in order to try to push the techniques further." Nobody seemed to care for highly technical papers—and these are top-notch students at the point of joining the elite at the frontiers of economic research.

A few remarks by the Columbia students would suggest that they are mathematically inclined. The first-year students complain about the lack of problem sets. Allen(1) thinks that "math for math's sake is nice." And Jane(1) regrets the fact that there is no high-level theorist on the faculty. Marking these students as mathematical or technocratic economists, however, makes no sense in light of all their other remarks about the relevance and applicability of economics. Their concern appears to be that they miss out on what the profession considers to be important for success—namely, problem-solving abilities and mathematical excellence.

Most of the students are looking beyond the mathematics for the relevance in economics. They want to gain knowledge about the economy and economic policy, knowledge they know will *not* help them in their careers. The Columbia students do, and so do the Harvard and MIT students. They reveal their preference in the choice of economists whom they respect most. Arnold(1) of MIT, for example, likes Rudiger Dornbusch because "he makes really meaningful, real contributions" (adding that he is technically adept as well).[3] Larry Summers, who did not make the list of most-respected economists in Chapter 3, gets mentioned several times by both MIT and Harvard students.[4] Laurel(3) of MIT likes Summers because "he takes on policy issues and takes on what's going on in the economy—he just goes right at it." Don(4), also of MIT, favorably compares Summers's empirical approach with the more technical approach of Jerry Hausman.[5] Brian(1) of Harvard likes Jeffrey Sachs[6] because "he is concerned with what is actually going on out there."

The Chicago students seem to take exception to this preoccupation with the empirical and the relevant in economics. Even though they select Gary Becker as one of their model economists on grounds that he will apply economic reasoning to any imaginable topic, the other choice is Robert Lucas, who allegedly does not care about institutions. When Chiang(4) says that "we don't care about institutions," he does not appear to be conflicted. Bill(4) does not mind his limited knowledge of the real economy; he even takes delight in saying that he "can care less" about the "inflation rate, the debt, and all those things." Harold(4) considers policy boring; the third-year students brag that "the stuff people do here [at Chicago] is irrelevant in terms of policy."

In their willingness to be aloof from the real world, the Chicago students distance themselves from the other students. This is not to say that Chicago students profess to be technocrats—they strongly prefer the more intuitive approach of Gary Becker over the highly mathematical approach of Lars Hansen.[7] Yet they do not mind life in the ivory tower. Many of the Harvard, Columbia, and MIT students, on the other hand, feel imprisoned.

Diversity

When Colander and I began the study, we were most interested in finding out how opinions of students change while they advance through graduate school. We were not expecting major differences in opinions across the separate schools. Even before we tabulated the numbers, we began to suspect that diversity could become the big story. The conversations with Harvard and MIT students, in particular, produced a strong impression of their living in separate worlds, but the numbers do not sharply divide the two groups. The only notable difference is the greater range of opinions among Harvard students.

The contrast that the numbers bring to light is that between Chicago students on one side and all the other students on the other. Tables 2.6 and 2.7 (Chapter 2) are especially striking. None of the Chicago students consider rational expectations unimportant; 38 percent of Harvard students do. No one from MIT disagrees with the proposition that fiscal policy can be effective; 44 percent of the Chicago students do. The monetarist idea that inflation is merely monetary draws no objection from Chicago, but nearly half from Harvard disagree. There are even strong disagreements on the micro questions, usually considered to be the mainstay of solidarity among economists. The students' responses to questions on the minimum wage, tariffs, and discrimination unmask such solidarity as a myth.

The conversations show that the numbers only scratch the surface. The differences run deep. When people look for (dis)agreements among economists, they tend to reduce what they write and say to a few propositions about the economy. In that way they can conclude, for example, that Milton Friedman is Adam Smith in disguise. This is a simplistic way of viewing the discourse of economics. More is involved. Differences among the students are manifested not only in their economic opinions but also in the way they discuss them. The students talk differently, like different economists, and the students *know* that they, as well as the full-fledged economists, are different.

Notice, first of all, the manner in which they express their disagreements. When I ask the fourth-year students at Chicago about efficiency wages,[8] Harold(4) says, "That's totally flushed down the toilet." The others laugh. Bill(4) subsequently dismisses Joe Stiglitz, a Keynesian economist who a few days before had presented a paper about efficiency wages. "He got laughed at." Both Bill(4) and Kareem(4) give what appears to be the Chicago line on the subject—"you cannot logically pull efficiency wages out of a maximization model"—but when Kareem(4) hints at the possibility of involuntary unemployment, he is overruled by loud laughter. Laughter is also the response when Dong(1) of Chicago mentions Keynes as an economist he appreciates. Likewise, the first-year Harvard students laugh heartily when Len(1) jokingly suggests Barro. When Larry(4) of MIT mentions Barro, he is almost apologetic—"would I get stoned if I said Barro?"—and he quickly adds that he hates Barro's ideology. It is as if he is anticipating the derision of his fellow students.

These are no cool, detached arguments in search of the truth. As any practicing economist knows but may be reluctant to admit, the sneer,[9] joke, gossip, and laughter are effective communicative (or rhetorical) devices in conversations with fellow economists. Laughter at hearing the name of Keynes or Milton Friedman or Robert Barro communicates one's general position.[10] Gossip helps to sort out what to think of other economists and their work, and the sneers and jokes solidify established opinions. The students clearly have grasped the import of these devices, especially in order to differentiate themselves from others.

Throughout the conversations, the students try to differentiate their school. When the Harvard students talk about diversity in their ranks, they claim a distinct identity for the Harvard program. They, as well as the Columbia and Chicago students, perceive the MIT program as superior, but Julie(1) of Harvard thinks that because of their diverse backgrounds, Harvard students are "probably better in terms of what we think economists should be."

The Columbia students do not articulate a clear profile for their school. The Chicago students, on the other hand, are most explicit. They know they are not the best, but they identify themselves with the message that Robert Lucas gives them their first day in school. Rick(1) explained.

I remember the first day when we had our orientation. Lucas's very first words, were "I think that the University of Chicago is the best place in the world to do economics." He went on to say, "We here at Chicago believe that what we do matters and is more important than events in Washington." [They laugh.] That may be a little bit of an exaggeration, but, boy, was it good to hear that.

Paul(3) recalls Lucas saying, "We take economics seriously, and that makes Chicago different from everywhere else." They do not identify this serious economics with monetarism; Milton Friedman has faded into the background of their vision. They do not identify with a conservative political ideology either, even though they are overall more conservative than students at the other schools. No, when they speak of taking economics seriously, they identify a Chicago attitude toward *argumentative strategy*, or the way of doing economics. Herbert(3) describes the strategy as "a commitment to being very parsimonious in fundamental assumption." The most fundamental assumption is, of course, that of rational individual behavior according to the neoclassical definition. Herbert believes that MIT students are looser with this assumption— "less disciplined," as Mike(3) puts it. They admire Becker because he is willing to go all the way with the neoclassical argumentative strategy.

Because of their commitment to the neoclassical strategy, the Chicago students consider themselves different, more serious about economics than those at other schools. They revel in their position as "true believers." Paul(3) perceives himself to be part of the loyal opposition in economics; Mike(3) talks of a role that Chicago people get to play in life because they are willing to give predictable criticisms of antimarket and antirational arguments.

The MIT students do not appear to be very conscious of their identity as MIT economists—at any rate they do not talk much about it. They are certainly looser than Chicago students with the fundamental neo-classical assumptions, at least according to the Chicago group's percep-tions. Laurel(3) of MIT claims that "most of us would like to have a theory of bounded rationality," and Rob(3) believes that there is a "departmental ethos" against rational expectations. The fourth-year stu-dents address the MIT identity when they speak of the uniformity in their school. Don(4) identifies an MIT research style: "You are supposed to have a theoretical section and an empirical section." Harvard, according to him, has more highbrow theorists. He also thinks that Harvard has people "who don't really think about much and kind of agree with stuff." A few moments before, however, Phil(4) had made a similar observation about the MIT faculty: "[T]here's a certain orientation here— people should be doing what sells."

All these differences are poignant. Most striking, however, is the contrast in overall sentiments that the conversations convey. After talking with the Harvard and MIT students and reading Colander's conversations with Columbia students, I was quite affected by the undertone of ambivalence and cynicism. These students are not happy and confident with economics. The loyalty and commitment of the Chicago students came like a fresh shower. At first I could not believe my ears. I tried to get them to vent their frustrations and criticisms. Their response was tepid; the dominant sentiment was that of conviction and commitment to the Chicago approach.[11] (We found a similar enthusiasm among graduate students at George Mason with whom we conducted separate conversations. These students had a clearly defined purpose in the form of the public-choice and Austrian programs there.)

The frustrations of non-Chicago students concern especially the discrepancy between what they expected from economics and what they found. They are all bogged down by what they perceive as an excessive emphasis on techniques, the limited relevance of the material, and the lack of discussion of the assumptions and (for the Harvard students) of alternative approaches.

The MIT students appear to be most accepting of the techniques, an attitude perhaps explained by a comment from Charles(2): "People come here because they like to do technical models, usually." Yet they are also most cynical. Josh(3) of MIT describes his time at graduate school as "a pretty blah experience, a pretty mediocre experience." Paula(3) "got sick of talking about economics after a while." Laurel(3) is worn out. It is tempting to dismiss these comments as reactions to a demanding program. The fourth-year students, however, suggest that more is at stake—the way economics is being done, for example. Claire(4) does not think much of the articles published in the *Journal of Political Economy* and has a low opinion of the famous economists who present papers in the money workshop at MIT. Wendy(4) tells how she was depressed after one particular seminar, wondering, "What's the profession coming to? This person is one of the biggest people in the field and it just seems like the worst thing we've ever seen, and worse yet, we didn't understand three-quarters of it." None of the other students take issue with Claire(4) and Wendy(4). Part of their cynicism stems from mixed feelings about life as an academic. They say they feel pressured into academic life, but several of them say the lifestyle of the faculty at MIT is unappealing. Peter(4) thinks that "they work too hard."

The Chicago students are humbled by the graduate school experience, but they do not fight the economics they are taught as much as the others do. Bill(4) is impressed by the discovery that, unlike the faculty at his undergraduate school, the Chicago people "believe in what they study." He and his fellow students find strength in their identity as mavericks, projecting themselves as the only ones truly committed to the neoclassical paradigm. They admire Milton Friedman, Gary Becker, and Robert Lucas because they dared to stick to their guns in spite of strong opposition within the profession. According to Harold(4), "They come up with ideas. People at other schools say, 'Look how ridiculous these ideas are!'—and then years later do it also." And even though their career aspirations are modest compared with those of MIT students, Chicago students draw inspiration from being part of the Chicago tradition. Carlos(4), pointing to the successes of that tradition, predicts that a Nobel Prize is awaiting someone in the current student body.

The argument is often made that frustration and cynicism are "normal" sentiments of people who undergo graduate training and that they do not reflect serious problems in the program. Yet they are not inevitable. Reports from those who attended graduate school at the time of the Keynesian revolution after World War II demonstrate that exciting intellectual experiences are possible for graduate students.[12] The Chicago students believe in what they do and are excited about it. Their experience shows that graduate school does not have to be frustrating and intellectually stupefying.

Socialization

In its preprofessional days—let's say before 1885 when the American Economic Association was founded—economics was a field open to anyone. Now the Ph.D.'s in economics stand guard over the subject, barring entry to anyone who does not conform to their standards. In the words of John Maloney, "Economics becomes a profession when 'who chooses economics?' becomes a less important question tha[n] 'who does economics choose?'"[13] Those who are chosen are those who make it through the initiation rituals of graduate school. Colander and I presumed that this means that students are "made"—socialized—into professional economists (and so the title of this book).

Yet the statistical survey fails to tell us whether the students change their beliefs because of graduate school. They do change—who does not in that stage of life?—but clear patterns do not emerge.[14] The numbers tempt us to conclude that the socialization of students is easily exaggerated.

The interviews, however, suggest that such a conclusion is premature. Without being prodded, the students bring up the issue of socialization themselves. (The Chicago students are again the exception.) The first-year students of Harvard, for example, talk extensively about being socialized. Len(1) believes that "if you do nothing but constrained optimization models for nine months, that socializes you not to think of problems that you cannot deal with through a constrained optimization approach." Already in their first year they figure out that, in the words of Vicky(1), "you need to protect yourself from being discredited," and they accept a lot they don't really believe in. According to Brian(1), they "are being socialized into something, but nobody in the faculty seems to know what that is, except they were socialized themselves five years ago." He talks quite eloquently about brainwashing: "You are deprived of sleep, you are subjected to extreme stress, bombarded with contradictory convictions—you end up accepting anything." Claire(4) of MIT feels "semisocialized into the profession" in the sense that she now understands that doing academic research is the thing to do, whereas she was planning to do policy work. Other MIT students talk about the pressure not to take courses with Michael Piore, a nonneoclassical economist, and to pursue a career at a major research institution even if they would prefer a job at a teaching college.[15]

The Chicago students needed some encouragement before they would address the socialization experience. Susan(2) does not care for the term brainwashing: "They are trying to convince you. This is an intellectual experience." In a brief exchange, David(2) comes to acknowledge that "if there is any brainwashing at all, it is not in terms of policy implications, but in terms of what economics is." Susan(2) subsequently accepts that they "follow one line," adding quickly it is the best line to follow. Mike(3) is willing to admit there is some pressure to conform. When Edward(3) speaks of self-selection, he objects, saying, "It's also the other students." Harold(4) presents the intriguing possibility that "all the brainwashing done [was] done in [his undergraduate school], which had a neo-Keynesian approach to macroeconomics."

More than the others, Chicago students profess that Chicago has changed their views. Ralph(4), for example, was led to believe as an undergraduate that he could do stabilization policy. Now he doesn't believe that's true. Paul(3) says that reading "paper after paper about 'Gee, isn't it amazing how this kind of cynical interest-group type of explanation seems to explain the observed policy effects a lot better than a sort of public-interest type of model' . . . leads you to a presumption against government intervention, independent of ideology." Yet neither Paul nor Ralph nor the other students are ready to attribute their change of mind to a socialization process. The explanation for this may be that they now believe the Chicago line. Unlike their counterparts at the other schools, the Chicago students do not look with disbelief on what they are supposed to accept. Their conversations lack the ironic tone that the others have.[16]

Yet the outsider sees numerous indications of a socialization process in the Graduate School of Business at Chicago. Even an insider sees it:

Melvin Reder, a professor at Chicago, observes that "together with the qualifying examinations, the Ph.D. theory courses constitute an *acculturation* process, normally lasting one to two years, whose end result is an economist with the Chicago style of thought."[17] The conversations exhibit a few instances of the acculturation process, as Reder calls it. John(1), who did his undergraduate work at MIT, repeatedly finds himself defending his non-Chicago preferences (such as not liking Lucas's message at the beginning of the year and not caring for Milton Friedman). Several times his comments meet with laughter. I had the distinct impression that he was marked as the odd man out, unlike Dong(1), the Chinese student who surprised everyone with his preference for Keynes. In general, the expression of doubts and non-Chicago values evoke strong reactions. Only an unusually tough person would be able to hold up in such an environment. Herbert(3) appears to be such a person. His interest in psychology does not square with the Chicago line, but he appears to be able to negotiate a critical distance that is not offensive to his fellow students. He is the exception.

Socialization is painful. The conversations show it. The faculty with whom we talked at the various schools are inclined to attribute the pain to the mental and social adjustment that graduate school requires. These professors say graduate school is tough for many students because they are no longer big fish in a small pond, as they were in college. And indeed several students tell about such an experience; Tony(1) of MIT is an example. But more is happening.

The conversations indicate that part of the pain is cognitive. The students have their eyes set on the "real world," where policy matters and where people have psychological and sociological dimensions. They are now learning to forget about that real world and think solely in terms of dynamic optimization problems—at least that is how they perceive what is happening to them. Accordingly, graduate training subjects the students to what I would call a rhetorical transformation. Outside graduate school, the rhetoric that people use when they talk about the economy is organic—the economy is an organism inhabited by real people who are often involved in battles between good and evil:[18] "The U.S. is engaged in a trade war with Japan"; "investors panicked on October 19, 1987"; "consumers lose confidence"; and "the administration is out of control." Graduate school bans this organistic, personalistic rhetoric and replaces it with the abstract, mechanistic, and mathematical rhetoric of academic discourse. People become "optimizers." Trade wars become "exchanges in a two-goods, two-factors-of-production model with constant technology." And panicky investors become "buyers and sellers who operate under information constraints in a stochastic environment." In this view of the world, technological constraints, endowments, and random factors reign. For many students, learning the academic rhetoric is like learning a new language. It is painful. Without the old language, they are deprived, as Brian(1) of Harvard so aptly describes the experience. They are far from sure that they like the new rhetoric.[19]

Economists as Characters

Another cause of pain apparent in the conversations is confusion as to what life as an economist is about. The students have mistaken the identity of economists and are now coping with their error. For instance, whenever Colander and I venture to identify them as technocrats, the students, with a few exceptions, demur. Yet they have voluntarily enlisted in a program that in their perception is making them into technocrats. Similarly, they are most uncomfortable about the career direction in which they feel pushed. When asked in the survey why they chose economics, the majority of students mention either the desire to engage in policy formulation or the enjoyment of economics as undergraduates. Now they feel the pressure to seek an academic career.

Identification follows the question "Who are you?" Socrates loved to pose the question to his interlocutors. Whatever the answer was, he would proceed to demonstrate that the person was really someone different from the identity he claimed for himself. Socrates would have found easy prey in U.S. graduate students. When they answer "I am an economist," they think of traits that do not match those their graduate program projects. They are finding out that as economists they are being cast in a role they did not expect. Their identity as economists is an imposed or socially constructed identity—to use a literary term, a *character*. (I do not intend its psychological meaning as conveyed in remarks like "That person has no character" or "we should check out her character." As I use the term "character" here, I am referring to its sociological and dramatic meanings.[20])

We think in terms of social characters. When someone does something unconventional at a dinner party, the comment that the person "is an artist" will be self-explanatory. The Artist is a character; anyone identified as such is expected to dress "interestingly" and behave "differently." The Artist is a social construction, a series of shared presuppositions about how the Artist behaves. We can also think of the Artist as a character in a play enacting a role. In this dramatic sense, the person is endowed with moral and dispositional qualities that the reader or viewer derives from what the character says and does. We attribute characteristics and thus typify individuals, whether they like it or not.

May We Become Intellectuals, Social Activists, or Teachers?

The prevalent character that the students want to enact appears to be that of the Intellectual. This character gets associated with single-minded pursuit of the truth and the love of ideas. The Chicago students evoke the romantic in the Intellectual when they extol the virtue of their heroes, Milton Friedman, Gary Becker, and Robert Lucas. Andrew(1), for example, admires Milton Friedman because "he was prepared to stick himself out on a limb and come up with all these ideas when everyone else was saying the opposite." Intellectuals like to talk, to explore, to enter new territory—unbound by tradition and discipline. At least that is how the Harvard students appear to imagine themselves. They want to talk about the assumptions and explore alternative approaches. Ed(1) who has the stigma of being a technocrat, actually likes to cross disciplinary boundaries and tread in the fields of philosohy and social sciences. Harry(3) of MIT reveals the same desire when he confesses to admiring George Akerlof because of his "ability to sort of expand the horizons of what economics is about."

But graduate school suppresses the character of the Intellectual.[21] As one student points out, economics is a discipline. Submission to the discipline requires compromising certain intellectual values. Some students do not mind the disciplining. "Why should we study in graduate school issues for which there's no demand at the time?" asks Larry(4) of MIT. "Like whether we should go to communism or something like that." Claire(4) seems to agree when she declares that "economics is a field in which there isn't a lot of just thinking to be done." Later, though, she expresses her dismay about the thinking that contemporary practices produces. And they finally agree that Harvard students are more diverse. According to Claire(4), they "are interested in art and we're not. They also seem to have diverse political beliefs and very different personalities." Her tone is regretful. Only the Chicago students do not seem to have lost their grip on the Intellectual as a possible character for them to enact. They find inspiring examples among the faculty and have a sense of being part of an influential intellectual tradition.

Another character that emerges in the comments of the students is the Social Activist. This is a character inspired by economists such as Karl Marx, John Stuart Mill, John Maynard Keynes, and Milton Friedman. They are economists who acted upon their social concerns and who used the ivory tower as a base from which to spread their wisdom. Many of the graduate students have their example in mind. John(1) of Chicago (who was an MIT undergraduate) wants to go to Washington and "work maybe for the Congress or the CBO and help them to assess actual policy." Andrew(1) wants to return to his native England and spread the ideas he learned at Chicago. Paul(3) of Chicago admits to being "kind of an idealist," with "vague ideas of changing the world a little bit." The first-year Harvard students talk about ambitions outside the world of economists in the so-called real world—Julie(1) reports two students who want to *rule* the world. The character of the Social Activist also manifests itself in praise for economists who seek to influence worldly affairs, such as Jeffrey Sachs, Rudy Dornbusch, Marty Weitzman, and Larry Summers.

But graduate school downplays the Social Activist as the character for economists to assume. The Chicago students, for example, learn that serious economists stay away from policy—and stay off the plane to Washington. At least that is how they interpret Lucas's famous opening speech. Likewise, MIT students come to believe that "policy is for simpletons." Claire(4) of MIT had imagined herself in the role of the Social Activist, but now she knows that "those who can't do economics do policy." Lester Thurow and John Kenneth Galbraith, two outspoken economists with public profiles, frequently come up as characters that serious economists are not supposed to emulate. Serious economists, the students learn, do research at research universities. "Research really is the lifeblood of these kinds of organizations," Laurel(3) of MIT says, "and they're interested in the prestige of the program."

Some students want to become the Teacher. They may concur with George Stigler, who sees in the teacher "a mysterious person." A good teacher, Stigler preaches, has the task "to fan the spark of genuine intellectual curiosity and to instill the conscience of a scholar—to communicate the enormous adventure and the knightly conduct in the quest for knowledge."[22] It sounds heroic, but graduate school does little to nurture and enhance this character. At MIT in particular, the Teacher is apparently made out to be an inferior character. The MIT students would not dare tell their faculty that they aspire for a life as a Teacher at a good liberal arts college.

No, Thy Role Will Be That of the Academic Professional

If graduate school downplays and negates the roles of Intellectual, Social Activist, and Teacher, into what character is it making the students? Is it the professional? The students suggest as much when they speak of graduate school as vocational training and talk about the techniques with which they are becoming equipped.

The characterization of economists as professionals, however, is unsatisfactory. As Colander and I point out in Chapter 1, economists like to identify themselves as professionals, but they are quite unlike doctors, for instance, who are a species of prototype professional. The concept

of "profession" invoked in its original meaning the vow that its prac-
titioners took. The profession was understood to be a calling that could
be followed only after intensive training by individuals who had already
professed. Doctors have kept the sense of calling alive—if not in their
hearts then at least in their proclamations. They continue to take the
Hippocratic oath before they go out and heal the sick. Needless to say,
vows have never been a part of the professional practice in economics.
And (as the students are learning), serious economists do not go out
and apply their skills to improve the lives of others. Doctors are for
hire; prestige in the outside world determines to a great extent their
status in the medical profession. Serious economists are academics; public
prestige can actually hurt their professional standing. (Thurow and
Galbraith are the examples.) Finally, doctors are much less reticent than
economists in their talk about the monetary benefits of their profession.

A more appropriate characterization of the role that is presented to
the students is that of the Academic Professional. As prospective Academic
Professionals, the students learn the tools of the trade; they learn
furthermore that they will apply those tools to impress, edify, and
perhaps entertain their fellow economists. Academic Professionals write
for academic journals, attend academic conferences to address fellow
Academic Professionals, work hard to get academic tenure, and generally
dedicate their lives to academia. Academic Professionals are careerists
who judge the performance of themselves and colleagues on the basis
of where they teach, where they publish, and how many items they
add to their curriculum vitae each year.

The character of the Academic Professional suppresses many of the
values and qualities that the students see in the characters they would
like to be. The overriding commitment of the Intellectual, for example,
concerns the pursuit of ideas and truth; if that pursuit demands the
excursion into foreign territory, such as history or sociology, the Intellectual takes the trip. By contrast, Academic Professionals who trespass
into the world outside academia—or even within academia outside the
economics department—put their tenure and professional standing at
risk. They are therefore committed first to interests of their own profession.
Academic Professionals are expected to be Kuhn's normal scientists—
that is, scientists who will work with the current tools of research
approved of by other normal scientists. The MIT students reveal this
aspect of the character when they justify the choice of their theses topics.
Harry(3) does takeovers, not because he wants to find out what is going
on in the economy but because of a paper of someone else. Josh(3) and
Rob(3) may have found inspiration for their topics in the outside world,
but the crucial step was finding a way of fitting the topics into a state-
of-the-art model and using state-of-the-art techniques. Paula(3) "stum-

bled" into her topic in a class she took. Ultimately, mastery of the technique is what matters to their lives as Academic Professionals. They are not expected to question the fundamental assumptions or to develop serious interest in alternative approaches. They are, after all, at a professional school—Claire(4) calls it a trade school.

The students also learn that the Academic Professional avoids interests that distract from the ultimate purpose in life—the production of scientific papers. Thus the Teacher has to be a secondary character, and the Social Activist represents a dangerous distraction that can compromise one's professional reputation.

Although some of the students appear to adapt well to the role of the Academic Professional, most of them keep an ironical distance. Brian(1) of Harvard thinks it "odd to see people consider grad school as they would law school or business school and think of economics as a profession." Chuck(2) of MIT can see being cynical: "It *is* a game— I mean, the tenure. You know what it is—you're an academic." Cynicism invades the conversations with MIT, Harvard, and Columbia students, because they are holding out against a role that is being imposed on them. Chicago students are shielded from this mood; they see themselves on a mission in the profession.

A Lost Generation?

According to the economics discipline, the realm of preferences, attitudes, and beliefs is forbidden to serious scholars. Yet questions about the world of economists inevitably drew Colander and me into the prohibited territory. And why not? Why would economists not look beyond the constraints under which consumers, workers, and institutions operate and explore a realm that turns out to be so illuminating for their own world?

In the realm of beliefs, students exhibit cynicism and a lack of faith in the approach they are learning. They are not unique in this. Common conditions throughout the Western world are the cynicism and lack of faith associated with the unraveling of "modernism," the twentieth-century cultural movement that invested faith in science as the successor to God. In economics, Paul Samuelson and others propagated the faith in the 1940s and 1950s. They, like philosophers, mathematicians, architects, painters, and physicists, believed in abstraction and formalism as the means to establishing universal truth in science and universal beauty in the arts. Few today still believe in the absolute powers of science—the students do not—but the commitment to abstraction and formalism remains. This combination—the loss of faith in science and the continuing commitment to modernist expressions—is called post-modernism. The conversations with graduate students express a general mood of the times.[23]

Colander and I can hardly expect that research like ours will change the discipline. No matter how disturbing our findings are, they will not suffice to move the professional elite—just as the sight of withering trees and the inhaling of smog will not move many people to change their style of life. Yet the stories of these students are saddening. Many of these students entered graduate school with lofty ideals, and it is sad to see those being crushed. And it is sad to sense the students' disillusionment with the discipline—and their resignation to the role of Academic Professional.

Is our sadness exaggerated? Some will argue that students' cynicism is the inevitable byproduct of graduate training. Admittedly, any training can have that effect—my dog and I were traumatized by the dog training I put us through. (Come to think of it, our problem was another case of mistaken identity. I thought the training would simply make him into a well-behaved dog. Instead, most of the routines seemed to prepare him for dog shows—to become an academic dog, as it were—and neither of us particularly cared for those.)

But the problem is bigger than the training as such. First, whatever one may think of their methodological and political ideology, the Chicago students (and the George Mason students) tell us that graduate school does not have to suppress intellectual desires and crush ideals.

Furthermore, disillusionment and cynicism are not conditions limited to graduate students. Many members of the profession appear to lack faith in what they do. They will confess, usually at unguarded moments, that their highly sophisticated research produces ultimately meaningless results—but they will demand their students follow their lead anyway. "Of course this assumption is absurd," a well-known economist noted during a recent seminar, "but, hey, isn't all we do absurd and utterly unrealistic?" People laughed, and he continued solving the model. When I told a friend about the unhappy conclusion to which this research was leading me, he told me about a private conversation with a mathematical economist. The fellow apparently did advanced research in signal extraction methods and had received much academic recognition. He did not believe, however, that he was getting anywhere. The best use he could think of for his economics technique was "to build a better stereo speaker." He apparently was serious. Such comments—and one elicits them with little effort—suggest that the shield behind which the professional elite enforces current practice is thin. Although irony and cynicism reinforce the shield, they also enhance the sadness about a discipline that is losing its intellectual vigor.

How long can irony and cynicism sustain the economics profession? When will we see the rebirth of the Intellectual, the Social Activist, and the Teacher as respectable characters in the world of economists? One cannot say, but the disillusionment of tomorrow's elite may hold a promise for the future.

9

Workmanship, Incentives, and Cynicism[1]

David Colander

The survey and the questionnaire effectively show us graduate education in economics at the elite universities. They reveal strengths in graduate economics education. The students are bright, perceptive, and interesting. There's a healthy diversity of the student body, and the programs are demanding and intellectually challenging.

But to the noneconomics observer, the survey and conversations also say that something is wrong with graduate economics education: The enormous division of views between Chicago and the other schools is disturbing. How can people studying a so-called social science have such major differences about the way the economy works? A second finding that will likely trouble the noneconomist is the perception students have that a knowledge of economic literature and economic institutions lacks importance. Is it reasonable for economics educators to place such slight emphasis on literature and institutions? A third concern is the sense of cynicism that came through in many of the written comments and in the conversations. The students knew what would get them ahead; they could do it, but for many the intellectual excitement of science wasn't there.

The lay reader might be shocked by these findings, but most economists won't be. Our findings were not unexpected. Students feel a lack of reality in what they study because, by design, there is little reality there; the focus on techniques and modeling precludes it. There are such differing views among schools because the views are built into the models and techniques the students learn. Students do not learn—and are not meant to learn—to question or to assess those models. The cynicism is a bit more difficult for economists to be complacent about;

187

graduate schools do not plan to instill cynicism, but cynicism is the natural outcome.

Our survey results will come as no surprise to most mainstream economists. In fact, conscious efforts have been made in the last thirty years to bring about the existing situation. For many economists, therefore, these results are neither shocking nor cause for concern. For them, graduate education is doing what it is supposed to be doing, just as economics is doing what it is supposed to be doing. To say that something is wrong with economics education would be to say that something is wrong with economics, and most mainstream economists don't believe that anything is wrong with economics as it is currently practiced.

To support their view, they point out that economics and graduate economics education are highly successful. Its graduates can get good jobs and in many cases are highly sought after. Economics is making advances in the understanding of the pure theory of markets. It is more unified than any of the other social sciences. In short, it has the outward manifestations of a highly successful discipline.

Thus, contrary to what the layperson might think, to argue that our survey points to something wrong with graduate economics education is to go against the mainstream view. We don't expect to hear this response often: "Oh, look at those results; now let's go out and change the discipline to make it more relevant." But we will hear this: "Oh, it's some more of those superficial Galbraithian critics who don't understand the need for clarity and formalism, taking easy potshots at the profession."

This chapter tries to justify my criticisms to those in the profession, but its other purpose is to explain to the lay reader the mainstream economics argument and to compare the different views that Klamer, I, and many critics of economics have with the mainstream view.

Let me begin by stating what my criticisms are not. They are not that what economics is doing is irrelevant, or that formalism and abstract models are bad. Seeming irrelevance and abstract formalism are necessary parts of any scientific inquiry. The question is this: Is a focus on formalism enough? Most mainstream economists believe that it is. I do not. I come to a different answer because my view of the methodology of science differs from the view held by most mainstream economists. Because I don't accept the methodological foundations of science that the mainstream accepts, I find myself in the difficult position (and it is a difficult position for an economist) of agreeing with the layperson. Economics as it is currently practiced and taught is seriously flawed, and because it is flawed, graduate education is flawed.

Methodology and the Survey Results

Because the differing views of the underlying methodological foundations of economics and the role and nature of empirical testing are central to my differences with the mainstream, some discussion of those foundations is needed. Most mainstream economists who are satisfied with the state of economics follow (probably implicitly, because few study methodology) some brand of Popperian or Lakatosian methodology of science, both of which are refinements of logical positivism.[2] A principle of these scientific methodologies is that economics (or any other science) is advanced by the empirical testing of well-specified propositions. According to positivism and its derivatives, that's what science is: You specify a hypothesis and you test it. All else is metaphysical sophistry that allows biases and subjectivity to enter the analysis. Good science—good economics—avoids that.

To be well specified, hypotheses must be clearly specified, and if hypotheses are to be clearly specified, students must learn the techniques to specify and test propositions precisely. Teaching students to do that is difficult, but that's the task graduate economics education has set itself. It must teach students how to specify hypotheses clearly and then how to model and test them. In this process, making reasonable assumptions and understanding economic reality in some broad vague sense are irrelevant. Empirical tests are relied upon to weed out the incorrect theories and extensions of a theory.

In the mainstream methodological view, there's no need for most researchers to have a broad picture of economics research, to know economic literature, or to know economic institutions. Each economist is working on a part of the puzzle—and what I have elsewhere called "the invisible hand of truth" will see to it that the pieces of the puzzle fit together.[3] Yes, the mainstream economists wish the students had a stronger sense of workmanship, but that's a problem in the students; it's not a problem of graduate economics education.

Methodology isn't much talked about in graduate schools, and so the underlying methodology must be deduced from what the graduate schools do and from what they teach. Chicago is unabashedly positivist. For Chicago, the later refinements are unnecessary. The other schools are less positivist, but the nature of what they teach still reflects the positivist outlook.

There is much to be said for the mainstream positivist methodology of science when there is an agreed-upon empirical test for the hypotheses being put forward. But when that consensus is lacking, as it often is in any branch of science, one is left with a wide range of reasonable hypotheses from which one cannot select on the basis of empirical testing. What happens then? A reasonable answer would be that some other selection process should supplement formal empirical testing of hypotheses. But that isn't what happens in economics. The mainstream position is that if it isn't empirically testable by the formal methods, it isn't science.

So what is the result? Students are presented with a contradiction. Many, if not most, of the interesting questions in economics are not empirically testable with econometrics. The closest equivalent I can think of is a story I heard about medical school interviews that were designed to reveal if students could handle stress. At the beginning of the interview, the student was asked to open a window. But the window was nailed shut, and when the student could not open it, he or she was berated— and then the interview started.

The human mind is amazing, and it can handle such contradictions. Students resolve the contradictions by (1) doing abstract theoretical work that will be empirically tested at a later date (which often never comes); (2) empirically testing what can't be empirically tested and coming up with results that convince few, but are formally impressive; (3) becoming cynical and leaving the economics profession; and (4) developing their own reasonable test criteria and learning on their own.

Telling students to do what can't be done, I argue, characterizes the current state of graduate education in economics. Students are forced to push empirical testing beyond its limits. They do so because they have no choice. If they want their Ph.D., they must empirically test. In reaction, many become cynical and lose their sense of pride in their work. After all, they are presented with a set of tools their first two years of graduate school and are told to use them in writing a dissertation in their last two years. If they are told to test, they will test as they were taught, whether the tests are appropriate or not.

Clearly, not all economists respond in the same way. Some simply do what can't be done and believe that it can. When professors and peers all say it can be done, some students can convince themselves they are doing it. They test and corroborate their results in an insulated environment, and then when economists at other schools are not convinced by these tests, the students attribute the skepticism to bias on the part of the other economists. This approach offers the least dissonance, but requires peer support of almost religious fervor. Chicago has excelled at this "solution," and that is why the Chicago students were the happiest with their education. What they were taught to do corresponded with what they were supposed to do.

The other schools, to a greater or lesser extent, see the process of empirical testing as more complicated. They admit this to the students, but don't give them the tools to deal with the more complicated reality. What these students are taught doesn't correspond with what they are supposed to do. The result is the cynicism we detected.

Some people work out alternative methods of choosing among theories, of informally processing nonformal empirical evidence, of integrating institutional knowledge with their formal analysis. As they do so, they become craftspeople. The results are impressive, and there are a number of mainstream economists whose work is almost universally admired. They have solved this dilemma. They are craftspeople, experts in their chosen field of specialty. They can deal with formalism, informalism, and common sense. I might not always agree with them, but I generally learn something from them, and deeply respect their views and ideas. My complaint is that graduate economics programs are not teaching students the craft of economics. The craftspeople in economics learned to do what they do on their own; they weren't taught it in graduate school. And that's what I'm saying is wrong with graduate education. It doesn't give students the tools they need to deal with the economic problems they will face.

I follow a sociological approach to methodology. Unlike the Popperian or Lakatosian methodologies, a sociological approach does not assume that scientists are searching for the truth. Truth is one of their goals but only one; professional advancement, recognition, and wealth are others of perhaps equal or more importance. *Good science is made possible by institutional conventions that make it in scientists' interest to follow reasonable conventions that are most likely to limit subjectivity and bias.* Good science, then, does not come naturally. It comes from limiting, through training, individuals' natural proclivity toward self-interest and instilling in them a yearning passion for the closest approximation to the truth that one can achieve. A sociological approach to methodology is not inconsistent with the mainstream positivist methodology. It is simply broader, and in specific instances it includes the Lakatosian methodology.

A sociological approach to methodology does not deny the importance and persuasiveness of empirical testing if an agreed-upon formal empirical test can be found and replication is possible. In such a case, this formal test guides, and should guide, scientists' actions. But the sociological approach accepts that empirical testing is an art and cannot be used as a decision rule for many hypotheses. Positivism says science ends with formal empirical testing; if formal empirical testing is impossible, no science is possible. A sociological approach says that science does not end with formal empirical testing—that there are reasonable ways of processing information upon which people can agree. A sociological approach to methodology expands the domain of science, avoiding, whenever possible, subjective bias.

An economist using a sociological approach will recognize formal empirical testing as itself an agreed-upon convention. It is convincing because people are taught that it is convincing and because it corresponds with their instincts. But it can be biased and subjective, as can all other types of tests. So the issue isn't formal empirical testing versus nonformal empirical testing; the issue is the nature of the appropriate empirical test.

My particular sociological approach to methodology reflects my economic training. It carries economists' assumption of economic rationality to its logical conclusion. Positivism assumes individuals search for the truth, even if it is not in their self-interest. The sociological approach that I use, paradoxically, assumes scientists are the same type rational beings that neoclassical economics assumes all people are. To be a neoclassical economist whose methodology is positivism is to be inconsistent.

If no agreed-upon convention of processing information exists, self-interest guides choices of theories. When scientific conventions no longer guide scientists' actions, those conventions will be replaced by self-interest and cynicism. That is what I believe has happened in economics. Because the profession has not come to grips with what decision rules to follow when empirical tests are inconclusive, the profession has lost its bearings and has allowed self-interest to govern the choice of theories.[4]

This is the environment in a discipline in which self-interest dominates: Models are chosen on the basis of whether they will lead to a publishable article, not on the basis of how illuminating they are. One knows as little literature as possible, because to know literature will force one to attribute ideas to others. Formal empirical tests are not done to answer questions, but instead are done to satisfy reviewers and advisers. Pay, not the fulfillment of intellectual curiosity, becomes the scientists' reward.

In an economics discipline guided by self-interest, the sense of joy, of excitement, of trying to explain conundrums in the economy, has been replaced by an intricate game of one-upmanship. For many economists, research is not a way to deepen their understanding of the economy; it's a way of advancing in the profession. The sense of pride and of workmanship is gone—replaced with a cynical understanding of how to get ahead.

The students are quick to pick up on the way the profession works. They recognize that the way to advance is to do a model that is slightly different from one of the other models. As one student said, "You never take on some really risky thing . . . the payoff is too low." You don't try to relate your model to reality, to have it add something meaningful to economists' understanding—not because you don't want to, but because you don't have the time. To try to relate your model to reality means entering into an uncharted area, an area for which you have no training.

Graduate students need only look around and see who the young successful economists are and where the payoffs are. Learn the techniques—or better yet, advance a technique and then figure out a question to ask that can use that technique. The more interesting the question, the better off you are, but if you choose the questions first and then the technique, you're likely to flounder. As one perceptive Yale student wrote in answer to the question about what leads to success in economics, "Not too critical a mind."

I could present a wide variety of examples to show that economic theories are not testable by generally agreed-upon tests, but I think our survey results as to the differences in views of students at various graduate programs make such a discussion unnecessary. When students can differ as much as do those at Chicago from other students about what theories are correct, there can be no generally accepted empirical test. That doesn't mean that the evidence isn't empirically tested. It's been tested—and not surprisingly, both sides find that they are right, within a 99 percent confidence interval. In turn, I'm 99 percent confident that they both aren't right and that the techniques available don't provide an answer as to who is right.

In mainstream methodology, therefore, what most economists are doing is not science, which is why they fight so hard against anyone who claims that the propositions aren't formally testable. In sociological methodology, science without definitive formal testing is still possible; one simply must supplement the controlled formal empirical testing with reasoned judgments and sensible interpretations and understanding of all the available empirical evidence. The formal empirical tests must be supplemented by informal tests, making a wider range of empirical observations play a role in deciding among theories.

Models have a much different role in the sociological methodology than they do in the positivist methodology. In positive methodology, models are ways of deriving formal testable hypotheses. To do so, they must be extraordinarily precise and clear so that they will yield formally testable hypotheses. In sociological methodology, models serve an organizing role. They structure one's thinking about a problem and make it possible to consider the problem in an orderly fashion. To serve this purpose, they do not have to be precise; in fact, precision can destroy the purpose of the model by diverting one's focus from the general ideas to the technical aspects of the model—by making it more difficult to keep in the back of one's mind the applicability of the model. If this

sociological methodology were adopted, economics would be more meaningful, and graduate economics students would be less cynical.

What to Do About
the Current State of Affairs

The economics profession must establish a set of conventions to guide
students so they can deal effectively with a wider range of empirical
evidence—so they can learn to make reasoned, and reasonable, judgments
that employ the available empirical evidence. Unless something is done,
self-interest will guide economists' work. There is no invisible hand that
guides economists to search for the truth; scientific conventions established
over long periods work as an invisible hand, but these conventions
themselves must be guided. What is needed in economics is the estab-
lishment of a set of conventions that can guide scientific inquiry when
formal empirical testing cannot.[5]

Establishing Nonformalist Conventions

Establishing nonformal empirical, or sociological, conventions is much
more difficult than establishing formal empirical conventions because
the appropriate nonformal empirical conventions are quite different from
and even contradict good formal empirical conventions. For example

- The positivist convention is that there is no reason to know institutions; in fact, it can be harmful because too much institutional
  information can cause one to lose sight of the forest for the trees.
  Assumptions must be unrealistic. The sociological convention is that
  to talk reasonably about an institution, one must know it intimately;
  if one is to judge a model, one must know why the model's
  assumptions differ from reality and why making those assumptions
  does not do an injustice to the model.
- The positivist convention is that the latest literature embodies all
  that is worth knowing from earlier literature. To know economic
  literature is nice, but it is not part of formal scientific discovery.
  The sociological convention is that one must know the past literature
  of one's field. Only then can one know the variety of viewpoints
  and choose the viewpoint most appropriate for the problem at hand.
- The positivist convention is that one should know only the paradigm
  within which one works. Formal empirical testing will decide among
  competing theories. The sociological convention is that one must
  know all paradigms so that one can use common sense in choosing
  which approach sheds most light on a particular issue.

I could go on, but I think the point is made. Integrating good sociological conventions with positivist conventions will not be easy; it requires split personalities. On the one hand, one must maintain a narrow scientific specialization; on the other hand, one must maintain a humanistic breadth. A good economist must do both simultaneously.

How Did Economics Evolve into Its Current State?

There has been a continual pull in economics between the positivist scientific conventions and the broader sociological conventions. Thus, to understand the current situation in economics, one must understand its history. Adam Smith was sociological; David Ricardo was formalist. The German historical school was sociological; Leon Walras was formalist. Alfred Marshall was sociological; Paul Samuelson is formalist. The ongoing history of economics is one of a swing between the two approaches.

In the early 1930s in the United States, the sociological approach dominated. Students learned economic literature and institutions. In the late 1930s, John Hicks and Paul Samuelson demonstrated the power of formal positivism and started economics along its present path. They showed that many of the previous economic views were biased and confused, and they added clarity to a wide range of economic propositions. Yet the sociological conventions still lingered, and students in the 1940s and 1950s received training in both traditions. By the late 1960s, the formalists dominated the profession, and today this domination is almost complete.

An important reason for their domination was the development of econometrics. In the 1960s and 1970s, with the progress of computers, the possibilities of formal empirical testing expanded enormously. Econometrics developed as a way of formally testing hypotheses and added another skill for economists to master. The curriculum was squeezed, and slowly the teaching of sociological conventions was pushed out. History of economic thought was eliminated as a requirement; economic history was eliminated; the teaching of any institutional material was eliminated; and the teaching of reasoned judgment was eliminated as being potentially biased. Students in the 1960s still received some of this training (their professors were from that tradition), but the upcoming younger economists increasingly had less. The emphasis shifted to technical skills. Applied economics came to mean less and less familiarity with the institutions in an area or field, and more and more knowledge of how to work with data sets.

In the 1950s and 1960s, this change was not seen as a loss; it was believed that econometrics would offer economics a formal empirical test that could rid it of many of the subjective biases inherent in nonformal argumentation. Consistent with that belief, economic literature and economic institutions were purged from the graduate economics curriculum and replaced with the teaching of techniques that would better allow economists to set up testable hypotheses and with econometrics that would better allow economists to test their theories. Unfortunately, the development of high-speed computers worked counter to, rather than in support of, making economics reflect the real world.

When foundations gave universities grants to set up "applied" seminars and to encourage students to do "applied" work, "applied work" no longer meant real-world work. "Applied" quickly came to mean "also trained in econometrics," and it added another technical expertise that economists were expected to have.

But high-speed computers did not make economics more applied. Although they improved economists' technical ability to test theories, computers reduced economists' ability to judge the appropriateness of their theories. Before the existence of high-speed computers, economists had to dirty their hands when they did applied economics. They had to work through the data—organizing it, sometimes even collecting it— but generally dirtying their hands. It was slow, tedious work, but it had a byproduct: It gave economists who did it a sense of the data, the problems with the data, and the institutions they were studying. They knew the institutions—they had to in order to get their data.

Today, self-collection of data is rare. Instead, an economist gets a computer tape of some panel data and tests and uses the information on that tape. This is an extremely efficient way to handle large amounts of data, but it involves an enormous loss of interpretive information. What's missing are the comments, the sensibility of the survey collector, the knowledge of whether the person answered truthfully or not, or how robust the data are. Some economists have that sense, and when one hears their arguments, they are convincing. But the majority do not fill in the gaps; they rely on the information as fed to them by the tapes, and thus they no longer have a sense of the real-world institutions they are studying.

In short, unless economists train themselves, they get little feel for the way the world works; instead, they learn the way their model of the world works and how knowledge of that model will advance them in their profession.

Graduate and Undergraduate Economics Training

Some of the mainstream economists with whom I have discussed this issue agree that there is a problem with economics education, but they argue that the problem lies in undergraduate, not graduate, education. Although they lament the focus on technique in graduate education, they claim they must bring the students up to speed because undergraduate education has not done its job. They point out that undergraduate natural science majors learn the techniques. Why can't undergraduate economics majors do the same? These arguments have some merit, especially for those who still follow a positivist methodology, but they are not a possibility, given the institutional structure of U.S. education. To see why, we must consider the interface between graduate and undergraduate education.

Economics is in a position different from the natural sciences. Because most undergraduate natural science departments can assume that at least a sizable minority of their majors plan to pursue science careers, they can structure the program to prepare students for graduate school. Economics departments cannot take this approach. Most undergraduate economics students have no intention of becoming scientists. They're going into business and have a consumer's interest in economics, not a producer's interest. The reality is that most students who major in economics are actually business majors in disguise. At schools where there is a business program, the number of economics majors drops dramatically. Liberal arts schools, where most economics majors are enrolled, would be doing a serious disservice to the majority of their majors if they taught a curriculum that would bring students up to speed in techniques used in graduate school. Not only would they be doing a serious disservice, they would lose, probably, 90–95 percent of their economics majors.

Put bluntly, the large demand for economics professors exists because of economics' relationship to business. Were undergraduate schools to make economics a true pre–graduate school preparation, the demand for economists to teach in these undergraduate schools would decline significantly—so much so that many of the new Ph.D.'s in economics would be unable to find jobs. Teaching economics is what most Ph.D. economists do.

The same pressures to teach real-world economics are felt in economics programs at schools where there are business departments. The demand for their services comes from servicing business school students, and if they are to get majors, they must keep the level of technique they teach far below that of graduate schools.

This does not mean that undergraduate economics programs don't use mathematical techniques. Many use techniques as a way of regulating the number of majors. If there is a shortage of majors, lower techniques; if there is a surplus of majors (depending on the political relationship the department has with the dean), raise techniques. But we're talking quantum levels below the techniques used in graduate school.

Undergraduate economics training could focus on economic literature and institutions and on reasonably interpreting nonformal empirical data. This approach would be useful for business students and would make undergraduate economics an integral part of an economics education. But who is to teach these courses? Outgoing graduate students have a strong desire to teach what they've learned in graduate school, and at present they are ill-prepared to teach in such a program. Instead, these new teachers initially design undergraduate programs to mimic graduate programs. It is only when they are faced with the reality of teaching students who are completely indifferent to what the teachers are doing that they acquire, through on-the-job training, a knowledge of economic institutions sufficient to get by in the classroom. But it's no thanks to their graduate training. Graduate economics students receive little useful training for teaching undergraduates.

Many of the top liberal arts schools that I know lament what is going on in graduate schools. What the graduate schools are teaching their students is not especially useful for what their students will be required to teach when they take up classroom teaching themselves. We hire their graduates because the graduate schools have a monopoly (the top schools call themselves the cartel) and because they get the brightest students. We hire from the best graduate schools because they serve as a screening device, not because of what they teach their students.

Providing undergraduate education is the largest job that the economics profession does. Graduate programs in economics depend upon the demand for undergraduate economics courses to justify their budgets to university administrations. They supply the graduate students to teach the courses (at bargain wages) and once in a while supply upper-level professors to teach an undergraduate course. For many graduate programs, a shortfall of graduate students will bring the dean upon their heads, not because of what it means for the graduate program but for what it means for the undergraduate program. Covering the undergraduate program is how the graduate programs "earn their keep." Graduate students are the input that keeps the undergraduate programs going— and thereby keeps the graduate departments going.

Thus, at each level, there is a need to rely on the demand from undergraduate students interested in business to maintain the current demand for economists. Were the undergraduate economics curriculum designed to prepare students for what they are taught in graduate economics, graduate programs would have to shrink by at least 50 percent. My suspicion is that faced with this reality, most economists would not choose the shrinkage option. Another option—running separate tracks for pre–graduate school majors and students who aren't going on to graduate school—isn't actually an option for most schools because the number of potential candidates for graduate school is so small that the administration can't justify a program designed only for them. So undergraduate economics education will remain what it is: a general introduction to economics—a mix of lowbrow theory, institutional knowledge, and economic reasoning—because that is what the demand is for. And so most undergraduate economics majors will remain ill-prepared for graduate school.

This state of affairs brings about two reactions. The first reaction is that graduate programs know that undergraduate programs are not preparing students for graduate school and don't require their entrants to have studied economics. Although an undergraduate major is almost essential for graduate studies in fields such as chemistry, physics, and engineering, it is not necessary in economics. Graduate schools accept many students who have no background in economics, and although it is somewhat of a limitation for the students, in our survey it was very apparent that for graduate students in economics, a mathematics background was a better background than an economics undergraduate background. In fact, I'm told that individuals who can't get a Ph.D. in math are directed to apply to economics, where they not only can get a Ph.D. but can be a star.

The second reaction is that the word goes out as to what is required in graduate schools, and undergraduate majors with good interpretive skills shy away from graduate economics programs. They hear from their undergraduate advisers that unless they are willing to go through training that will seem to them like jumping through hoops, they should not go to graduate school in economics. The only students who apply are those who think they can put up with—or who actually enjoy—jumping through hoops; many of the brightest students with excellent interpretive skills drop out. As a number of students told us when they commented on our survey results: "If you think the responses you got were of concern, you should talk to so-and-so, who dropped out." The selection process is screening out those individuals with the interpretive skills to deal effectively with reasonably interpreting nonformal empirical evidence. Students who go into and get through graduate economics programs are those who will accept technical modeling for its own sake. And these will become the next generation of teachers.

So the institutional situation is as follows: Undergraduate economics programs are, of necessity, general nontechnical programs; it is left to graduate programs to teach both the technique and the sensibility. Graduate programs teach technique, leaving students to learn interpretive skills and sensibility on their own. Most don't; they become undergraduate teachers, and institutional content in interpretive skills is given an even lower ranking in the next generation.

There is no easy way out of the current state economics finds itself in. It is a self-reinforcing state that will require Herculean efforts to change, because change goes against the very interests of the individuals who would be required to make that change. Unfortunately, history provides few examples of such changes from within. Instead, institutions go through the motions of implementing change, but they do not change. That seems to be the path chosen by the profession.

In response to our survey, the AEA established a commission (primarily made up of graduate-level economics professors) to study graduate education. Spending hundreds of thousands of dollars, they conducted surveys of a large number of groups to see if major changes were necessary. I have not seen the survey, let alone its results, but I will make a nonformal empirical prediction about the findings: Those results will be that there is some reason for concern about the nature of graduate economics education but that, fundamentally, graduate education is sound. It is doing what it intended to do, and what it should do, subject to minor changes. Perhaps, if my empirical prediction is correct, some positivist economists who choose theories on the basis of predictability might take seriously the need for change.

Notes

Preface

1. Charles J. Sykes, *Profscam: Professors and the Demise of Higher Education* (Washington, D.C.: Regnery Gateway, 1988).

2. Arjo Klamer, *Conversations with Economists* (Totowa, N.J.: Rowman and Allanheld, 1983).

3. David Colander and Arjo Klamer, "The Making of an Economist," *Journal of Economic Perspectives* (Fall 1987): 95–111.

Chapter 1

1. Axel Leijonhufvud, "Life Among the Econ," *Western Economic Journal* (September 1973): 327–337.

2. Mitchell's remarks appear in Joseph Dorfman, *Economic Mind in American Civilization, 1918–1933* (New York: Viking Press, 1959), p. 210. We thank Bob Coats for referring us to this warning.

3. Thomas Hill, "Inaugural Address," *Addresses at the Inauguration of Thomas Hill, D.D., as President of Harvard College* (Cambridge, Mass., 1863), pp. 36–37. Quoted in Richard J. Storr, *The Beginning of the Future* (New York: McGraw-Hill), p. 39.

4. Quoted in Bernard Berelson, *Graduate Education in the United States* (New York: McGraw-Hill, 1960) p. 19.

5. Quoted in Storr, *The Beginning of the Future*, pp. 59–60.

6. We should note that this situation is peculiar to the United States. In other countries, the separation between the academic and the real worlds is less strong. In Portugal, for example, economists in the government are often prominent academics as well. In the Netherlands, Klamer was taught monetary theory by the vice president of the Dutch Central Bank. Such arrangements are far less prevalent in the United States.

7. This consideration of the number of economists relies heavily on Harry Landreth and David Colander, *History of Economic Theory* (Boston: Houghton Mifflin, 1989). The figures for the number of economists and the breakdown of types of economists are estimates rather than exact. The order of magnitude is correct, but there is enormous difference in the numbers depending on the source. For example, estimates of the number of economists range from 88,000 to 160,000 (in 1982). The data come from unpublished estimates by the National

Science Foundation, *The Guide to Graduate Study in Economics* (Wry Owen and Larry Cross, editors); the Census Bureau; and the American Economic Association. Other sources that have been useful for this composite sketch of the economics profession are Herbert Stein, *American Economic Review* (May 1986): 1–9; and John Siegfried and Jennie Raymond, "A Profile of Senior Economics Majors in the U.S.," *American Economic Review* (May 1984): 19–25. Because much of the data is for years that cannot be compared with one another, we have estimated ratios and projected the data to 1987. Thus these data should be seen as estimates.

8. *U.S. Statistical Abstract*, Bureau of the Census, 1986.

9. *An Assessment of Research-Doctorate Programs in the United States Social and Behavioral Sciences*, National Academy of Sciences, 1982.

10. A. W. Coats, "Economics in the U.S.: 1920 to 1970" (undated manuscript).

11. Siegfried and Raymond, "A Profile of Senior Economics Majors in the U.S.," pp. 19–25.

Chapter 2

1. Robert Kuttner, "The Poverty of Economics," *Atlantic Monthly* (February 1985): 74–84.

2. Klamer, *Conversations*; Richard Whitley, *The Intellectual and Social Organization of the Sciences* (London: Oxford University Press, 1984); A. W. "Bob" Coats, "The Sociology of Science: Its Application to Economics," Duke University Mimeo, 1985; Donald McCloskey, *The Rhetoric of Economics* (Madison: University of Wisconsin Press, 1986).

3. George Stigler and Claire Friedland, "The Citation Practices of Doctorates in Economics," in *The Economist as Preacher* (Chicago: University of Chicago Press, 1982), pp. 192–222. (First published 1975.)

4. Dropouts are not included in the survey. However, at most of these schools, the dropout rate is relatively low, which suggests to us that the admissions procedures are succeeding in weeding out students who cannot accept the process.

5. The percentages can add up to more than 100 percent because some students chose more than one goal.

6. Reported in the *Committee on the Status of Women in the Economics Profession March 1987 Newsletter*, p. 4.

7. Ward's hierarchy was as follows: (1) micro and macro theory, and econometrics; (2) international trade, public finance, money and banking; (3) labor, industrial organization, and economic history; (4) history of economic theory, economic development, and comparative economic systems. Benjamin Ward, *What's Wrong with Economics* (New York: Basic Books, 1972).

8. The question was phrased as follows: "Which characteristics will most likely place students on the fast track? Circle one." In our interviews, we asked students how they interpreted "fast track" and found that almost all students believed it to refer to success in the academic profession.

9. Bruno Frey et al., "Consensus and Dissension Among Economists: An Empirical Inquiry," *American Economic Review* (March 1984): 986–994.

10. Stigler, *The Economist as Preacher*.

11. Perceptions often differ from reality. Robert Solow pointed out to us that he never made such a statement. The likely source for the statement is a quotation from Dale Jorgenson as reported in a *Business Week* article.

Chapter 4

1. As we pointed out in Chapter 2, Solow says he never made this remark.

2. Robert Heilbroner, *The Worldly Philosophers: The Lives, Times, and Ideas of the Great Economic Thinkers* (New York: Simon and Schuster, 1980).

3. Martin Weitzman, *The Share Economy: Conquering Inflation* (Cambridge, Mass.: Harvard University Press, 1984).

4. Albert Hirschman, *The Passions and the Interests: Political Arguments for Capitalism Before Its Triumph* (Princeton, N.J.: Princeton University Press, 1977); and *Exit, Voice and Loyalty: Responses to Decline in Firms, Organizations, and States* (Cambridge, Mass.: Harvard University Press, 1970).

5. John Maynard Keynes, *The General Theory of Employment, Interest, and Money* (New York: Harcourt Brace Jovanovich, 1936).

6. Charles did his undergraduate work in England.

7. Patrick Minford stands out among English economists because of his endorsement of new classical economics.

Chapter 5

1. At the time of this conversation, Amartya Sen was still at Oxford University. In 1987 he joined the Harvard department. Alfred Chandler is a business historian at Harvard Business School. Phil Mirowski, an economist from Tufts University, had given the Political Economy Lecture a few weeks before these conversations.

2. A year after this conversation, Solow was awarded the Nobel Prize for his contributions to growth theory.

3. The National Bureau of Economic Research (NBER) employs graduate students as research assistants.

4. Weitzman, *Share Economy.*

5. Klamer, *Conversations.*

Chapter 7

1. Milton Friedman and and Rose Friedman, *Free to Choose: A Personal Statement* (New York: Harcourt Brace Jovanovich, 1980).

2. Adam Smith, *An Inquiry into the Nature and Causes of the Wealth of Nations,* edited by R. H. Campbell and A. S. Skinner (Oxford: Clarendon Press, 1976). (First published in 1776.)

3. Milton Friedman, *Price Theory* (Chicago: Aldine Publishing Co., 1976).

4. Gerard Debreu, *Theory of Value: An Axiomatic Analysis of Economic Equilibrium* (New York: Wiley, 1965).

Chapter 8

1. Talk is also crucial in the making of knowledge in the natural sciences. See, for example, G. Nigel Gilbert and Michael Mulkay, *Opening Pandora's Box* (Cambridge: Cambridge University Press, 1984); and Karin Knorr Cetina, *The Manufacture of Knowledge: An Essay on the Constructivist and the Contextual Nature of Science* (Oxford: Pergamon Press, 1981).

2. Howard S. Becker, et al., *Sociological Work: Method and Substance* (Chicago: Aldine Publishing Co., 1970).

3. Rudiger Dornbusch is an international economist at MIT who is frequently consulted by governments and institutions.

4. Lawrence Summers got tenure at Harvard University before he turned thirty and was an economic adviser to presidential candidate Michael Dukakis in the 1988 campaign.

5. Jerry Hausman is an econometrician at MIT and recipient of the J. B. Clark award (given to honor the most promising economists under forty).

6. Jeffrey Sachs is another young economist who got tenure at Harvard before turning thirty. Most of his work is on international trade; he has a big and somewhat controversial reputation outside academia because of his role in the negotiations on the debt of the Third World, mainly in his capacity as consultant to the government of Bolivia.

7. The Chicago students discuss the work of Lars Hansen, a neoclassical economist, quite extensively in Chapter 7.

8. An argument that is used in Keynesian analysis to justify rigid wages.

9. Donald McCloskey has argued that the sneer is important in academic life. A Chicago economist educated at Harvard, he wishes that both schools would stop their sneers. I would argue that the sneer has a legitimate role in conversation. (See Arjo Klamer and Donald McCloskey, "The Rhetoric of Disagreement," *Rethinking Marxism*, forthcoming.)

10. The sneering that second-year Chicago students made in the direction of Robert Solow, an MIT economist, was not surprising. I was surprised, however, when Edward (3) expressed his respect for Solow, mentioning in particular his contribution to growth theory. I later found out that Robert Lucas gives a seminar on growth theory in which he takes Solow's work as the point of departure.

11. In case there is a suspicion of bias in the interviewing, note that I do not subscribe to the Chicago approach.

12. See especially William Breit and Roger W. Spencer, *Lives of the Laureates* (Cambridge: M.I.T. Press, 1986).

13. John Maloney, *Marshall, Orthodoxy and the Professionalisation of Economics* (Cambridge: Cambridge University Press, 1985), p 57. This is an instructive book on the transformation of economics into a profession.

14. We now recognize that the survey is not well designed to test the extent to which students change their opinions. A longitudinal study, in which students are surveyed at various stages, would give more insight.

15. As Chapter 3 shows, many additional comments scribbled on the survey further support this consciousness of students being socialized—of having "to

jump through a number of hoops," as one Stanford student wrote, or of having to play by the rules of the game.

16. One hears irony in a contrast between what is asserted and what actually is the case.

17. Melvin Reder, "Chicago Economics: Permanence and Change," *Journal of Economic Literature* (March 1982): 9 (my italics).

18. Let me point out that rhetoric, as used here, is by no means derogatory in the sense of "mere rhetoric." Rhetoric, as McCloskey and others, including the author, have shown, characterizes any form of communication; it emerges in metaphors, stories, arguments, appeals to authority, and other devices that people use to get their point across to others. See Arjo Klamer, Donald McCloskey, and Robert Solow, eds., *Consequences of Economic Rhetoric* (Cambridge: Cambridge University Press, 1989).

19. I am only hinting at a large issue, namely the discrepancies in rhetorical practices. *Consequences of Economic Rhetoric* contains several studies that explore the rhetorical differences between academic and common economics discourse.

20. "Character" is similar to "ethos" as used in rhetorical analysis. Because of its vagueness, the term "character" had gone out of use in literary and philosophical discourse; partly because of its vagueness, it is being revived. Alastair MacIntyre, for example, uses the term in *After Virtue* (Notre Dame, Ind.: University of Notre Dame Press, 1981). I also found very useful an article by the legal scholar Jerry Frug, "Argument as Character," in *Stanford Law Review* 40 (April 1988): 869–927. Craufurd Goodwin applies the notion of the character, without actually calling it that, in his illuminating article "The Heterogeneity of the Economists' Discourse: Philosopher, Priest, and Hired Gun," in Klamer, McCloskey, and Solow, *The Consequences of Economic Rhetoric,* pp. 207–220.

21. The Scholar is another possible characterization.

22. George Stigler, *The Intellectual and The Marketplace* (London: The Free Press, 1963), p. 14.

23. I have elaborated on this theme in Arjo Klamer, "The Advent of Modernism in Economics" and "New Classical Economics: A Manifestation of Late Modernism," unpublished papers, Project on Rhetoric of Inquiry, University of Iowa, Iowa City, Iowa 52242.

Chapter 9

1. My views have been refined by discussion and useful criticism of an earlier draft of this chapter by Hal Varian and Robert Solow. I suspect we still differ substantially, but their critical comments were helpful in shaping this chapter.

2. I present a more extended discussion of methodology in Harry Landreth and David Colander, *History of Economic Theory* (Boston, Houghton Mifflin, 1989). In a nutshell, Positivism assumes researchers discover "true" theories. The Popperian methodology is that researchers can never know if theories are true. The best that they can do is to *falsify* theories. The Lakatosian methodology points out that it is hard to be sure when a theory is falsified. The *hard core*

of a theory is accepted without testing. Only the peripheral implications are tested. They all assume that researchers are searching for the truth.

3. The "invisible hand of truth" is a concept discussed in a chapter of that title in David Colander and A. W. Coats, eds., *The Spread of Economic Ideas* (Cambridge, England: Cambridge University Press, 1989).

4. For my view that economists' self-interest, more than politics or empirical findings, guided the evolution of macroeconomic theories, see David Colander, "The Evolution of Keynesian Economics," in *Keynes and Public Policy*, edited by Omar Hamouda and John Smithen (Aldershot, England: Edward Elgar, 1988), pp. 92–100.

5. To some degree, the development of Baysian econometrics is moving in the direction of establishing an alternative, more believable, formal empirical test, but it is still in its infancy and, most likely, will simply present econometric tests in a more honest fashion rather than expand the domain of empirical testing.

About the Authors

Arjo Klamer is the author of the highly successful *Conversations with Economists*, selected by *Business Week* as one of the top ten business books of 1984. He is currently an associate professor at George Washington University. Together with Donald McCloskey and Robert Solow, he recently edited *Consequences of Economic Rhetoric* (Cambridge University Press, 1989).

David Colander is one of the youngest economists ever to be awarded a Distinguished Professorship in Economics. Besides having written over thirty articles, he has edited or written ten books, including *The Spread of Economic Ideas* (co-edited with A. W. "Bob" Coats, published by Cambridge University Press, 1989). He has taught at Columbia, Vassar, and the University of Miami; has been a consultant for Time-Life Films and Congress; and has been a visiting scholar at Oxford and an Economics Policy Fellow at the Brookings Institution. He is currently the Christian A. Johnson Distinguished Professor of Economics at Middlebury College.

Index

ABD's. *See* All but dissertation done
Abel, Ken, 93, 96
AEA. *See* American Economic Association
AER. *See American Economic Review*
Akerlof, George, 42(table), 76, 84, 146, 153, 180
All but dissertation done (ABD's), 11
American Economic Association (AEA), 1, 5
  commission on graduate education, 200
  founded (1885), 176
  job-listing service, 8–9
  membership, 8
American Economic Review (AER), 111, 148
American Enterprise Institute, 8
Amherst College, 78
Aristotle, 125
Arrow, Kenneth, 41, 42(table), 43, 97
Asian students, 29, 57, 109, 136

Barro, Robert, 83, 88, 92, 98, 106, 157, 158, 173
Baysian econometrics, 206(n5)
Becker, Gary, 98, 99, 107, 133, 138, 139, 140, 145, 146, 148, 149, 151, 159, 162, 164, 165–166, 174
  graduate student ranking and opinion of, 42(table), 160, 171, 172, 176, 180
Becker, Howard S., 170
Behavior according to conventions, 23(table)
Bird, Larry, 75

Blanchard, Oliver, 65, 84, 85
Blinder, Alan, 106
Boston College, 68
Boston University ranking, 10(table)
Boulding, Kenneth, 38, 42(table)
Brookings Institution, 8
Brown University ranking, 10(table)
Buchanan, James, 135, 150
Bureau of the Census, 7
Business cycles, 143, 144, 161, 162
Business school students, 197, 198

Cagan, Phillip, 123
California Institute of Technology ranking, 10(table)
Cambridge controversy, 124
Career plans, 71, 77–78, 79–80, 91, 102, 121–123, 134, 163–164, 165, 176, 179, 180–181
Carter, Jimmy, 111
Chandler, Alfred, 95, 203(n1)
China, 136
Claremont College ranking, 10(table)
Cochrane, John, 145
Colander, David, 57, 169, 170, 175, 176, 179, 181, 183, 184, 188
Columbia University, 6
  graduate students, 13, 29, 111, 113, 183
  graduate students, conversations with, 57, 109–119
  graduate student experience, 109–111, 112, 114–115, 118–119, 120–121, 173, 175
  graduate student opinions, 21–23(tables), 26–27, 38, 39, 45, 47–

52(tables), 54–56(table), 171, 172.
  See also subentry graduate
  students, conversations with
graduate student ranking and
  opinions of economists, 41–
  42(tables), 125–126
and Harvard University
  comparison, 109, 119
and MIT comparison, 109, 173
ranking, 10(table), 109
and University of Chicago
  comparison, 110
Comparative economics, 17(table)
Connections with prominent
  professors, 18(table)
Conservatives, 14, 38, 90, 141
Conversations with Economists
  (Klamer), 38, 156
Cornell University ranking, 10(table)
Corporate finance, 9
Cost mark-up pricing, 23
Council of Economic Advisors, 6
Cynicism, 71–72, 97, 100, 175, 176,
  183, 184, 185, 187–188, 191, 194

Data Resources Incorporated (DRI),
  164
Debreu, Gerard, 42(table), 149, 153,
  158
Demsetz, Harold, 149
Diamond, Peter, 65, 75
Directly Unproductive Activities
  analysis, 124
Dissertation topics, 16, 74–75, 102,
  123–124, 182–183
Division of labor, 107
Dornbusch, Rudiger, 63, 65, 84, 85,
  171, 181
DRI. *See* Data Resources Incorporated
Duke University ranking, 10(table)
Dunlop, John, 104

Eckstein, Otto, 54–56(table)
Econometrica, 148
Econometrics. *See* Statistics and
  econometrics

Economic assumptions, 23, 92, 94–
  95, 96–98, 106–108, 111–112,
  124–126, 130–132, 140–144,
  150–151, 154–157, 159–163
Economic development, 17
Economic history, 163
Economics, 82–83, 184–185, 191, 194,
  200
conventions to be established, 194–
  195
graduate education, likes and
  dislikes, 13, 18–19, 25–27, 38,
  44–46, 47–52(tables), 60–61, 71–
  74, 88–89. *See also* Socialization
  process
graduate school, first, 6
graduate schools, 3, 5, 6, 7, 9, 11–
  12, 13, 27–28, 108, 178, 187,
  188, 198, 199, 200
graduate schools, ranking, 9,
  10(table)
graduate student questionnaire
  (1985), 13, 14, 28–36, 37, 59,
  87–88, 127
graduate students, 5, 13–14, 24–25,
  27–28, 37–38, 53, 172–176, 179–
  185, 187
graduate students interests, 14–19
graduate students profile, 14, 110
jargon, 4, 113
journals, 8, 82, 111, 132
literature, 1, 7, 18(table), 27, 28,
  98, 101, 111, 112, 148, 165, 192,
  194, 198
professionalization, 3, 4–7, 13,
  181–183
research institutes, 8
satire of, 4
scientific status, 20–21, 24, 65–66,
  81–82, 96–98, 183, 188, 189
specialty courses, 9
undergraduate training, 9, 11, 110,
  197–198, 199
See also Columbia University;
  Harvard University;
  Massachusetts Institute of
  Technology; Methodology;

Stanford University; University of Chicago; Yale University
Economists, 3, 4, 12, 169, 181–183, 184, 188, 196
  applied, 106, 195, 196
  British, 78, 97
  business, 7, 8
  careers, 5, 6–7, 8, 9, 12, 15, 197
  government, 8, 15, 95
  mainstream, 189, 193, 196
  M.A.'s, 7, 11
  number of, 7, 11
  opinions about, 37–38, 40, 59, 64–65, 67–68, 75–76, 78, 83–84, 93, 95, 97–99, 102–105, 106, 108, 125–126, 129, 135–136, 138–140, 151–153, 160, 162, 171–172, 173, 174, 176, 180, 181
  Ph.D.'s, 7, 11, 28
  ranking of, 41–43
  research, 6, 15, 40, 78, 192
  salaries, 7–8
  successful, 46, 53, 54–56(table), 193
  women, 7
  See also Professors; individual names
Economy, 46
  knowledge of, 17, 18(table), 19–20, 28, 164, 170, 171, 172
  opinions on, 20–25, 133–134, 187
Edgeworth, Francis, 3
Efficiency, 140
Efficiency wages, 92, 96, 150, 159, 160–161, 173
Exit, Voice and Loyalty (Hirschman), 67

Farber, Hank, 75
Fast-track. See Success, perceptions of
Feldstein, Martin, 42(table)
Findlay, Ronald, 42(table)
"Firefighting," 8
Fiscal policy, 22(table), 25, 172
Fischer, Stanley, 42(table), 65, 78, 85

Fisher, Frank, 66–67, 69
Forecasting, 8, 114
Foreign students, 11, 29, 57, 109, 129, 136, 154
Formalism, 188, 195
France, 102
Freeman, Richard, 93
Free to Choose (Friedman and Friedman), 135
Frey, Bruno, 19
Frey Study of American economists, 19(table)
Friedland, Claire, 20
Friedman, Benjamin, 92, 106, 138
Friedman, David, 147
Friedman, Milton, 80, 111, 112, 123, 130, 134, 135, 140, 141, 145, 146, 149, 151, 157, 162, 173
  graduate student ranking and opinion of, 42(table), 152, 176, 178, 180

Galbraith, John Kenneth, 5, 13, 63, 104, 182
  graduate student ranking and opinion of, 38, 42(table), 64, 128, 181
General Theory of Employment, Interest, and Money, The (Keynes), 68
George Washington University, 10(table), 132
German historical school, 195
Gold standard, 102
GPA. See Grade point average
Grade point average (GPA), 9
Graduate students. See Career plans; Columbia University; Dissertation topics; Harvard University; Massachusetts Institute of Technology; Political orientation; Stanford University; University of Chicago; Yale University; under Economics
Great Britain, 69, 70, 97, 102
Green, Jerry, 105, 107

Grossman, Sanford, 42(table), 68, 105

Hansen, Lars, 83, 139–140, 142, 143, 158, 172
Hart, Oliver, 42(table), 75
Harvard University, 6, 68, 80, 81, 160
  and Columbia University comparison, 109, 119
  graduate student experience, 88–89, 98, 100–101, 175, 176–177, 179
  graduate student opinions, 20, 21, 22–23(tables), 24, 25, 41, 44–45, 46, 47–52(tables), 54–56(table), 137, 170, 171, 172. See also subentry graduate students, conversations with
  graduate student ranking and opinion of economists, 41, 42(table), 171, 173
  graduate students, 13, 24, 29, 53, 89–90, 95, 100, 173, 180, 181, 183
  graduate students, conversations with, 57, 87–108
  and MIT comparison, 85–86, 89, 95–96, 100, 102, 173, 174
  ranking, 10(table)
  and University of Chicago comparison, 101, 155, 158
Hausman, Jerry, 42(table), 84, 85, 171
Hayek, Friedrich, 108
Heilbroner, Robert, 64
Heritage Foundation, 8
Hicks, John, 42(table), 195
Highbrow theory, 11
Hilbert, 160
Hilbert space, 158
Hill, Thomas, 6
Hirschman, Albert, 67
History of economic thought, 9, 17(table), 89, 91, 109, 162–163, 195
Hume, David, 117
Hungary, 103

Imperfect competition, 23
Income distribution, 22(table), 116, 159
Indiana State University, 104
Industrial organization, 9, 17, 74
Inflation, 21, 22(table), 25, 111, 123, 130, 152
Inquiry into the Nature and Causes of the Wealth of Nations, An (Smith), 144
Intellectuals, 180, 184
Interdisciplinary interaction, 16, 146, 166, 180
International trade, 9, 17(table)
Intuition, 63, 133, 138, 139, 170, 172
IS/LM model, 85, 88, 136–137, 144, 145

Jevons, William Stanley, 3
Johns Hopkins University, 6, 10(table)
Journal of Economic Perspectives, 1
Journal of Political Economy (JPE), 82, 148, 175
JPE. See Journal of Political Economy

Keynes, John Maynard, 64, 92, 97, 131, 146
  graduate student ranking and opinion of, 41, 42(table), 43, 68, 126, 136, 173, 178, 180
Keynesian economists, 173, 176. See also Neo-Keynesian economics
Klamer, Arjo, 38, 57, 169, 170, 176, 179, 181, 183, 184, 188
Knight, Frank, 153, 162
Kornai, Janos, 103
Kreps, David, 105, 107
Kuhn, Thomas, 182
Kuttner, Robert, 13
Kydland, Finn, 98, 99, 143
Kydland-Prescott model, 143

Labor, 17(table), 70, 74–75, 91, 161
Lakatosian methodology, 189, 191, 205–206(n2)

Law and economics, 17(table)
Leijonhufvud, Axel, 4, 170
Leontief, Wassily, 13, 54–56(table)
Lewis, Karl, 42(table)
Liberals, 14, 38, 71, 90, 150, 153
Libertarians, 38, 137
"Life Among the Econ"
    (Leijonhufvud), 4
Locke, John, 117
London School of Economics, 110
Lowbrow theory, 11
Lucas, Robert, 23, 92, 98, 99, 103,
    104, 106, 125, 129, 134, 139,
    140, 141, 142, 143, 145, 146,
    148, 156, 157, 163, 173–174
    graduate student ranking and
    opinion of, 42(table), 54–
    56(table), 77, 84, 151–152, 160,
    172, 176, 178, 180, 181

McBain, Howard Lee, 6
Macroeconomics, 9, 16, 17(table), 25,
    63, 65, 69, 73, 83, 84, 85, 88–
    89, 92, 109, 110, 111, 112, 119,
    131, 136, 138, 142, 143, 145,
    146, 154, 156, 157, 158, 159,
    160, 177
Maloney, John, 176
Malthus, Thomas, 126
Mankiw, Greg, 99, 101
Marglin, Steve, 90–91, 93, 106
Marshak, Jacob, 153
Marshall, Alfred, 162
Marx, Karl, 41, 42(table), 43, 66, 125,
    180
Marxism. See Political economy,
    Marxist
Massachusetts Institute of Technology
    (MIT)
    and Columbia University
    comparison, 109, 173
    graduate student experience, 60–61,
    71–74, 78–79, 174, 175, 177, 178
    graduate student opinions, 20, 21,
    22(table), 23, 24, 25, 44, 46, 47–
    52(tables), 54–56(table), 171, 172.

See also subentry graduate
    students, conversations with
    graduate student ranking and
    opinion of economists, 41–
    42(table), 65, 75–76, 171, 173,
    175, 186
    graduate students, 13, 24, 29, 53,
    59, 85, 180, 183
    graduate students, conversations
    with, 57, 59–86, 181
    and Harvard University
    comparison, 85–86, 89, 95–96,
    100, 102, 173, 174
    ranking, 10(table)
    and University of Chicago
    comparison, 69, 85, 86, 128,
    130, 131, 138, 146, 147, 155,
    158, 173, 174
Mathematics, 14, 18(table), 27, 39,
    40, 60, 61, 63, 64, 65, 67, 68,
    73–74, 80–81, 96, 99, 100, 104–
    105, 110–111, 112, 118, 130,
    132–133, 138, 147–148, 157–158,
    170–171, 199
Medoff, James, 93, 103
Methodology, 189–194, 197
Michigan State University ranking,
    10(table)
Microeconomics, 9, 16, 17(table), 27,
    66, 68, 69, 88, 89, 106, 109, 110,
    118, 124, 131, 134, 136, 154
Milgate, Murray, 68
Mill, John Stuart, 3, 125, 180
Minford, Patrick, 70
Minimum wages, 22(table), 25, 159–
    160, 172
Mirowski, Phil, 95, 203(n1)
MIT. See Massachusetts Institute of
    Technology
Mitchell, Wesley, 5
Models, 26, 28, 62, 65, 74, 83, 85,
    88, 94, 114, 119, 130, 131, 136–
    137, 142–143, 145, 161, 166, 175,
    187, 192–193, 194
Modigliani, Franco, 157
Money and banking, 9, 17(table),
    22(table), 161

Myrdal, Gunnar, 42(table)

National Bureau of Economic
    Research (NBER), 5, 8, 101,
    203(n3)
National Science Foundation, 15
NBER. *See* National Bureau of
    Economic Research
Neoclassical economics, 20, 21(table),
    23, 24, 39, 44, 66, 76, 82, 90,
    91, 92, 97, 103, 105–106, 111,
    123, 140, 145, 155, 174, 192. *See*
    also Political economy,
    neoclassical
Neo-Keynesian economics, 11, 154,
    177
Neo-Marshallian economics, 11
Newsweek, 104, 135
New York Times, 104
New York University ranking,
    10(table)
Nobel Prize, 111, 135, 150, 153, 176,
    203(n2)
Northwestern University ranking,
    10(table)

Ohio State University ranking,
    10(table)
Okun, Arthur, 42(table), 75
Optimal control theory, 110
Optimizing model, 39
Oxford University (England), 110

Pareto optimal, 159
Passions and the Interests, The
    (Hirschman), 67
Phelps, Edmund, 123
Phillips curve, 111, 112, 152, 156
Piore, Michael, 62, 63, 64, 82, 83,
    103, 177
Polanyi, Karl, 42(table)
Policy, 25–26, 39, 40, 61–64, 80, 89,
    97, 112, 115–116, 117–118, 141–
    142, 143, 146, 150, 159, 165,
    171, 172, 181
  jobs, 15, 79, 134, 165, 180

Political economy, 9, 17, 124
  Marxist, 17, 64, 66, 68, 152, 153
  neoclassical, 17
Political orientation, 14, 38, 71, 90,
    115–117, 137
Political theory, 125
Popperian methodology, 189, 191,
    205–206(n2)
Positive and normative economics,
    20, 21(table), 24, 151, 159, 189,
    191, 194, 195, 197, 200
"Positive Economics" (M. Friedman),
    130
Positivism, 189, 191, 192, 193, 194
Prescott, Edward, 98, 99, 143, 148
Price rigidities, 23, 74
Price Theory (M. Friedman), 149
Princeton University, 6, 10(table), 80
Professional standards, 46
Professors, 43–44, 45, 100, 101, 118
Public finance, 9, 17(table)
Purdue University ranking, 10(table)

Radicals, 14, 38
Rand Corporation, 8
Rational expectations, 23, 63, 66–67,
    76, 92, 106, 108, 111, 123, 146,
    157, 162, 172
Rationality assumptions, 23(table),
    66–67, 76, 131, 132, 140, 155–
    156, 174, 192
Reading in other fields, 16. *See also*
    Interdisciplinary interaction
Recession, 111, 112
Reder, Melvin, 178
Relevance of material, 14, 26, 46,
    61–64, 69, 70, 101, 111, 114, 175
Research, 18(table), 121, 124, 181
Research assistantships, 101
Ricardo, David, 3, 42(table), 125, 126,
    138, 162, 195
Robinson, Joan, 42(table)
Rosen, Sherwin, 42(table), 162

Sachs, Jeffrey, 93, 171, 181
Samuelson, Paul, 97, 183, 195

graduate student ranking and
opinion of, 41, 42(table), 43, 54–
56(table), 68
Sargent, Thomas, 92, 98, 104, 106
SAT. *See* Scholastic Aptitude Test
Schelling, Tom, 107
Scholastic Aptitude Test (SAT)
scores, 9
Schumacher, E. S., 38
Schumpeter, Joseph, 42(table), 125,
126, 162
Self-selection, 24, 25, 68, 150, 177
Sen, Amartya, 42(table), 95, 203(n1)
Share Economy, The (Weitzman), 65,
104
Shultz, George, 80
Slutsky, Eugene, 42(table)
Smith, Adam, 125, 135, 136, 162,
173, 195
graduate student ranking and
opinion of, 41, 42(table), 43, 78
Social concern, 46, 114, 180–181, 183
Socialization process, 27–28, 91–92,
94, 97, 170, 176–179
Social sciences, 64, 82, 96, 99, 107,
108, 188
Sociology, 107–108, 125, 166, 170,
191–192, 193–194, 195
Socrates, 179
Solow, Robert, 18, 26, 42(table), 62,
74, 97, 99–100, 153, 156, 157,
203(n2)
Soviet economics, 102, 113
Spence, Michael, 42(table), 101, 107
Stanford University, 96
graduate student opinions,
21(table), 22–23(tables), 24, 45,
47–52(tables), 54–56(table)
graduate student ranking of
economists, 41–42(tables)
graduate students, 13, 24, 29
ranking, 10(table)
Statistics and econometrics, 9, 17, 46,
63, 64, 65, 68, 70–71, 73, 91,
95, 104, 109, 110, 119–120, 142,
190, 195–196, 206(n5)

Stigler, George, 14, 20, 42(table),
146, 151, 152, 153, 160, 163, 181
Stiglitz, Joseph, 42(table), 68, 112,
160, 161, 173
Stock market crash (1987), 127, 131,
133–134
Success, perceptions of, 17–18, 28,
39, 59, 112, 138
Summers, Larry, 75, 84, 89, 92, 93,
101, 102–103, 153, 171, 181

Tariffs and imports quotas, 22(table),
115, 172
Technocrats, 170, 172, 179, 180
Theory, 14, 26–27, 39, 43, 62, 69,
92, 94, 104, 106, 110, 112, 114,
115, 118, 131–132, 137, 156, 165,
171, 174, 188, 191, 193, 196
Theory of Value (Debreu), 153
Theses. *See* Dissertation topics
Thurow, Lester, 63, 64, 84, 103–104,
181, 182
Tobin, James, 42(table), 80, 126, 157
Townsend, Robert, 104, 148

Unemployment, 111, 112, 130, 137,
152, 161, 173
University of Arizona ranking,
10(table)
University of California–Berkeley,
10(table), 145
University of California–Los Angeles,
10(table), 68, 132
University of California–San Diego
ranking, 10(table)
University of California–Santa
Barbara ranking, 10(table)
University of Chicago, 20, 24, 145,
146, 189, 190
and Columbia University
comparison, 110
Graduate School of Business, 177
graduate student experience, 127–
129, 137–138, 144–149, 154–157,
173–174, 175–176, 177–178
graduate student opinions, 20, 21,
22(table), 23–24, 25, 28, 39, 40,

45–46, 47–52(tables), 54–
56(table), 170, 172, 173. *See also*
subentry graduate students,
conversations with
graduate student ranking and
opinion of economists, 41,
42(table), 43, 129, 135–136, 138–
140, 151–153, 160, 162–163, 173,
174, 176, 180
graduate students, 13, 29, 37, 38,
53, 127–128, 137, 180, 181, 183,
184, 193
graduate students, conversations
with, 57, 127–166
and Harvard University
comparison, 101, 155, 158
and MIT comparison, 69, 85, 86,
128, 130, 131, 138, 146, 147,
155, 158, 173, 174
ranking, 10(table)
reputation, 141, 149–150
and University of California–
Berkeley comparison, 145
and University of Minnesota
comparison, 158
University of Colorado ranking,
10(table)
University of Illinois ranking,
10(table)
University of Maryland ranking,
10(table)
University of Massachusetts ranking,
10(table)
University of Michigan ranking,
10(table)
University of Minnesota, 10(table),
158, 171
University of Pennsylvania ranking,
10(table)
University of Rochester ranking,
10(table)

University of Southern California
(USC), 10(table), 104
University of Texas ranking, 10(table)
University of Virginia ranking,
10(table)
University of Warwick (England), 127
University of Washington ranking,
10(table)
University of Wisconsin ranking,
10(table)
Urban economics, 17(table)
USC. *See* University of Southern
California

Varian, Hal, 149, 153
Veblen, Thorstein, 42(table)
Viner, Jacob, 16
Virginia Polytechnic Institute (VPI)
ranking, 10(table)
VPI. *See* Virginia Polytechnic
Institute

Walras, Leon, 3
Ward, Benjamin, 16, 17
Washington University ranking,
10(table)
Weitzman, Martin, 65, 84, 104, 181
Williams, Jeffrey, 102
Williams College, 78
Women, 22(table)
Worldly Philosophers, The (Heilbroner),
64

Yale University
graduate student opinions, 21–
22(tables), 39, 45, 46, 47–
52(tables), 54–56(table), 193
graduate student ranking of
economists, 41–42(tables)
graduate students, 13, 29, 38, 53
ranking, 10(table)